Transformative Pedagogies for Teacher Education

Critical Action, Agency, and Dialogue in Teaching and Learning Contexts

A Volume in
Transformative Pedagogies in Teacher Education

Series Editors

Ann E. Lopez
University of Toronto
Elsie Lindy Olan
University of Central Florida

Transformative Pedagogies in Teacher Education
Ann E. Lopez and Elsie L. Olan, Editors

Transformative Pedagogies for Teacher Education: Critical Action, Agency, and Dialogue in Teaching and Learning Contexts (2019)
edited by Ann E. Lopez and Elsie Lindy Olan

*Transformative Pedagogies for Teacher Education:
Moving Towards Critical Praxis in an Era of Change* (2018)
edited by Ann E. Lopez and Elsie Lindy Olan

Transformative Pedagogies for Teacher Education

Critical Action, Agency, and Dialogue in Teaching and Learning Contexts

edited by

Ann E. Lopez
University of Toronto

Elsie Lindy Olan
University of Central Florida

INFORMATION AGE PUBLISHING, INC.
Charlotte, NC • www.infoagepub.com

Library of Congress Cataloging-in-Publication Data

CIP record for this book is available from the Library of Congress
http://www.loc.gov

ISBNs: 978-1-64113-699-0 (Paperback)

978-1-64113-700-3 (Hardcover)

978-1-64113-701-0 (ebook)

Copyright © 2019 Information Age Publishing Inc.

All rights reserved. No part of this publication may be reproduced, stored in a retrieval system, or transmitted, in any form or by any means, electronic, mechanical, photocopying, microfilming, recording or otherwise, without written permission from the publisher.

Printed in the United States of America

CONTENTS

About the Series
  Ann E. Lopez and Elsie Lindy Olan vii

Series Foreword
  Christine Sleeter xi

Preface
  Ann E. Lopez and Elsie Lindy Olan xv

Acknowledgments xix

1. Understanding Student Diversity Through Intersubjectivity:
   Introducing Lesson Study in Teacher Education in Norway
   and the United States
   Nina Helgevold and Aki Murata 1

2. Examining Efficacy of Equity Education: Challenging
   Uncritical and Laminated Notions of Equity in
   Teacher Education
   Ann E. Lopez 19

3. Secondary Preservice Teachers Exploration of
   Inclusive Education
   Jennifer Lock and Petrea Redmond 37

4. Integrating Learning Spaces: Understanding Conditions That Enable Transformational Shifts in Teacher Education Programs and Practices
   Lisa J. Starr and Kathy Sanford 55

5. Rethinking the Intersectionality of the Zone of Proximal Development: The Challenges of Disruptive and Transformative Change to Improve Instruction
   Enrique A. Puig 69

6. Fidelity of Practice: The Challenge of Transformative Change in Teacher Professional Development
   Mary Hutchinson and Xenia Hadjioannou 87

7. Experience of Transformation: Educator Perspectives
   Amanda Jo Cordova, Encarnación Garza, Jr., and Juan Manuel Niño 103

8. Student Responses to Critically Compassionate Intellectualism in Teacher Education for Social Justice
   Amy Rector-Aranda 133

9. Enacting Social Justice Colloquia as a Key Component of a Transformative Teacher: Education Program
   Todd S. Hawley, Lisa A. Borgerding, and Kristine E. Pytash 153

10. Self-Study as a Transformative Methodology and Pedagogical Practice in a Writing Workshop
    Elsie Lindy Olan 169

11. Vulnerability Starts With Myself: Bilingual Teacher Educator Identity as Pedagogy
    Blanca Caldas Chumbes 183

12. Transforming Teacher Education: Nurturing Innovative Pathways of Collaboration Essential to Democratizing Teacher Education
    Edward Podsiadlik and Michelle Parker-Katz 197

13. We Don't Do This Work Alone: How Practitioner Demos Develop Digital Praxis in Teacher Education
    Cherise McBride, Lanette Jimerson, and Jabari Mahiri 213

About the Authors 231

ABOUT THE SERIES

Ann E. Lopez and Elsie Lindy Olan

Transformative Pedagogies for Teacher Education is a book series that feature the work of teacher educators across the globe that are engaging in alternative pedagogies grounded in social justice to meet the needs of students. This series is about praxis—connecting theory to educational practices that practitioners, scholars and activists can draw on as they seek to create meaningful and lasting change in the lives of students. The research, experiences and practices highlighted in this series foreground the voices and experiences of teacher educators who are working with teacher candidates and in classrooms; all on a journey to create more equitable practices no matter their contexts. We live in a world where borders are shrinking and people are on the move. As teacher educators, we must vow to include the richness that this diversity brings to education. Each author is committed to the cause and to the goals of equity, guided by their own experiences and contexts. The teacher educators who contributed to this series are unique in their own way, each sharing narratives and experiences that inform their journey. Their research reflect new and different ways to prepare teacher candidates to enter classrooms and schools that have vastly changed over the last 20 years. It is our hope that this project will encourage not only teacher educators and teacher candidates, but also educational leaders and policymakers to seek out alternative approaches to education to addresses the needs of students who have traditionally been marginalized.

Transformative Pedagogies for Teacher Education:
Critical Action, Agency, and Dialogue in Teaching and Learning Contexts , pp. vii–ix
Copyright © 2019 by Information Age Publishing
All rights of reproduction in any form reserved.

Transformative pedagogy empowers students to critically examine beliefs, values, and knowledge with the aim of developing new epistemologies, center multiple ways of knowing, and develop a sense of critical consciousness and agency. Singer and Pezone (2000) urge teacher educators not to become pessimistic and overwhelmed by societal and educational challenges, but seek out ways to engage in transformative actions. Grounded in the work of Dewey and Freire, the works in this series take a critical approach to education. Freire (1970) pedagogical aim was to ensure that the oppressed had educational experiences that allowed them to take control over their own lives. It is important for teacher candidates and teacher educators to work keep this at the forefront of their work given the current complexities of schooling. Freire believed that education should be a vehicle for hope for society at large. In this endeavour both educators and students should explicitly challenge social injustice and oppression. According to Freire, knowledge emerges through invention and re-invention, through the restless, impatient, continuing, hopeful inquiry human beings pursue in the world, with the world and with each other. The authors seek to enact teacher education in the traditions of Dewy (1961) who suggests the ideals of democratic education must translate into experiential learning, and pragmatic actions combined with reflective thinking. If we are to advance the education then theory must be connected to practice.

By examining our practices as teacher educators we engage in continuous learning that enables new knowledge to emerge in the hope of creating change in education and society. As Freire (1970) argues the role of the teacher is to ask questions by engaging in problem-posing methodologies, support students to discover new ideas, value their life experiences and include prior experiences as the basis for new academic understanding and social action, a process he refers to as conscientization.

Different and alternative transformative pedagogical approaches weave through this series. Through the frame of liberatory pedagogy (Freire, 1970), that focuses on raising critical consciousness and recognizes that education is political; culturally responsive pedagogy (Gay, 2010; Ladson-Billings, 1995a; Villegas & Lucas, 2008) which argues for the cultural references of students to be represented in all aspects of learning; participatory action research (Reason & Bradbury, 2001) that captures the voices and experiences of urban youths and advances practical knowledge in pursuit of social action; case studies (Merseth, 1994; Shulman, 1992) that bridge theory to practice divide; the voices of teacher educators working on the border; and disruptive pedagogy (Lee, 2014) authors share narratives, colaboring with the students sharing experiences in pursuit of teacher education to transform education and social change. Teacher educators share not only their aspirations for education, but also their vulnerabilities on the journey of liberatory education.

We hope that different approaches and pedagogies highlighted in this series will advance the work of educators committed to social justice and more equitable outcomes for students who are at the margins, a better society and a more democratic world. Indeed this is the aim of transformative education.

REFERENCES

Dewey, J. (1961). *Democracy and education: An introduction to the philosophy of education.* Oakland, CA: Macmillan

Freire, P. (1970). *Pedagogy of the oppressed.* New York, NY: Herder and Herder.

Gay, G. (2010). *Culturally responsive teaching: Theory, research, and practice.* New York, NY: Teachers College Press.

Ladson-Billings, G. (1995). Toward a theory of culturally relevant pedagogy. *American Educational Research Journal, 32*(3), 465–491.

Lee, B. (2014). Teaching disruptively: Pedagogical strategies to teach cultural diversity and race. In E. Fernandez (Ed.), *Teaching for culturally diverse and racially just world* (pp. 147–166). Eugene, OR: Cascade Books.

Lucas, T., Villegas, A. M., & Freedson-Gonzalez, M. (2008). Linguistically responsive teacher education: Preparing classroom teachers to teach English language learners. *Journal of Teacher Education, 59*(4), 361–373.

Merseth, K. K. (1994). Cases and case method in teacher education. In J. Sikula (Ed.), *Handbook of teacher education* (2nd ed., pp. 722–744). New York, NY: MacMillan.

Reason, P., & Bradbury. H. (2001), Introduction: Inquiry and participation in search of a world worthy of human aspiration. In P. Reason & H. Bradbury (Eds.), *Handbook of action research* (pp. 1–14). Thousand Oaks, CA: Sage.

Shulman, L. S. (1992). Toward a pedagogy of cases. In J. L. Shulman (Ed.), *Case method in teacher education* (pp. 1–32). New York, NY: Teacher College Press.

Singer, A., & Pezone, M. (2000). A response to Annette Hemming's 'high school democratic dialogues: Possibilities for praxis'. *American Educational Research Journal, 38*(3), 535–539.

SERIES FOREWORD

Christine Sleeter

Transformative Pedagogies for Teacher Education arrives at a time when such a book is not only welcomed, but also much needed. Currently teacher educators who are committed to social justice face numerous challenges.

For one thing, all over the world student populations continue to diversify as migrants seek economic opportunity and refugees flee violence. As a result, educators struggle to figure out how to teach their increasingly diverse students in countries ranging from Greece and Italy, to South Korea, from Australia and New Zealand, to India. For example, in the United States, by 2013, public school students were 50% of color; as this book went to print, there was no racial/ethnic student majority (National Center for Education Statistics, 2016), and in the context of growing economic inequality, a majority of students came from families living in poverty (Layton, 2015).

The growing diversity of students, often enmeshed within growing economic inequality, presents urgent challenges that go beyond attempts to frame policy. In Greece, for example, the national law promoting cross-cultural education uses vague wording that allows for a wide range of interpretations, while normalizing segregation and obsessing on cultural differences (Mitakidou, 2011). Canada, which national policy frames as bilingual and multicultural, grapples with its foundation in settler colonialism, and its casting of differences in terms of language and culture but not race (Haque, 2014). European Union policies that purport to include

Roma students often fail to impact how students are actually treated in schools and classrooms (Miskovic & Curcic, 2016).

For teachers and teacher educators, multiculturalism as lived out in schools and communities presents urgent challenges, particularly in contexts of backlash against immigration. For example, Eksner and Cheema (2017) report interviews with Muslim youth who grew up in Germany where currently about 5% of the population are members of ethnic communities that identify as majority Muslim. The authors write that,

> Youths marked as Muslim experience intersectional "othering" as being marked as (1st, 2nd, 3rd) immigrants, ethnocultural "others" and because of their assumed religious membership. "Othering" of youths marked as Muslim is based on certain visible markers (e.g., phenotype or name) and works via the ascription of both religious membership (i.e., being born into a Muslim family) and religious orientation (i.e., de facto beliefs), both of which are discursively connected to conservative and radical political and cultural beliefs and practices. (pp. 161–184)

Their "othering" is underscored by media representations that stereotype and oversimplify the students' communities, and implicitly link Islam with terrorism.

For teacher educators, the question becomes: How do we prepare teachers to respond proactively and constructively to their students, given larger contexts of difference and power within which children and youth live? And how do we do this work in contexts where neoliberalism has increased the privatization of education, policies have deprofessionalized teaching and shortened teacher education (e.g., Zeichner, 2008), and testing regimes narrowly constrain what students are to learn?

While this book arrived during a time of challenges and changes, it also arrives at a propitious time of growing knowledge about culturally responsive and social justice teaching, as well as work on behalf of schools as sites for liberation and justice. For example, in the United States, the research on the academic and social impact of ethnic studies on children and youth (Sleeter, 2011) has been instrumental in supporting grassroots mobilizing in numerous school districts to institutionalize ethnic studies teaching in schools. Conferences are regularly held in which teachers and teacher educators share progressive and activist practices and learn from each other. Examples include the National Association for Multicultural Education and the Teacher Activist Groups in the United States, and the Korean Association for Multicultural Education's annual conference. Indigenous communities in many parts of the world are reconstituting education as tribal-centered and aimed toward cultural reclamation, empowerment, and self-determination (e.g., McCarty & Lee, 2014).

Transformative Pedagogies for Teacher Education resonates well with Milner's (2008) extrapolation of several core principles from social movements to the work of transforming teacher education. First, Milner writes that activists must establish a common agenda and vision. Social justice–minded teacher educators and their collaborators must develop enough conceptual convergence that despite differences, they can work as a unified collective. *Transformative Pedagogies for Teacher Education* represents an important part of that process of developing a common collective vision. Even though the chapters speak to various innovations within different teacher education programs, they are similarly anchored in a vision that values differences, dialog across those differences, critical analysis of unequal power relations, and the potential of teachers learning to work in collaboration with their students.

Second, Milner (2008) argues that social movement work takes account of contexts, realities, and resources. There is no one formula; local work is necessary. This principle is beautifully embodied in this book, in which authors speak from their own work with programs in specific contexts, while sharing insights that others may draw on, learn from, and perhaps adapt.

Third, Milner (2008) points out that movements connect "pro-action, re-action, and prediction" (p. 340) using evidence of impacts of past practices and trends to make a case for changes for the future. Many of the chapters in this book not only describe innovative practices, but also report data on the transformative impact of their work, data that can guide future developments.

Finally, movements involve persistent long-term work. In that sense, the series in which *Transformative Pedagogies for Teacher Education* appears represents numerous teacher educators coming together to dialogue, share strategies, and draw strength and inspiration from each other for the long haul of transforming teacher education. I commend this book to readers, who, by engaging with it, become part of the dialogue and ongoing collective transformational work.

REFERENCES

Eksner, H. J., & Cheema, S. N. (2017). "Who gere is a Real German?" German Muslim youths, othering, and education. In J. A. Banks (Ed.), *Citizenship education and global migration* (pp. 161-184). Washington, DC: American Educational Research Association.

Haque, E. (2014). Multiculturalism within a bilingual framework: A retrospective. *Canadian Ethnic Studies, 46*(2), 119–25.

Layton, L. (2015, January). Majority of U.S. public schools students are in poverty. *The Washington Post.* Retrieved from www.washingtonpost.com/local/education/majority-of-us-public-school-students-are-in-poverty/

McCarty, T. L., & Lee, T. S. (2014). Critically culturally sustaining/revitalizing pedagogy and Indigenous education sovereignty. *Harvard Educational Review 84*(1), 101–124.

Milner, H. R., IV. (2008). Critical race theory and interest convergence as analytic tools in teacher education policies and practices. *Journal of Teacher Education, 59,* 332–346.

Miskovic, M., & Curcic, S. (2016). Beyond inclusion: Reconsidering policies, curriculum, and pedagogy for Roma students. *International Journal of Multicultural Education 18*(2), 1–14.

Mitakidou, S. (2011). Cross-cultural education in Greece: History and prospects. In C. A. Grant & A. Portera (Eds.), *Intercultural and multicultural education* (pp. 83–97). New York, NY: Routledge.

National Center for Education Statistics. (2016, May). Racial/ethnic enrollment in public schools. *The Condition of Education.* Retrieved from nces.ed.gov/programs/coe/indicator_cge.asp

Sleeter, C. E. (2011). *The academic and social value of ethnic studies.* Washington, DC: National Education Association.

Zeichner, K. M. (2008). *Teacher education and the struggle for social justice.* New York, NY: Routledge.

PREFACE

We are living in challenging times. Populism and nationalism are on the rise, public education is under attack, xenophobia, racism, and other forms of exclusion have found space in the popular discourse. Educators play an important role in challenging the rhetoric of division and hate, while offering action and possibilities for change. Schools have always played an important role in the social and political discourse and the times in which we are living are no different. Teachers, students, teacher educators, along with communities all have an important role to play in the pursuit of equity and justice in society. This volume is about teaching and learning that critically examines education and offers different perspectives on ways that teacher educators can engage with teacher candidates and have meaningful impact on the educational outcomes of students. The volume is grounded in critical approaches drawing on the work of Freire and other critical thinkers who argue for the critiquing of power in schooling and the development of practice that empowers educators to transform how they teach.

Transformative pedagogies call for the development of students as critical thinkers, participatory and active thinkers, and creators of alternative possibilities of social reality (Nagda, Gurin, & Lopez, 2003). As societies become more diverse, it is imperative that teachers are prepared to engage with students from different communities in ways that enhance their learning and value their experiences. Teachers who are unaware of cultural influences on learning, the structure and substance of inequality often find it difficult to understand students whose experience do not resemble their own (Darling-Hammond, 2011). Teachers, and in particular new teachers, must be supported to develop practices that support the implementation of critical ideas in the classroom. Teachers must be given the practical tools they need to transform their good intentions into effective actions (Zeichner, 2009). This is what this second book in this volume seeks to do through the work of authors from different contexts, locations, and approaches. Authors expand on ways to connect theory to practice, drawing on research as well as their own experiences. They wrestle with challenging issues in teacher education, posit new epistemologies and examples from practice that others can learn from. Schools must become more effective in meeting the needs of a more culturally, racially, linguistically, socioeconomically diverse school population, as well as confront all forms of exclusion (Darling-Hammond, 2011).

There is an urgent need for schools and faculties of education to adequately prepare teachers for the racial and ethnocultural diversity that exists today in advanced economies (Dlamini, 2002). Teachers interact daily with students in their teaching and learning contexts whose experiences and backgrounds are different from their own. This reality calls for teacher education that support the development of skills and knowledge in new teachers allow them to enter schools with a mindset to see difference as an asset. There continues to be inequity in outcomes for students from different backgrounds in many advanced economies, while some emerging economies are seeking to advance more equitable and socially just approach to education. Technology has allowed the shrinking of borders and sharing of ideas. As many emerging economies seek to disrupt colonial legacies particularly in education, practical pedagogical examples that disrupt power in education and respond to sociocultural and political realities, teacher educators in those contexts will also find this volume useful.

The goals of this volume and approach are worth reaffirming. The main goals are to:

- Highlight possibilities for action in the preparation of teachers in increasingly diverse and changing contexts
- See schooling as conduit in support of global diversity and competence
- Support teacher educators on their journey to engage in teacher education that is socially just, culturally responsive and respond critically to the growing and diverse needs of students and communities
- Provide a platform where teacher educators' empirical research, as well as their lived experiences in teaching and learning contexts can inform education systems, policies and practices

The approach of this volume is to provide space where teacher educators and others who work directly with children can share their stories of success and learn from the challenges on their journey. We all recognize the need to move beyond theorizing and offer practical suggestions to teachers that will inform pedagogy, curriculum, and practice in meaningful ways. Teachers and teacher educators must also do their part by engaging in critical self-reflection about what they need to learn and unlearn in order to meet the needs of diverse learners. In each chapter authors from varying contexts draw on research and experience to examine ways that teacher educators respond to the development of teacher candidates. They present frameworks of transformative pedagogies in teacher preparation programs and as well as school contexts that all educators can learn from. It is important to enhance this work and move towards critical actions where teachers and stakeholders critically examine their acquisition of skills and knowledge, interpretations and assumptions, and discontent with curricula and institutional practices while taking action. They identify disruptions that lead to their transformations and transformative learning and teaching. These implementations, collaborations, discussions, practices, and reflections are descriptive of their experiences, inquiries and opportunities within diverse school settings where they can take action, and venture into culturally responsive leadership in their school settings. This book about praxis and will be of benefit for all those involved in education.

Ann E. Lopez

Elsie Lindy Olan

REFERENCES

Dlamini, S. N. (2002). From the other side of the desk: Notes on teaching about racism when racialized. *Race Ethnicity and Education,* 5(1) 51–66.
Darling-Hammond, L. (2011). Studying diversity in teacher education. In A. Ball & C. Tyson (Eds.), *Studying diversity in teacher education* (pp. ix–x). New York, NY: Rowman and Littlefield. Published in Partnership with AERA
Nagda, B. A., Gurin, P., & Lopez, G. (2003). Transformative pedagogy for democracy and social justice. *Race and Ethnicity in Education,* 2(3) 165-191.
Zeichner, K. (2009). *Teacher education and the struggle for social justice.* New York, NY: Routledge.

ACKNOWLEDGMENTS

Every publishing endeavor takes times and the support of others. As we complete book 2 in the series we would like to thank those who have supported this effort. The series as we indicated in the first book, the series is dedicated to teachers, teacher educators and others who work with teacher candidates in teacher education programs and in schools to prepare them to enter increasingly diverse schools and communities. Their contributions drawing on their experiences from various contexts have made this a rich experience. We thank the authors who contributed chapters to this book for going on this journey with us, their enduring patience, and responding to the numerous e-mails.

The art work on the cover is by Natalia Ortiz to whom we owe a debt of gratitude for her artistic vision. We thank the anonymous reviewers who reviewed the chapters and provided valuable suggestions for improvement. Thanks to our families for their support throughout this process. They are an important part of the journey. And as always, Ann acknowledges the guidance of her grandmother for her inspiration and who taught her to challenge injustice everywhere and find joy in learning.

CHAPTER 1

UNDERSTANDING STUDENT DIVERSITY THROUGH INTERSUBJECTIVITY

Introducing Lesson Study in Teacher Education in Norway and the United States

Nina Helgevold and Aki Murata

Introduction

One of the major challenges facing teacher education in the 21st century is supporting teachers to manage the complexities of classroom teaching and the creation of positive learning environments for diverse communities of students (Ball, 2013; Darling-Hammond & Lieberman, 2012; Feiman-Nemser, 2001). As global demographic changes affect local classrooms, teachers today must be prepared to teach an increasingly diverse population of students, who represent different cultures, languages, races, performance levels, religions, and socioeconomic levels. Ladson-Billings (2001, p. 14) describes this challenge as follows:

Transformative Pedagogies for Teacher Education:
Critical Action, Agency, and Dialogue in Teaching and Learning Contexts, pp. 1–18
Copyright © 2019 by Information Age Publishing
All rights of reproduction in any form reserved.

> Not only [will teachers encounter] . . . multiracial or multiethnic [students] but they [students] are also likely to be diverse along linguistic, religious, ability, and economic lines. . . . Today teachers walk into urban classrooms with children who represent an incredible range of diversity

Field practicum holds promise in providing preservice teachers (PSTs) targeted experiences with diverse students (Anderson & Stillman, 2013; Cochran-Smith et al., 2015; Sleeter & Owour, 2011). Without focused guidance, practicum experiences can actually work to further reinforce the misunderstanding and widening the gap (Akiba, 2011; Anderson & Stillman, 2013; Darling-Hammond, Hammerness, Grossmann, Rust, & Shulmann, 2006). As one way of addressing this challenge, the study presented in this chapter illustrates how PSTs understood and made sense of the challenges of teaching diverse students during field practicum with lesson study (LS).

The two authors are university teacher educators who have used their own courses and programs as research sites. By incorporating LS, we aimed to focus PSTs' attention to the challenges of teaching in classrooms with diverse students. Previous research has found that novice teachers tend to be more preoccupied with their own teaching and survival in classrooms, and that they have difficulties in shifting their attention from themselves to their students (Richardson & Placier, 2001). Despite the differences between the two programs, our aim was to see if, and how, LS could support intersubjectivity development among PSTs, by focusing their attention on the learning experiences of diverse learners.

We argue that intersubjectivity can be an essential support for teachers as they engage and teach students whose backgrounds may differ from their own. In the process of gaining intersubjectivity, teachers become more aware of student experiences and understanding and adapt their teaching to meet the needs of students. Intersubjectivity "concerns the degree to which interlocutors in a communicative situation share a perspective" (Wertsch, 1998, p. 111). Rommetveit (2003) suggests through "attuning to the other" and through leaving our own private outlook on the situation, we are able to construct "a partially shared social reality" despite different perspectives. In teaching, this means teachers share students' reality in classrooms (Helgevold, 2016). We investigated how PSTs developed intersubjectivity with their students by analyzing the data from focus group interviews before and after targeted field practicum with lesson study. We asked the following research questions:

> *Do PSTs develop intersubjectivity with their students through LS, evidenced by (1) changes in their talk about student diversity, and (2) changes in their talk about classroom teaching?*

The findings of the study, outlined in the sections below, will aim to shed light on how PSTs make sense of teaching in diverse classrooms, and how working with diverse students in a targeted manner can help shift their understanding of diversity.

A secondary focus of this chapter is the authors' reflection on their own assumptions about diversity and about PSTs in the research process. As teacher educators, we need to continually and critically examine institutional programs and practices, and how our own beliefs and values are embedded in these practices. The both authors were trained as teachers, before becoming teacher educators. We come from different cultural backgrounds, teaching and conducting research in two different countries, representing different school systems and student populations. This cross-cultural research setting created an ideal context to reflect on our intersubjectivity as teacher educators with the PSTs as well as with each other on the topic of student diversity.

Backgrounds and Perspectives

Preparing PSTs to Teach Diverse Learners

Despite concerted efforts within the field of teacher education, there is little consensus on how best to support novice teachers' work with the complexities of teaching and the creation of positive learning environments for diverse children (Taylor & Sobel, 2001). Although teacher education courses have often addressed topics on the multicultural classroom and inclusion in specialized courses, the effects of these on PSTs' understanding of diversity is unclear (Hollins & Guzman, 2005; Taylor & Sobel 2001; Villegas & Lucas, 2002). Garmon (2004) suggests that the attitudes and beliefs held by PSTs when entering teacher education programs will serve as filters for subsequent learning, and in addition, these act as ideological anchors for teaching decisions and behaviors (Gay, 2010). When PSTs have limited experiences working with people from different backgrounds, the examination of beliefs and attitudes about cultural diversity is essential in order to build a better understanding of how the development of inclusive classroom practices can be supported (Gay, 2010). In this chapter we understand inclusive education as *a principled approach to education*, which involves the process of increasing participation for all students, as well as reducing their exclusion from "the curricula, cultures and communities of local schools" (Ainscow & Miles (2008, p. 20)

Villegas and Lucas (2002) present six characteristics of a culturally responsive teacher. These include the teacher being socioculturally conscious, holding affirming views of students from diverse backgrounds, sees themselves as both responsible for and capable of educational change, understands how learners construct knowledge, knows about the lives of their students, and uses this knowledge to design instruction. They argue that these qualities, or strands, must be "consciously and systematically woven throughout the learning experiences of prospective teachers in their coursework and fieldwork" (p. 21). In order to prepare teachers for a multicultural society, teacher educators must articulate a vision of teaching and learning in a diverse society, examining and revising the curriculum in light of this vision, while deepening their own knowledge, understandings, conceptions, and practices of diversity (Milner, 2010).

In a recent overview of research, Cochran-Smith et al. (2015) claim that in order to prepare PSTs for classrooms with student diversity, more studies are needed that go beyond "assuming that changing teacher candidates' beliefs necessarily leads to different behaviors and actions in their classrooms" (p. 117). Consequently, there is a need to better understand how PSTs can be supported in the development of a repertoire of culturally responsive and socially just teaching practices with which they can address the needs of diverse student population. Studies that investigate how teacher preparation influences professional practice by engaging PSTs as reflective and inquiring professionals have made useful contributions to the field. These studies focus on how PSTs' understanding of teaching is informed through analyzing the data of classroom practices (Cochran-Smith et al., 2015). To gather and analyze data of classroom practices is a core element in LS, which was used as both a learning and research context in this study.

Lesson Study

Lesson study originated in Japan, over 100 years ago, with the aim to support teachers' exploration and implementation of effective teaching practices with primary focus on student learning (Chokshi & Fernandez, 2004; Lewis, Perry, & Murata, 2006; Murata, 2011). Throughout the 1980s and 1990s, LS helped shift a didactic stance to more student-centered teaching practices among Japanese teachers (Lewis & Tsuchida, 1998; Murata & Takahashi, 2002). During the last 15 years, it has also received global attention (Murata, 2011; Fujita, Hashimoto, & Hodgson, 2004). As a model of professional development, LS provides context for teachers to expand their knowledge of teaching through an organized cycle of (a) goal setting, (b) curriculum analysis, (c) lesson planning, (d) teaching a lesson while being observed (research lesson), and (e) debriefing and reflecting in an open and collaborative setting (Fernandez, 2005). The growing body of research on LS in preservice education suggests that the cycle of teaching embedded in LS helps PSTs make connections between different aspects of classroom practices, while at the same time, developing a deeper understanding of each practice (Amador & Weiland, 2015; Helgevold, Næsheim-Bjørkvik, & Østrem, 2015; Murata, 2011).

Research Background and Design

For this study, we worked with PSTs in two different teacher education programs in Norway (University A) and in the United States (University B), in which LS was introduced as a part of their field practicum experiences.[1] The two programs differed in several dimensions. The PSTs at University A were undergraduates in their second year of teacher education. As a group, they were younger than students at University B who already held bachelor's degrees. Students from University A were all ethnic Norwegians, thus representing a homogeneous teaching force (Banks et al., 2005). They will be teaching in classrooms that are, due to labor immigration and refugees from different parts of the world, becoming more diverse. To qualify teachers to work in diverse classrooms therefore has a high priority within Norwegian teacher education.

The PSTs at University B typically had some informal teaching experiences prior to attending the teacher education program. While majority of the PSTs was Caucasian (approximately 75%, and other 25% were Black, Asian, and Latinos), because the university was located in an urban area, the students in their practicum classrooms were highly diverse in terms of race, culture, language, and ethnicities.

Notwithstanding these differences, both programs aim at preparing PSTs for teaching in diverse classrooms. We wanted to collect data, to possibly identify common developmental shifts as preservice teachers gained intersubjectivity with their students. At University A, participants were 15 PSTs taking subject content courses (mathematics, natural science, English as foreign language (ELF), physical education), while at University B, 16 PSTs all enrolled in the elementary-level teaching credential program.

At University A, the LS process was primarily facilitated by the mentor teachers in the practicum classrooms with guidance from university researchers. The LS cycle involved teaching the same lessons twice to different groups of students, revising the original lesson after collecting and analyzing student learning data from the first lesson. In the research lessons, the PSTs at University A collected data on *case pupils* (Dudley, 2013). "Case pupils" represent or typify learner groups whom the teacher finds important to observe and understand in the research lessons (RL). "Case pupils" can be students with different cultural backgrounds, second language learners, disengaged students or students that represent different academic attainments. Teachers plan the RL for the whole class but keep their "case pupils" in mind, specifying what they hope each will be doing at key points in the lesson. PSTs at University A chose their "case pupils" in collaboration with their mentor teachers.

At University B, LS was embedded in the mathematics teaching methods course in which the instructor facilitated the process. The PSTs followed the lesson study cycle described above, while they also conducted preassessments prior to planning research lessons, to understand students' current thinking of the lesson topics.

Both groups of PSTs collected student data during lesson observations, in addition to assessing student understanding outside of the lessons, to reflect on learning experiences from students' perspectives.

At both universities, the PSTs were interviewed before and after their LS experiences in small focus groups. For this study, we have extracted and analyzed the sections of the interviews where the PSTs highlighted issues of student diversity (see Appendix A). In the preinterview, the PSTs were asked to comment on a classroom situation where a teacher describes her diverse classroom as challenging. They were also given a topic to teach in this classroom, and discussed how to introduce the topic. In the post interviews, we extracted the data where PSTs reflected on the RL they had planned and taught as a part of their LS project.

Throughout the analysis, we wanted to understand whether and to what extent PSTs' talks about teaching in diverse classroom was influenced by their LS experience. Would collecting data and observation support them in critical reflections on their own teaching practices and their own understanding of student diversity? In analyzing the focus group interviews we referred to Matusov and Smith's (2007) framework describing PSTs' narratives about Latino students. In the framework, they categorize two narratives or ways of talking to reflect intersubjectivity: *problematizing* (considering how students think and perceive reality) and *subjectivizing* (involving students finding answers to problems). The framework also included talks that reflected non-intersubjectivity—that is *objectivizing* (not considering students' perspectives in understanding the situation), and *finalizing* (expressing certainty about a student without the student's perspective). Drawing on this framework, we analyzed PSTs' discussions in the interviews, focusing especially on the categories; subjectivizing and problematizing (intersubjectivity talks). Table 1.1 summarizes how these talks developed from pre- to postinterviews.

Table 1.1 shows significant increases in both groups' intersubjectivity talks over the course of LS. The reasons why PSTs at University B showed higher levels of intersubjectivity talks in both pre- and postinterviews could possibly be explained by three factors. First, they were older students with

Table 1.1.
PSTs' Intersubjectivity Talk Development

	Preinterview	Postinterview
University A	25%	66%
University B	54%	85%

more life experiences, second, they have been in field practicum regularly for nine months in classrooms with diverse student population prior to LS, and third they have taken courses on social justice and equity in education, in which they were exposed to a critical lens when considering classroom diversity. In the following sections, examples will illustrate how PSTs' growing awareness of students' perspectives helped generate deeper reflection on their own teaching. Section 4.0 and 4.3 points to experiences relating to PSTs from both universities, while section 4.1 highlights experiences from University A, and section 4.2 highlights experiences from University B.

Complexities of Teaching Diverse Students

In the pre-interviews, PSTs were uncertain about how to work with diverse students in the classrooms. When asked to comment on a *case*, PSTs from University A all discussed how teaching diverse students would be challenging. A statement from an EFL student at University A represents challenges put forward:

> I see it as a very big challenge, to get the lesson to work, the differences are so big, I hardly know, where is the academic level, it is difficult. It shouldn't be too low for those who demand more, and it shouldn't be too high for those who struggle to understand, and in addition to academic levels there are minority language speakers and those with reading difficulties. (University A)

The PSTs also expressed concerns about how, within a larger group of students, to meet individual needs with ranged academic levels. The following quotation from a science student at University A illustrates this concern,

> I don't know how to divide myself into 20 parts, and I am thinking the focus (here) is very much on those who need support, to put it that way, or the weaker students, but I do realize that it is very boring for those who are more clever and need other challenges. (University A)

PSTs at University B, while older and with more classroom experiences, also shared their uncertainty about teaching diverse learners. One student expressed:

> I feel like in *any* discipline, not just in math, you're always gonna have a wide range of student abilities and extra factors coming in ... like, there's a difficult language, and then, you have students who are all gonna learn it differently, and then math on its own can be difficult. (University B)

When PSTs only notice differences among their students or between students and themselves, the idea of meeting the needs of all students may be daunting. The key to bridge this difference is to gain intersubjectivity with students. In the following sections, we will highlight how gaining insight into students' experiences and thinking in the lesson supported PSTs' in reflecting how to teach in a more inclusive manner.

4.1 Focusing on Possibilities Instead of Limitations

During the LS, PSTs observed their students closely. This challenged PSTs' conceptions of students, helping them think differently about students and classroom situations. In the post-interview, the PSTs in EFL at University A discussed how they experienced the changes they had made in the second RL and ways that this improved the level of participation of all the students. One male student pointed:

> Those who raised their hands were relatively strong, but in the last lesson, we saw that also the weaker students were active. Impressively much.... We didn't expect that, that the ADHD and the one with dyslexia were very, very active, and really engaged in this lesson. (University A)

This example shows how the LS process, with its inclusion of student observations and interviews, challenged PSTs preconceived expectations about *"weaker"* students. Similarly, as expressed underneath by a female PST in science, University A, PSTs' ideas about students' participation and learning in lessons in general were confronted during LS:

> Sometimes when you are up front, you think you know who has learned something and those who don't seem to pay attention haven't learned anything. Together with my mentor teacher, I had picked out a case pupil who rarely participates during lessons. I thought that he hadn't learned anything during that lesson, because it looked like that. When I interviewed him he had really learned a lot. Then I interviewed another case pupil, a girl who was really active in the same lesson, and she had not grasped what it was

all about. So you can't conclude that the ones who are the most active have learned the most, At least that is what many of us think, at least that is what I have been thinking. (University A)

In preinterviews, especially at University A, PSTs predominantly discussed student diversity in terms of static characteristics, such as ADHD students or language minority students, the focus being on what the students could *not* do instead of what might be possible. In the post-interviews, after LS, the PSTs discussed student diversity in a more fluid manner. In both groups (University A & B), PSTs expressed their surprise at experiencing what the students had been able to do in the lessons (which they had not expected), and how exciting these new-found possibilities were. The teachers began to understand what the students could do by what they had experienced in the lessons. This helped the PSTs go beyond the 'labels' previously assigned to the students and to have affirming views of diverse students (Villegas & Lucas, 2001).

4.2 Student Thinking to Inform Teaching

LS teams at University B taught lessons on geometry for their elementary-school students, predetermined by the course instructor. They incorporated activities that invited the students to reason spatially, while the formats and levels of reasoning varied across the grade levels taught. For example, the kindergarten students sorted various shapes into rectangles and non-rectangles, and the fifth-grade students created their own rules for categorizing various shapes and guessed each other's rules by looking at the shapes in the categorical groups. After teaching the research lesson, in post-interview, the PSTs in the kindergarten class discussed student thinking in the lesson in terms of what they had anticipated and what was surprising: Below are some examples of what from PSTs indicated as surprising moments for them:

> I think a square and a rectangle were confusing [for students]. For the most part. Except we didn't know that the width of the rectangles was going to affect them so much, or at least I didn't foresee that. (University B)

A PST in a Grade 1 class, when describing her experience in the research lesson, said:

> [What] we didn't expect was … I mean you were talking about the shapes, like, the two different kinds of shapes in each picture, but then they (students) were like doing subclassifications! Just seeing these responses that I didn't expect, really informed me. (University B)

PSTs were learning about student thinking of the content topic by experiencing the very thinking itself, by taking the opportunity to think deeply about possible ways students thought about the content. This occurred during the planning of the lessons. Teaching the lesson opened up yet another window to extend their understanding of student thinking, leading to new learning. The PSTs were also learning how to target their teaching to the level where students were, and how well-targeted lessons would be a key to student engagement. A PST in a Grade 1 class at university B discussed how she changed the research lesson plans based on the data she had collected on student thinking.

> [We] totally revamped our idea for what the actual lesson could be, and it was a good thing that we shifted it to better match our students. But it definitely just took a little bit more brainpower. (University B)

While in teacher education programs, PSTs may learn about the importance of student thinking in planning their lessons. However, without the actual experiences of collecting data on students' current thinking, incorporating the information into their planning, teaching the actual lesson, and experiencing high levels of student engagement in lessons, the acquired knowledge (the importance of student thinking) may not be authentically connected to their actual teaching practices. PSTs can experience and understand the critical role of student thinking in their teaching, and therefore become more aware of how to adapt their teaching in order to meet student diversity.

4.3 Open-Ended Teaching

The increased level of intersubjectivity shown in Table 1.1, might have supported PSTs to embrace new teaching approaches that were more open-ended and inclusive. PSTs also experience challenges in shifting teaching practices (e.g., Cohen, 1990: Gusky, 2002; Stein & Wang, 1988), and face further challenges if they had not experienced this kind of teaching during their own education as students.

At University A, PSTs tended to design more traditional, teacher-led lessons in their first research lessons. A common experience across the teams was that these lessons were too prescriptive. The students were given too much information and procedural directives which resulted in students losing track of what they were supposed to do, and consequently many of them lost interest in the lesson. The following example, from one of the EFL female students upon reflecting on the experience, shows this:

> My group didn't understand the task to start with. We had divided a text into chronological parts. In the first round of the group-work, they didn't understand that they were going to make sentences out of the examples, and even if some of them are cognitively strong students, even they just underlined what was wrong, so they misunderstood the task. (University A)

The LS team revised their second research lesson based on observations and students' feedback from the interviews from the first lesson. As a result, this second lesson had more open-ended tasks, thus allowing more space for students' own ideas and thoughts. As one of the male students in the same group noted:

> And we clearly noticed how the focus was different in the two groups, in the first group they automatically did what they already knew, but in the second lesson their focus was on something new which was more exciting and they had a better time, and it was more interesting for them to study the content than the technicalities. (University A)

Open-ended and less explicit instruction was something PSTs at University B had learned in their mathematics teaching methods course. Instead of the teacher being the primary holder of the knowledge and explaining the procedures in lessons, the content was introduced through a problem, and students develop understanding of the concept by solving the problem. With this approach, it is crucial for teachers to be able to anticipate student thinking, facilitate different ideas in the course of discussion, and connect student ideas with core mathematics concepts. It requires teachers to know the content well, as well as typical student learning progressions, possible errors students make as they develop understanding, different ways to present problems, and how learning can be supported.

In the beginning of the course, planning lessons was not easy for PSTs at University B. They were just becoming aware of their role in creating space for student thinking and the facilitation of learning in the lesson space. One PST commented:

> Even just trying to write it up, like describe what we *thought* they were thinking, was kind of hard. Like, I remember doing that, and we were like, "how are we going to talk about this pattern?" (University B)

Thus, creating space and having the students share ideas was insufficient. As teachers, they needed to be able to make connections between student ideas and further connect them to the mathematics content at hand. While feeling uncertain, PSTs pushed themselves to teach open-ended lessons with the support provided by the structure of LS. The group structure necessitated adhering to the planned lesson, and with the support of their peers, PSTs tried new ways of teaching, which might not have happened if they worked alone.

After teaching RLs, in postinterview, PSTs shared their experiences with open-ended teaching. They enjoyed hearing student ideas and experiencing student learning in a more authentic manner, for the first time for many of them. As one PST noted:

> we noticed the spectrum of skills the students were bringing to the table ... there was room for all of them to participate and bring their different skills ... all students could engage in the lesson and kind of take it to wherever their level was. (University B)

Teaching started to become a shared journey with the students, as student thinking was considered central in the open-ended process. Another PST commented:

> I'm thinking [now] about how to get kids to a place where they're taking on more responsibility and they're more independent. And so one way that I was thinking about ... getting to a point kids are talking to each other, not just to me. I thought that was a big ... *still* a big area of growth for me. (University B)

The open-ended teaching experiences presented PSTs with different possibilities for the future. By developing intersubjectivity and understanding student thinking, PSTs considered students an integral part of classroom instruction and the process of teaching and learning. This heightened students' experiences informed the teaching of PSTs in more-authentic ways.

The LS experience challenged and influenced PSTs' "static" understanding of students and they became more engaged as inquiring professionals (Cochran-Smith et al., 2015) through collecting and analyzing data from the classrooms. Detailed observations from research lessons made PSTs become aware of students' experiences and perspectives. They considered their own teaching, at a deeper level, including affordances and constraints for their students, and this developed a more nuanced and dynamic view of both the students and teaching in diverse classrooms. As a result, more open-ended teaching gave additional room for students to explore and incorporate their own ideas and thoughts. The PSTs were beginning to see themselves as both responsible for and capable of educational change (Gay, 2010; Villegas & Lucas 2002).

Teacher Educators' Reflections

The two authors of this chapter are teacher educators, working at institutions of higher education in two countries (Norway and the United States) with different professional capacities, with PSTs with different cultural and educational backgrounds. We are both committed to bringing social justice to our education systems, and as a part of our effort, including issues of equity into our courses with PSTs. Issues on diversity in education are often raised as issues on social justice, race, ethnicity, gender and ability. In this study, we have chosen a different approach to diversity; to study PSTs' intersubjectivity development through LS as a focused field practicum. We believe this approach will guide our understanding and learning about how PSTs make sense of teaching of diverse students across different educational contexts, thus support us as teacher educators in examining our teaching practices for PSTs with diverse learners in mind (Milner, 2010; Villegas & Lucas 2002).

Working cross-culturally, we had to articulate (more than when we worked with others with similar respective cultural background) and explain what we were seeing in the data to each other. That, in turn, made us further realize about our own assumptions about the topic, and possible biases and preconceived ideas about the research subjects. For example, Murata (2011) considered race as an utmost important issue to address when bridging the gap between teachers and students based on her work in urban U.S. schools, thus focused her attention to PSTs' talk on race. This was not the case in Norwegian schools. Helgevold (2016) foregrounded issues with second-language learners in the classroom as a challenging issue among the Norwegian students, but became aware of the Norwegian PSTs use of a "labeling" language to describe individual students in the classrooms. This language was more prominent among the Norwegian than PSTs in the U.S. Was this way of talking something the PSTs adopted from more-experienced teachers in practicum? Was this an issue to be discussed with mentor teachers and practice schools? Multiple ongoing discussions occurred on these nuanced differences in the data, and that pushed us to become more aware of core ideas about PST development. This was also a way to develop intersubjectivity between ourselves.

Another layer of intersubjectivity development was with PSTs in the study. As we delved into analyzing the data, we came to understand how PSTs were trying to articulate their own understanding of diversity in their effort to teach students whose backgrounds were different from their own. While we do not exactly know each PST's and student's background and therefore the social distance in between, we could use the PSTs' perspectives on this issue to better understand the challenges they identified and focus on their experiences, instead of quickly judging what was missing from their talk. This challenged our assumptions of PSTs, and we started to focus on the possibilities they are presenting in their talk instead of the limitations they had. We could empathize with the PSTs and how our work with PSTs is similar to their work with students of different backgrounds in classrooms. Instead of objectivizing PSTs as voiceless research subjects, we came to see their development and hope for future improvement. We also came to realize that developing intersubjectivity with our PSTs is integral to continuously improving our work.

Working with PSTs from two different educational contexts, we were pressed to make sense of the similar yet different patterns they showed in their intersubjectivity development. Both groups developed intersubjectivity, but the knowledge developed differently across the groups, because of their varied ages and experiences, and the way the two programs guided their progresses. While there are some characteristics shared within the groups, individuals naturally go in and out of the group patterns. Working in this manner, it reminded us how embracing diversity does not mean ignoring individual's membership to a group. By recognizing diversity as an essential issue in education, we tried to find ways to critically approach and include issues of diversity instead of trying to eliminate the differences in our study.

Just as LS helped PSTs in our study experience student thinking in the lessons, it helped us experience PSTs' thinking in the teaching process. By listening to what they said in terms of their developing knowledge on teaching in the interviews, we could learn how they were making sense of their changing roles as teachers and developing knowledge about their students. The process of LS guides teachers through a cycle of teaching, and the data collected in the process could provide valuable information on teacher learning on many fronts.

Using LS itself does not guarantee instructional changes, and we have also learned different ways we should support PSTs to guide their learning throughout the process better. For example, we found that if the lesson is not open-ended enough, the PSTs could focus their attention on surface-level learning of students, which did not deepen their understanding of student learning in a meaningful way. As discussed in the introduction, without focused guidance, LS, as with any other experiences we provide for PSTs, could further reinforce misunderstandings about student diversity and widen the gap (Akiba, 2011; Anderson & Stillman, 2013; Darling-Hammond et al., 2006) between teachers and students. Reflection on the teacher educators' role in teacher education is essential for a number of reasons. In this case of facilitating the LS in such a way that PSTs deepen their knowledge about how to teach subject content, using new teaching methods, and without gaining knowledge about intersubjectivity with their students. As teacher educators, moving our focus towards our colleagues to build shared intersubjectivity could also provide the foundation for new ways of working with diversity, not only within the classroom but also into the field of education.

NOTE

1. We originally started as a part of a larger research study that introduced LS in a teacher education programs in Norway, while additional funding made it possible to collect data from the sample of U.S PSTs for comparative analysis. The Norwegian author translated the transcriptions of the Norwegian interviews into English.

REFERENCES

Ainscow, M. & Miles, S. Prospects (2008) Making Education for All inclusive: where next? *Prospects, 38*(1), 15. Retrieved from https://doi.org/10.1007/s11125-008-9055-0

Akiba, M. (2011). Identifying program characteristics for preparing pre-service teachers for diversity. *Teachers College Record, 113*(3), 658–697.

Anderson, L. M., & Stillman, J. A. (2013). Student teaching's contribution to pre-service teacher development: A review of research focused on the preparation of teachers for urban and high-needs contexts. *Review of Educational Research, 83*(1), 3–69.

Ball, D. L. (1993). With an eye on the mathematical horizon: Dilemmas of teaching elementary school mathematics. *The Elementary School Journal, 93*(4), 373–397.

Banks, J., Cochran-Smith, M., Moll, L., Richert, A., Zeichner, K., LePage, P., Darling-Hammond, L., Duffy, H., & McDonald, M., (2005). Teaching diverse learners. In L. Darling-Hammond & J. Bransford (Eds.), *Preparing teachers for a changing world: What teachers should learn and be able to do* (pp. 232–275) San Francisco, CA: Jossey-Bass.

Cochran-Smith, M., Villegas, A. M., Abrams, L., Chavez-Moreno, L., Mills, T., & Stern, R. (2015). Critiquing teacher preparation research: an overview of the field, Part II. *Journal of Teacher Education, 66*(2), 109–121.

Chokshi, S., & Fernandez, C. (2004). Challenges to importing Japanese lesson study: Concerns, misconceptions, and nuances. *Phi Delta Kappan, 85*(7), 520–525.

Cohen, D. (1990). A revolution in one classroom: The case of Mrs. Oublier. *Educational Evluation and Policy Analysis, 12*(3), 311–329.

Darling-Hammond, L., & Lieberman, A. (Eds.). (2012). *Teacher education around the world. Changing policies and practices.* London, England: Routledge.

Darling-Hammond L., Hammerness K., Grossmann P., Rust, F., & Shulmann, L. (2006). The design of teacher education programs. In L. Darling-Hammond & J. Bransford (Eds.), *Preparing teachers for a changing world.* San Francisco, CA: Jossey-Bass (The Jossey-Bass Education Series).

Dudley, P. (2013). Teacher learning in lesson study: What interaction-level discourse analysis revealed about how teachers utilised imagination, tacit knowledge of teaching, and fresh evidence of pupils' learning, to develop practice knowledge and so enhance their pupils' learning. *Teaching and Teacher Education, 34,* 107–121.

Feiman-Nemser, S. (2001). From preparation to practice: Designing a curriculum to Strengthen and sustain teaching. *Teacher College Record, 103*(6), 1013–1055.

Fernandez, M. (2005). Learning through microteaching lesson study in teacher preparation. *Action in Teacher Education, 26*(4), 37–47.

Fujita, H., Hashimoto, Y., & Hodgson, B. R. (2004). *Proceedings of the Ninth International Congress of Mathematics Education.* Norwell, MA: Kluwer.

Garmon, M. A. (2004). Changing preservice teachers' attitudes/beliefs about diversity what are the critical factors? *Journal of Teacher Education, 55*(3), 201–213.

Gay, G. (2010). Acting on beliefs in teacher education for cultural diversity. *Journal of Teacher Education, 61*(1–2), 143–152.

Gusky, T. R. (2002). Professional development and teacher change. *Teachers and Teaching: Theory and Practice, 8*(3.4), 381–392.

Helgevold, N. (2016). Teaching as creating space for participation—Establishing a learning community in diverse classrooms. *Teachers and Teaching, 22*(3), 315–328.

Helgevold, N., Næsheim-Bjørkvik, G., & Østrem, S. (2015). Key focus areas and use of tools in mentoring conversations in initial teacher education. *Teaching and Teacher Education, 49*(7), 128–137

Hollins, E. R., & Guzman, M. T. (2005). Research on preparing teachers for diverse populations. *Studying teacher education: The report of the AERA panel on research and teacher education*, 477–548.

Ladson-Billings, G. (2001). *Crossing over to Canaan: The journey of new teachers in diverse classrooms. The Jossey-Bass Education Series.* San Francisco, CA: Jossey-Bass.

Lewis, C., Perry, R., & Murata, A. (2006). What is the role of the research in an emerging innovation?: The case of Lesson Study. *Educational Researcher, 35*(3), 3–14.

Lewis, C., & Tsuchida, I. (1998). A Lesson is like a swiftly flowing river. *American Educator.* Retrieved April 24, 2019, from https://www.ncetm.org.uk/public/files/34863/swift+flowing+river.pdf.

Matusov. E., & Smith, M.P. (2007). Teaching imaginary children: University students' narratives about their Latino practicum children. *Teaching and Teacher Education, 23,* 705–729.

Milner, H. R. (2010). What does teacher education have to do with teaching? Implications for diversity studies. *Journal of Teacher Education, 61*(1–2), 118–131.

Murata, A. (2011). Introduction: Conceptual overview of Lesson Study. In L. C. Hart, A. S Alston, & A. Murata (Eds.), *Lesson study: Research and practice in mathematics education: Learning together* (pp. 1–12). New York, NY: Springer.

Murata, A. & Takahashi, A. (2002). Vehicle to connect theory, research, and practice: How teacher thinking changes in district-level Lesson Study in Japan. In D. L. Haury (Ed.), *Proceedings of the twenty-fourth annual meeting of North American chapter of the international group of the Psychology of Mathematics Education,* pp. 1879–1888.

Richardson, V., & Placier, P. (2001). Teacher change. In V. Richardson (Ed.), *Handbook of research on teaching* (4th ed.). Washington DC: American Educational Research Association.

Rommetveit, R. (2003). On the role of "a psychology of the second person" in studies of meaning, language, and mind. *Mind, Culture and Activity, 10*(3), 205–218.

Sleeter, C. E., & Owuor, J. (2011). Research on the impact of teacher preparation to teach diverse students: The research we have and the research we need. *Action in Teacher Education, 33*(5–6), 524–536.

Stein, M. K., & Wang, M. C. (1988). Teacher development and school improvement: The process of teacher change. *Teaching and Teacher Education, 4*(2), 171–187.

Taylor, S. V., & Sobel, D. (2001). Addressing the discontinuity of students' and teachers' diversity: A preliminary study of preservice teachers' beliefs and perceived skills. *Teaching and Teacher Education, 17*(4), 487–503.

Villegas, A. M., & Lucas, T. (2002). Preparing culturally responsive teachers rethinking the curriculum. *Journal of Teacher Education, 53*(1), 20–32.

Wertsch, J. V. (1998). *Mind as action*. New York, NY: Oxford University Press.

APPENDIX: EXCERPTS FROM INTERVIEW PROTOCOLS.

Preinterview

The following case was given as a handout (The case was adjusted for the Norwegian students taking subject content courses in natural science, English as foreign language and physical education):

Lisa is a new third grade math teacher. What concerns her most is how to provide all her students the opportunity to learn as much as possible.

Lisa: The students in my class have very different attitudes about school in general and math in particular, ranging from those who are highly motivated to learn to those who don't seem to care in the slightest. Of course, this doesn't just affect their grades but also levels of focus and the learning environment generally. Some of them are so interested in math that they do extra math at home. These students get good support and follow-up from their parents. Others don't seem to do any math work at all, either at school or at home. Part of what is especially difficult is that many of my students do not seem to be prepared to learn the 3rd grade material. I also have six students who have reading difficulties and five whose first language is not English and who have only been living in the U.S. for a short time. How can I help my students learn?

1. What are your own feelings about this situation? Does anything strike you as especially difficult?
2. What kinds of issues do you think Lisa will encounter when she teaches a class of children with many different needs?

3. What do you think Lisa means when she talks about students who are not prepared to learn third grade material?
4. What kinds of question do you think Lisa should be asking herself?
5. How would you plan this lesson?
6. What do you think would be a reasonable learning objective for the first lesson?
7. What would you keep in mind when deciding how to teach this topic?
8. What would you expect to be especially difficult for third grade students learning multiplication for the first time?
9. How will you assess whether the students have achieved your learning objectives?

Postinterview

1. How did you go about making sense of the student interview data?
2. In planning lessons, did you have several lesson ideas? If so, please describe them. Why did you choose the lesson that you chose? Where did the ideas come from and how did you decide which one to use for the research lesson? How did you use the information gained from student interview to inform lesson planning?
3. Did you find it challenging to anticipate student responses to each question/problem you posed when writing the lesson plan? Please give one example from your group discussions and describe how you came to the several anticipated responses written in your lesson plan.
4. How did the debriefing of the lesson go? What did you learn from your peers' observation (if you taught the lesson) or by observing your peer teach the lesson you had planned together?
5. What did you learn most from LS?

CHAPTER 2

EXAMINING EFFICACY OF EQUITY EDUCATION

Challenging Uncritical and Laminated Notions of Equity in Teacher Education

Ann E. Lopez

Introduction

All across the globe societies are becoming more diverse due to population shifts and schools are becoming more ethnically, racially and linguistically diverse (Lopez, 2018). In Australia, Canada and the United States the percentage of racialized people is increasing and represent a large percentage of the students in public schools. Educators at all levels are called on to respond to this new reality to ensure that students from diverse backgrounds experience success in schools. Educational practices and policies predicated on the assumption of homogeneity are no longer meaningful or appropriate in today's reality. Teachers are in classrooms where languages and cultures are different from their own. Darling-Hammond (2011) suggests that teachers must become aware of these cultural influences on learning.

Transformative Pedagogies for Teacher Education:
Critical Action, Agency, and Dialogue in Teaching and Learning Contexts, pp. 19–35
Copyright © 2019 by Information Age Publishing
All rights of reproduction in any form reserved.

These changes necessitate teachers becoming more equitable in their approach so that all students can see themselves and their experiences represented in the curriculum. This has precipitated calls for more attention to be paid to equity in education at all levels. Attempts at equity education have taken on various forms and perspectives. Lee (2009) for example suggests that equity within the Canadian context has often come to mean a superficial response to diversity in the form of dances, clothing, dialect, and food without examining power relations. Improved educational outcomes for students, particularly racially and ethnically diverse students who are underserved by the education system, require critical approaches to equity education.

Teacher education and the preparation of teacher candidates play an important role in this endeavor. While teacher candidates will not acquire all the knowledge that they will need to work with diverse students in their teacher education programs, it is important that they develop the habits of mind to teach students who are different from them. Grant and Gibson (2011) suggest that students from diverse communities require different educational approaches and practices and teacher education programs have a duty to prepare future teachers to effectively engage with diverse communities and students.

Addressing culturally, ethnically, linguistically, racially diverse and other aspects of difference has become a focus for critical scholars and researchers through frameworks such as antiracist education, anti-oppressive education, critical multicultural education, culturally responsive pedagogy and other forms of equity pedagogies. Education provides an opportunity for people with challenging circumstances to improve their chances in life. In that regard, many see education as a way of leveling the playing field. Diverse communities have lost confidence in the ability of public schools to serve the needs of culturally, ethnically, linguistically diverse students (Nieto, 2004) and this trust must be restored. A positive relationship between schools and the communities they serve benefits students and the community. Auerbach (2010) suggests authentic school-community partnerships include respectful alliances among educators, families, and community groups. This involves relationship building which is crucial, dialogue and sharing of power, all key ingredients in developing socially just, democratic schools.

Schooling structures and practices in many Western countries continue to represent the knowledge and experiences of those who hold power, and exclude the knowledge and experiences that reside in diverse communities. To address this disparity that is often represented in the curriculum, pedagogy and leadership practices, educators in many countries have sought to implement various equity initiatives. In Canada for example, starting in the 1970s the Ontario provincial government implemented various initiatives to address educational inequities, particularly for students of color. In 1979 the Ontario Ministry of Education developed a *Policy on Race and Ethnocultural Equity* (Mock, 1989) and in 1993 the *Antiracism and Ethnocultural Equity in School Boards*. The intent of the *Antiracism and Ethnocultural Policy* (1993) was outlined as follows:

> The intent of antiracist and ethnocultural equity education is to ensure that all students achieve their potential and acquire accurate knowledge and information, as well as confidence in their cultural and racial identities. It should equip all students with the knowledge, skills, attitudes, and behaviors needed to live and work effectively in an increasingly diverse world, and encourage them to appreciate diversity and reject discriminatory attitudes and behavior. (p. 1)

In 2009 the Ontario Ministry of Education introduced *Ontario's Equity and Inclusive Education Strategy* which was later updated in 2014. The strategy provided a framework for teachers, teacher educators and school administrators to address issues of equity in their daily work. The strategy among other things called for:

> An equitable, inclusive education system is one in which all students, parents and other members of the school community are welcomed and respected, and every student is supported and inspired to succeed in a culture of high expectations for learning. (p. 5)

Three priorities were highlighted in *Ontario's Equity and Inclusive Education Strategy* (2009, 2014). These include increasing student achievement, closing gaps in student achievement, and increasing public confidence in publicly funded education. A key element of the strategy was the recognition that achieving equity must be understood as a journey, not as a destination. The work equity and inclusive education must be ongoing to ensure that schools continue to provide caring, inclusive, safe, and accepting environments that support the achievement and well-being of every student. Educators are urged to think of equity and inclusive education is an ongoing process that requires shared commitment and leadership in response to the ever-evolving, complex issues and concerns of communities and schools (Ontario Equity and Inclusive Strategy, 2009, 2014). Teacher education has been a focus of equity initiatives as it is important that new teachers develop a deep understanding of the issue for lasting and sustainable change to occur. In this chapter drawing on research that I conducted with teacher candidates in a large teacher education program in Southern Ontario, Canada my experiences as a classroom teacher, school administrator, administrator in a teacher education program and teacher educator, I explore what it means to engage in equity education from a critical perspective, the impact of neoliberalism on the equity agenda, and approaches to support the development of teacher candidates toward a critical and unlaminated forms of equity education (Lopez, 2013, 2019). I use the term laminated forms of equity to describe approaches and polices that are framed and placed on walls, in documents but are not acted on and that do not bring about real change in the lives of students.

Critical Approach to Equity

The term "equity" is widely used, but rarely understood (Solomon, Singer, Campbell, Allen, & Portelli, 2011). Equity is premised upon the recognition that all children have different identities and lived experiences and there must be a commitment to meet the needs of all students so that they can grow up and have a successful life (Blankenstein & Noguera, 2015). Given the increasing diversity in schools it is important to re-examine what we mean by equity education, how teachers understand, operationalize and embed in their daily work (Lopez, 2013) The notion of equity that is foregrounded in this chapter is a critical one that examines what is "taken for granted" (Simon, 1992, as cited in Solomon et al., 2011), and "raises questions about the social and political implications of the often unexamined daily practices of teachers" (Solomon et al., 2011, p. 20).

Issues of equity are important to students, communities, parents, policy makers, educational leaders, teachers, and teacher educators. Apple (1996), Freire (1993 and 1973) and other critical scholars call for injustices to be named and addressed, power to be challenged, and educators to engage in activism and resistance to the status quo. As equity initiatives proliferate in education, Ladson-Billings (2014) warns against lack of criticality and initiatives that merely represent masked neoliberal approaches to education that do not challenge the status quo, but appropriate terms such as "equity," "diversity," and "culturally responsive" to be more appealing. Ladson-Billings urge educators to ensure that their work has a critical edge that pushes students to "consider critical perspectives on policies and practices that may have direct impact on their lives and communities" (p. 78). She also called for educators to move away from gestures such as "adding some books about people of color, having a Kwanzaa celebration, or posting diverse images" (p. 79) as examples of critical work.

Equity Versus Equality

The concept of equity can be conceptualized in different ways and is sometimes taken to be synonymous with equality. It is important for teacher candidates to understand this distinction. Many enter the teaching profession having succeeded in an education system and society based on meritocracy. They bring ideas of creating "equality" in society as a cause to take up in pursuit of a more just world. Many teacher candidates prior to entering teachers college have never examined the difference between equity and equality, and believe that treating everyone equally is a way to address injustices in society. Attempts to operationalize equitable practices and pursuit of fairness can be challenging for some as an equitable understanding of fairness often seems counterintuitive as it does not necessarily entail equal treatment (Solomon et al., 2011). It cannot be overstated how important an understanding of this distinction is, particularly for teachers and teacher candidates who are called on to make decisions in classrooms everyday that impact the lives of students and their educational outcomes.

The Ontario Ministry of Education (2016) posits that equity is a "condition or state of fair, inclusive and respectful treatment of all people." Equity does not mean treating people the same without regard for individual differences. The Toronto District School Board (TDSB, 2014, 2018) notes that equity is "providing each and every student with the conditions that support achievement and well-being. It is about supporting not only the students who are falling behind, but raising the bar for all students" (p. 1). The TDSB (2014) which has been at the forefront of many equity initiatives in K–12 public education in the Province of Ontario, offers the following distinction between equality and equity. Equality is the:

> Achievement of equal status in society in terms of access to opportunities support, rewards, and economic and social power for all without regards to race, color, creed, culture, ethnicity, linguistic origin, religion, sex, gender identity, gender expression, sexual orientation, family status or marital status. (p. 30)

Equity on the other hand:

> Ensures equality of opportunities and outcomes for all by responding fair and proportionality to the needs of individuals. Equity is not the same as equal treatment because it recognizes a socio-cultural power imbalance that unfairly privilege some while oppressing others and therefore focusses on redressing disparity—meeting individual needs to ensure fair access, outcomes and participation that results in equality, acknowledging historical and present systemic discrimination against identified groups and removing barriers, eliminating discrimination and remedying the impact of past discrimination and current oppression. Equity practices ensure fair, inclusive and respectful treatment of all people, with consideration of individual and group diversities and intersectionality of multiple social identities, access to privileges and impacts of oppression. Equity honors and accommodates the specific needs of individuals. (p. 32)

Maitzegui-Onate and Santibanez-Gruber (2008) suggest that notions of equity must acknowledge the existence of unequal treatment in education processes, recognize education as basic right, and the fair distribution of "educational" assets must be safeguarded. They suggest further that if equity is not present in the educational system, students will be denied opportunities to achieve their full potential.

Inequities in Education

In many Western nations, poor, Black, Hispanic, and non-native English speakers are least likely to have access to quality education, and they are most likely to attend segregated low-quality schools (Braithwaite, 2017). Despite the good work of many dedicated and talented teachers, there is a crisis with inequality in public schools that denies poor children and children of color a high-quality education (Zeichner, 2009). If we are to advance notions of equity that are critical, particularly in teacher education, teacher candidates must become aware of the inequities that continue to exist in schools. Research show that despite the increased diversity in schools, teaching staffs remain predominantly White and middle class (Bradley-Levine, 2018; Ryan, Pollock, & Antonelli, 2009). While schools are becoming increasingly diverse, only a small percentage of teachers share similar backgrounds with their students, resulting in a significant teacher-student diversity gap (Trejo, 2017). We know from research when teachers reflect the demographics of students in their classrooms, students benefit. These benefits include more culturally relevant pedagogy, higher student expectations, and perspectives that challenge negative stereotypes of diverse students. Research in K–12 schools continue to show a positive correlation between teachers of color and improved academic performance by students of color who have these teachers in their classrooms (Achinstein & Ogawa, 2011).

Inequities in education persist in many countries despite efforts at equity education. In Canada for example, research show that Black students are being suspended at a higher rate and are not achieving the same academic success as White students. Research conducted by James and Turner (2017) with the Toronto District School Board, Canada's largest school Board shows that Black students are being suspended more compared to other students, and are being streamed into lower academic[1] classes at a larger rate than other students. The data reveal that by the time Black students graduate from high school, 42% of them have been suspended at least once compared to only 18% of White students. Over the years, the disproportionately high rates of suspension and expulsions of Black students, Indigenous students and students with disabilities have been identified as ongoing issue. The implementation of the Ontario Safe Schools Act (2000) under a former Conservative government saw the issue of school suspensions entering the public discourse as it related to Black, Indigenous, and students with special needs. Ruck and Wortley (2002) examined the perceptions of differential treatment relating to school disciplinary practices by high school students of Black, South Asian, Asian, White, and "other" (Aboriginal, Hispanic, and mixed-race) racial backgrounds in Toronto. They found that racial minority students, particularly Black students were much more likely than White students to perceive discrimination with respect to teacher treatment, school suspension practices, the use of police by school authorities and police treatment at school.

Data released in 2013 by the TDSB showed that Black students were three times more likely than their White counterparts to be suspended from school (Rankin, Rushowy, & Brown, 2013). Fact sheet prepared by the Ontario Alliance of Black School Educators (2017) show the following data collected by the TDSB from the 2006–2011 cohort of students:

- While 11% of the student population in the cohort self-identified as Black, Black students are more than twice as likely as their White peers to be suspended at least once during high school.
- Over half of the Black students in this cohort (56%) identified two countries of origin—Jamaica (41%) and Somalia (15%). Nine percent of Black students are at least third generation Canadian, e.g., they were born in Canada to Canadian-born parents
- Black students are three times as likely than White students to be in the Essentials program of study and two and a half times as likely to be in Applied. By contrast, White students are one and a half times as likely than their Black peers to be in the Academic program of study.
- A greater proportion of Black students than their White peers are identified with non-gifted special education needs. Only 0.4% of Black students are identified as gifted, compared to 4% of their White counterparts. Conversely, 16% of White students are identified with other special education needs compared with 26% of Black students.
- Black students have a drop-out rate almost twice that of their White peers, while the graduation rate of Black students is 15 percentage points below that of their White peers.
- White students are almost twice as likely to leave high school and attend an Ontario university than their Black peers. Black students don't apply to go on to postsecondary education at almost the same rate as White students go on to Ontario universities.

Up until recently school boards in Ontario did not collect data based on race. Following the lead of the TDSB, two more school boards have agreed to collect race based data which will yield more comprehensive statistics from across the Greater Toronto Area. Some scholars (see Dei, Mazzuca, McIsaac, & Zine, 1997) have argued that students of color are being "pushed out" of school by practices that do not reflect their lived experiences. Similar conditions exist in the United States and other Western countries.

While graduation rates for students of color in the U.S. have increased over time, inequalities by race have persisted (Chapman, Laird, Infill, & KewalRamani, 2011). Black and Hispanic students are both more likely than whites and Asians to be poor and to attend low-performing schools. Black and Hispanic youth are more likely to earn a GED instead of a conventional high school diploma (Braithwaite, 2017). High dropout rates for some students of color persist and lack of readiness for college. African American students are less likely to be ready for college, especially those coming from high-poverty schools (Moore et al., 2010). In Australia, research has found that educational inequality has cost the Australian economy more than 20 billion dollars. This has contributed to the widening gap between rich and poor, Indigenous children and newly arrived migrants who are disproportionately represented in the lower percentile groups. The report from the Public Education Foundation (2018) found that students at the bottom of Australia's schooling system were falling further behind, despite increased spending on education, with their socioeconomic status and parents' education remaining key factors. Social structures in many Western countries continue to be based on biased, discriminatory and structural inequity which must be challenged in order to achieve equitable outcomes for those oppressed by the system (Solomon, et al., 2011).

Equitable Education and the Neoliberal Agenda

The promise of a better and more just society through increasingly inclusive and equitable public education has captured the educational imagination of critical educators through much of the 20th century (Kaur, 2012), but this promise has yet to be realized in many countries and education systems. Bringing about this change has not been easy as those who hold power seek to keep the status quo in place and ideologies undergirded by meritocracy flourish. Apple (2001) argues that efforts at creating more equitable education has been eroded with the rise of neoliberal ideologies that dominate educational discourses around the world. Education in many countries has been impacted by the rise of a neoliberal political, economic, and cultural agenda (Connell, 2013). This is manifested in calls for more standardization, reduce funding for public education, assaults on the teaching profession, and emphasis on accountability. Neoliberal educational strategies focus on high-stakes accountability, increased assessment, and school choice. As Braithwaite (2017) suggests under neoliberal education reform, schools are mandated to increase the number of assessments they administer and are penalized or rewarded according to student performance.

Drawing on examples from Australia Connell (2013) argues that under a neoliberal agenda "increasingly, education has been defined as an industry, and educational institutions have been forced to conduct themselves more and more like profit-seeking firms" (p. 102). Under a neoliberal education agenda, the focus of schools has shifted to serving the needs of individuals rather than the collective good of society. Neoliberalism ignores structural inequalities in access and opportunity, and shifts responsibility for high-quality education from the state to the individual, under an ideology that centralizes and confines power to capital and corporations (Solomon et al., 2011). Neoliberal policy ignores racial and socioeconomic inequalities, creates an illusion of meritocracy, where all students are perceived to have equal access to a high-quality education when in reality this is not so. Nonetheless, this perceived equality of opportunity drives an education agenda that some will never fear well by, and when they fail poor outcomes are attributed to families and individual decision- making, rather than the inequalities that exist in society. Good outcomes are attributed to individual merit and hard work (Braithwaite, 2017).

Under neoliberal reforms, the prevalence of testing has reshaped the curriculum in low performing schools to focus primarily on basic skills, while students in better-performing schools are exposed to a wider variety of knowledge and critical thinking skills (Giroux, 2012). Those with a neoliberal agenda view education as preparation for the workplace and the generation of capital. Within this construction of the role of education is the desire to educate new teachers with the skills and knowledge of how to become more competitive within a market-driven globalized economy (Solomon et al., 2011). The task for critical educators is to find space in this environment for equity, diversity and social justice. It is not easy. It can be done and must be done and how we educate teacher candidates is important in this effort.

Notwithstanding the onslaught of neoliberal education ideologies critical educators must continue to pursue equitable education goals and challenge inequities in education. This must be a shared effort that includes students, teachers, school leaders, teacher educators, parents, and community activists. As governments, schools and school boards highlight equity initiatives we must guard against what I refer to as *laminated forms of equity* (Lopez, 2013, 2014). These are policies that sound good on paper, they are framed, laminated and placed on walls in schools, but nothing changes materially in the lives and experiences of marginalized and underserved students.

Changing the attitudes of teachers toward students of color and those outside of the dominant culture is not only an ethical imperative, but an urgent one given the changing demographic landscape (Solomon et al., 2011). It is important that we engage in education practices that is transformative and create lasting change. Solomon et al argues that:

> Transformative schooling requires all stakeholders to work together to create educational spaces that engage with difference in non-reductionist ways, and that enable teacher candidates to critically process contradictions between their own past experiences and perceptions concerning social difference and social justice, and what they will be learning from others' diverse experiences and perceptions. The hope and logic underlying this work is that by holds that by fleshing out and grappling with these incongruities, shifting cognitive frameworks, and often ambivalent emotional variables considering difference, prospective teachers will develop enhanced critical thinking skills, which in turn will lead to a more inclusive world view and a desire to create progressive and socially just classroom environments. (p. 186)

Zeichner and Flessner (2009) suggest that teacher education programs must prepare teachers for the global demands of the 21st century, and that this preparation must be grounded in an anti-oppressive framework. Even though challenging, more and more teacher education programs are attempting to achieve this task by including urban education, social justice, diversity and equity in their programs.

Supporting Teacher Development Toward a Critical Approach to Equity

There is an urgent need for schools and faculties of education to adequately prepare teachers for the racial and ethnocultural diversity that exists in Canadian and other Western societies (Dlamini, 2002). We need to develop a diverse body of students who will enter the teaching profession. This starts in the classroom. As Kohli and Pizzaro (2016) assert, the approaches of predominantly White teaching staffs in schools are often condescending and reflect a lack of commitment to the academic success of Black and Latina/o students and to their community. It is against this backdrop of changing demographics and shifting sociocultural contexts that these approaches are situated.

The following approaches are grounded in critical notions of equity to support teacher candidates on their journey. Paris (2016) urges teacher educators to think about how teacher candidates are prepared to disrupt foundational racism, foster racial equity, and advance an asset and strength-based approach to teaching and learning. Paris suggests that radical and critical approaches to teaching and learning have been obscured in teacher education, for practices that support less radical forms such as "tolerance," "diversity," and "inclusion." I agree with Paris that more critical approaches must be embedded across teacher education programs in all aspects of teaching and learning.

I outline three approaches that I believe will support teacher candidates to develop critical approaches to equity education. In this process teaching skills, strategies and pedagogical moves are grounded in the political, ideological and moral commitments of teacher candidates (Paris, 2016). Firstly, that teacher candidates should be encouraged to engage in critical self-reflection. In this process opportunities are provided for teacher candidates to examine what they bring to the classroom in the form of their personal histories, identities, values and beliefs. According to Solomon and Levine-Rasky, (2003) beliefs guide teachers' classroom practices and inform their pedagogical choices, assessment design and interaction with students. It is important for teacher candidates and teacher educators to engage in self-interrogation to excavate biases and assumptions that they may hold about people who are different from them. Social distancing and dissonance have created challenges for some teacher candidates to proactively engage in critical equity education. Narrowing this gap requires shifting of perspectives, understanding one's social location, experiences and privileges. This might necessitate unlearning for some teacher candidates which can create discomfort. We learn from and through discomfort. Space must be created where teacher candidates can engage in the journey of deep self-reflection, leading to action.

Dewey (1933) suggested that reflection is an important aspect of learning and argued that experience alone does not necessarily lead to learning. Dewey identified three attributes of reflective teachers: open-mindedness, responsibility, and wholeheartedness. These are important attributes that teacher candidates must develop to take on the many challenging issues they will face in schools. Freire (1973) noted that reflection is important in developing critical consciousness where learners become actors, not observers, and authors of their own decisions. Mezirow (1990) suggests "transformative reflection" involves looking at what is known with a view towards understanding how it can become better leading to a change in personal understanding and behavior. As they engage in this critical reflection, teacher candidates are encouraged to use journals not only to write their thoughts down, but so they can look back and see their own evolution and process. Reflection as part of a cycle of learning involves planning, action, and evaluation (Kolb, 1984).

Second, I suggest supporting teacher candidates to become advocates and proactively engage in social justice activism becoming advocates for educational equity. Teacher advocacy is the ethical pursuit of social justice and critical practice (Bradley-Levine, 2018) which requires teachers to take a political stance (Marshall & Anderson, 2009). Achinstein and Athanases (2005) suggest when teacher candidates become advocates for students, this can lead to the development of positive relationships with communities. Picower (2012) suggests that "teacher activists" are "educators who work for social justice both inside and outside of their classrooms" (p. 562). Towards this goal Picower identified what she refers to as "commitments." These "commitments" allow teacher activists to pursue social justice on behalf of their students. They involve the belief that education can simultaneously emancipate and oppress students. In this regard teacher activists organize their classrooms to be democratic and caring learning spaces, utilizing place-based and culturally relevant instructional approaches to empower students.

Teacher activists take action outside of the school and work with parents to create change (Lopez, 2016), and seek solidarity with other teachers through collective struggle on behalf of their students rather than themselves (Stern & Brown, 2016). When teachers become engaged with communities this can take a variety of forms. Sometimes they become "personally involved with an issue or movement; promoting social justice through personal intervention, program creation, or by extending the curriculum; or simply taking up cases to get just and equitable treatment for individual students" (Marshall & Anderson, 2009, p. 11). Bradley-Levine (2018) suggests that this type of activism takes place both within and outside of classroom and school spaces, and requires a willingness to vocally share one's political stance outside the classroom and school. Teacher candidates should be encouraged to become advocates through engagement with the course work, practicum placements and social causes in the community. Some come to teachers college with a habit of mind for advocacy for others it is a new journey.

Third, I recommend using critical incidents as a pedagogical tool to develop a critical approach to equity in teacher education classes. Critical incidents are moments of deep learning from practice that cause us to think and engage in deep reflection about things that trouble us (Griffin, 2003; Tripp, 2012). Critical incidents provide a deeper and profound level of reflection of an event or occurrence, because in addition to a detailed description of the event that created moments of deep learning, it also involves analysis and reflection on the meaning of the event (Griffin, 2003). Critical Incidents (Tripp, 2012) as a pedagogical tool give preservice teachers a way to think critically and reflectively about their practice.

Critical incidents can be posed as problems of practice that create learning and might pose more questions in the process. The purpose of utilizing this pedagogical approach is to create agency among teacher candidates to act within their sphere of influence in their classrooms to create change. Tripp (2012) outlined four essential ingredients in using "Critical Incidents" in teaching. These include (a) describe and explain the incident; (b) find a general meaning and classification for the incident; (c) take a position regarding the general meaning; and (d) describe the actions to be taken. Teacher educators are urged to support teacher candidates in examining critical incidents that they experience through critical lens. Critical incidents are highly charged moments that evoke real learning and can be transformative. Space must be provided for teacher candidates to debrief and deconstruct of their experiences. In my experience as a teacher educator examining these critical incidents particularly as they relate to issues of equity can lead to deep learning for teacher candidates.

Conclusion

Given the growing diversity in Canada and other Western countries, schools and educators have a duty to respond, not by promoting neoliberal ideologies and feel good approaches to equity, but by challenging in critical ways inequities that prevent some students from reaching their full potential. Diversity is an asset to nations and must be addressed in order to have a complete history of the knowledge that have impacted human growth and development (Dei, 1996). Teachers must become aware of the cultural influences on learning, the structure and substance of inequality (Darling-Hammond, 2011). Teacher education programs must ensure that teacher candidates develop strategies, to work with the diversity presented in classrooms (Hollins, 2008; Villegas & Davis, 2008) as well as the habit of mind (Hollins, McIntyre, DeBose, Hollins, & Touner, 2004) to work with students who are socialized differently from them. Grant and Gibson (2011) suggest that, "marginalized student populations require different dispositions, beliefs, and practices than that traditionally present in teacher education program" (p. 24). This requires critical and reflexive action by teacher candidates to become agentive in gaining a deeper understanding of students and more effective ways to teach them. Freire (1970/1993) remind educators that "to surmount the situation of oppression, people must first critically recognize its causes, so that through transforming action they can create a new situation, one which makes possible the pursuit of a fuller humanity" (p. 47). It is the hope that new teachers entering the field will carry with them a critical stance that challenges inequities (Lopez, 2011) and advocate for those who have been traditionally ignored or dismissed (Bradley-Levine, 2018). Solomon et al. (2011) ask: How do we know when society and schools are more equitable? They posit that in the event of such an equitable transformation, many of the problems experienced by minoritized, racialized, and low-income students would be eliminated, leading to greater success and inevitably to more equal representation and achievement in educational, social and political structures. (p. 17)

Critical equity work requires the commitment of teacher educators, school leaders, students, communities, and parents to bring about change.

NOTE

1. In Ontario students are streamed into three pathways, academic, applied, and workplace. Students in the academic stream are prepared for university, those in the applied stream are prepared for colleges, and those in the workplace stream are prepared to enter the workforce.

REFERENCES

Achinstein, B., & Athanases, S. Z. (2005). Focusing new teachers on diversity and equity: Toward a knowledge base for mentors. *Teaching and Teacher Education: An International Journal of Research and Studies, 21*(7), 843–862.

Achinstein B., & Ogawa, R. T. (2011). *Changed(d) agents: New teachers of color in urban schools*. New York, NY: Teachers College Press.

Apple, M. (1996). Power, meaning and identity: Critical sociology of education in the United States. *British Journal of Sociology in Edu*cation, *17*(2), 125–144.

Apple, M. W. (2001). Comparing neo-liberal projects and inequality in education. *Comparative Education, 37*(4), 409–423.

Auerbach, S. (2010). Beyond coffee with the principal: Toward leadership for authentic school–family partnerships. *Journal of School Leadership, 20*(6), 728–757.

Blankenstein, A. M., & Noguera, P. (2015). *Excellence through equity: Five principles of courageous leadership to guide achievement for every student*. Alexandria, VA: ASCD.

Bradley-Levine, J. (2018). Advocacy as a practice of critical teacher leadership. *International Journal of Teacher Leadership, 9*(1) 47–58.

Braithwaite, J. (2017). Neoliberal education reform and the perpetuation of inequality. *Critical Sociology, 43*(3), 429–448

Chapman, C., Laird, J., Ifill, N., & Kewal Ramani, A. (2011). *Trends in high school dropout and completion rates in the United States: 1972–2009*. Washington, DC: National Center for Education Statistics.

Connell, R. (2013). The neoliberal cascade and education: An essay on the market agenda and its consequences. *Critical Studies in Education, 54*(2), 99–112.

Darling-Hammond, L. (2011). Studying diversity in teacher education. In A. Ball & C. Tyson (Eds.), *Studying diversity in teacher education* (pp. ix–x). New York, NY: Rowman and Littlefield. Published in Partnership with AERA

Dei, G. S. (1996). *Anti-racism: Theory and practice.* Halifax, England: Fernwood.

Dei, G. S., Mazzuca, J., McIsaac, E., & Zine, J. (1997). *Reconstructing drop-Out: A Critical ethnography of the dynamics of Black students' disengagement from\school.* Toronto, ON: University of Toronto Press.

Dewey J. (1933). *How we think: A restatement of the relation of reflective thinking to the education process.* Boston, MA: D.C. Heath & Co.

Dlamini, S. N. (2002). From the other side of the desk: Notes on teaching about racism when racialized. *Race Ethnicity and Education,* 5(1), 51–66.

Freire, P. (1993). *Pedagogy of the oppressed.* New York, NY: Continuum. (Original work published 1970)

Freire, P. (1973). *Education for critical consciousness.* New York, NY: Seabury.

Giroux, H. (2012, October 16). Henry A Giroux: Can democratic education survive in a neoliberal society? *Truthout.* Retrieved December 13, 2015 from http://www.truth-out.org/opinion/item/12126-can-democratic-education-survive-in-a-neoliberal-society

Grant, C., & Gibson, M. (2011). Diversity and teacher education: A historical perspective on research and policy. In A. Ball & C. Tyson (Eds.), *Studying diversity in teacher education* (pp. 19–61). New York, NY: Rowman and Littlefield. Published in Partnership with AERA.

Griffin, M. (2003). Using critical incidents to promote and assess reflective thinking in preservice teachers. *Reflective Practice,* 4(2), 207–220.

Hollin, E. (2008). *Culture on school learning: Revealing the deep meaning* (2nd ed.). Mahwah, NJ: Lawrence Erlbaum Associates.

Hollins, E., & McIntyre, L., DeBose, C., Hollins, K., & Touner, A. (2004). Promoting a self-sustaining learning community: Investigating an internal model for teacher development. *International Journal of Qualitative Studies in Education,* 17(2), 247–264.

James, C. E., & Turner, T. (2017). *Towards race equity in education: The schooling of Black students in the greater Toronto area.* Toronto, ON: York University.

Kaur, B. (2012). Equity and social justice in teaching and teacher education. *Teaching and Teacher Education,* 28(2012), 485–492

Kohli, K., & Pizarro, M. (2016). Fighting to educate our own: Teachers of color, relational accountability, and the struggle for racial justice. *Equity & Excellence in Education,* 49(1), 72–84. doi:10.1080/10665684.2015.1121457

Kolb, D. A. (1984). *Experiential learning: Experience as the source of learning and Development.* Englewood Cliffs, NJ: Prentice-Hall.

Ladson-Billings, G. (2014). Culturally relevant pedagogy: Aka the remix. *Harvard Educational Review,* 84(1), 74–85.

Lee, E. (2009). Taking multicultural, anti-racist education seriously: An interview with Enid Lee. In W. Au (Ed.), *Rethinking multicultural education: Teaching for racial and cultural justice* (pp. 9–16). Milwaukee, WI: Rethinking Schools.

Lopez, A. E. (2011). Culturally relevant pedagogy and critical Literacy in diverse English classrooms: Case study of a secondary English teacher's activism and agency. *English Teaching Practice and Critique,* 10(4), 75–93.

Lopez, A. E. (2013). Embedding and sustaining equitable practices in teachers' everyday work: A framework for critical action. *Teaching & Learning,* 7(3), 1–15.

Lopez, A. E. (2014) Re-conceptualizing teacher leadership through curriculum inquiry in pursuit of social justice: Case study from the Canadian context. In C. Shields & I. Bogotch (Eds.), *International handbook of educational leadership and social (in) justice* (pp. 465–484). Dordrecht Heidelberg, New York, NY: Springer.

Lopez, A. E. (2016). *Culturally responsive and socially just leadership: From theory to action.* New York, NY: Palgrave MacMillan.

Lopez, A. E. (2018) Disruptive pedagogy: A critical approach to dealing with diversity in teacher education. In A. Lopez & E. L. Olan (Eds.), *Transformative pedagogies for teacher education* (pp. 157–174). Charlotte, NC: Information Age Publishing.

Maitzegui-Onate, C., & Santibanez-Gruber, R. (2008). Access to education and equity in plural societies. *Intercultural Education, 198*(5), 373–381.

Marshall, C., & Anderson, A. L. (2009). Is it possible to be an activist educator? In C. Marshall & A. L. Anderson (Eds.), *Activist educators: Breaking past limits* (pp. 1–30). New York, NY: Routledge.

Mezirow, J. (1990). *Fostering critical reflection in adulthood: A guide to transformative and emancipatory learning.* San Francisco, CA: Jossey-Bass.

Mock, K. R. (1989). Implementing race and ethnocultural policy in Ontario school boards. Retrieved from https://files.eric.ed.gov/fulltext/ED333066.pdf

Moore, G. W., Slate, J. R., Edmonson, S. L., Combs, J. P., Bustamante, R., & Onwuegbuzie, A. J. (2010). High school students and their lack of preparedness for college: A statewide study. *Education and Urban Society, 42*(7), 817–838.

Nieto, S. (2004). *Affirming diversity: The sociopolitical context of multicultural education* (4th ed.). Boston, MA: Pearson Education.

Ontario Alliance of Black School Educators. (2017). Black student achievement in the TDSB. Retrieved from http://onabse.org/YCEC-TDSBFactSheet1.pdf

Ontario Ministry of Education. (1993). *Antiracism and ethnocultural equity in school boards guidelines for policy development and implementation* Retrieved from http://www.edu.gov.on.ca/eng/document/curricul/antiraci/antire.pdf

Ontario Ministry of Education. (2009). Ontario's equity and inclusive education strategy. Retrieved from http://www.edu.gov.on.ca/eng/policyfunding/equity_quick_facts.html

Ontario Ministry of Education. (2014). Ontario's equity and inclusive education strategy. Retrieved from http://www.edu.gov.on.ca/eng/policyfunding/equity_quick_facts.html

Ontario Ministry of Education. (2016). Ontario's equity and inclusive education strategy. Retrieved from http://www.edu.gov.on.ca/eng/policyfunding/equity_quick_facts.html

Ontario Ministry of Education and Training, Making Schools Safer. (2000). Retrieved September 14, 2005, from http://www.edu.gov.on.ca/eng/document.nr/00.12/polibg.html

Paris, D. (2016). On educating culturally sustaining teachers. *Teaching Works.* Retrieved from http://www.teachingworks.org/images/files/TeachingWorks_Paris.pdf

Picower, B. (2012). Teacher activism: Enacting a vision for social justice. *Equity & Excellence in Education, 45*(4), 561–574.

Public Education Foundation. (2018). *What price the gap?: Education and inequality in Australia*. Retrieved from https://publiceducationfoundation.org.au/wp-content/uploads/2018/04/Issues-Paper_What-Price-The-Gap.pdf

Rankin, J., Rushowy, K., & Brown, L. (2013, March 22). Toronto school suspension rates highest for black and aboriginal students. *The Toronto Star*. Retrieved from https://www.thestar.com/news/gta/2013/03/22/toronto_school_suspension_rates_highest_for_black_and_aboriginal_students.html

Ruck, M. D., & Wortley, S. (2002). Racial and ethnic minority high school perceptions of school disciplinary practices: A look at some Canadian findings. *Journal of Youth and Adolescence, 31*(3) 185–195.

Ryan, J., Pollock, K., & Antonelli, F. (2009). Teacher diversity in Canada: Leaky pipelines, bottlenecks, and glass ceilings. *Canadian Journal of Education, 32*(3), 591–617.

Simon, R. (1992). *Teaching against the grain: Texts for a pedagogy of possibility*. New York, NY: Bergin & Garvey.

Solomon, P. R., & Levine-Rasky, C. (2003). *Teaching for racial equity and diversity: Research to practice*. Toronto, ON: Canadian Scholars Press.

Solomon, P. R., Singer, J., Campbell, A., Allen, A., & Portelli, J. P. (2011). *Brave new teachers: Doing social justice work in neo-liberal times*. Toronto, ON: Canadian Scholars Press.

Stern, M., & Brown, A. (2016). "It's 5:30. I'm exhausted. And I have to go all the way to f*%#ing Fishtown.": Educator depression, activism, and finding (armed) love in a hopeless (neoliberal) place. *Urban Review, 48*, 333–354.

Toronto District School Board. (2014). *Helping students to succeed: Equity in the TDSB*. Retrieved from https://www.tdsb.on.ca/About-Us/EquityNew

Toronto District School Board. (2018). *Draft Equity Policy. Retrieved from* http://www.tdsb.on.ca/Leadership/Boardroom/Agenda-Minutes/Type/A?Folder=Agenda%2F20180327&Filename=180327+Equity+Policy+3360.pdf

Trejo, J. (2017). A reflection on faculty diversity in the 21st century. *Mol Biol Cell, 28*(22) 2911–2914. doi:10.109/mbc.E17-08-0505

Tripp, D. (2012). *Critical incidents in teaching: Developing professional judgment* (Classical Edition). London, England: Routledge.

Villegas, A., & Davis, D. (2008). Preparing teachers of color to confront racial/ethnic disparities in educational outcomes. In M. Cochran-Smith, S. Feiman-Nemeser, K. Demers, & D. McIntyre (Eds.), *Handbook of research on teacher education: Enduring questions in changing contexts* (pp. 583–605). Mahwah, NJ: Lawrence Earlbaum & Associates.

Zeichner, K. (2009). *Teacher education and the struggle for social justice*. New York, NY: Routledge.

Zeichner, K., & Flessner, R. (2009). Educating teachers for critical education. In M. Apple, W. Au, & L. Armando Gandin (Eds.), *International handbook of critical education* (pp. 296–311). New York, NY: Erlbaun/Routledge.

CHAPTER 3

SECONDARY PRESERVICE TEACHERS EXPLORATION OF INCLUSIVE EDUCATION

Jennifer Lock and Petrea Redmond

In contemporary classrooms, teachers are expected to design and facilitate inclusive learning environments for all learners (Subban & Mahlo, 2016). The growth of inclusive practice in schools began in the late 1970s (Costello & Boyle, 2013). This is a major shift, as noted by Rose, Meyer, and Hitchock (2005) "away from meeting disability-specific needs and toward providing 'changing' access to the general education curriculum for all students" (p. 11). As a result, teacher education programs are required to provide preservice teachers (PSTs) with appropriate educational opportunities to develop the knowledge and skills to effectively respond to the diverse needs of all children.

This chapter provides an overview of a single case study that examined the online collaborative transformative learning experience that was established with preservice teachers, teacher educators and practicing teachers dialoguing about contemporary pedagogical approaches for a diverse and changing classroom. The purpose of the online collaboration was to introduce secondary preservice teachers (PSTs) to the reality of inclusive pedagogies required to effectively teach across a range of differences within their classrooms. *The research examined the* concerns and knowledge of secondary PSTs regarding inclusion of students with special educational needs in secondary classrooms. The results of the study highlight the need for PSTs to have greater opportunities to question and explore what inclusive education is, to determine what that means for practice, and to identify how they can be responsive to diversity in contemporary learning environments.

Inclusion in Education

Contemporary secondary classrooms in all discipline areas include students from a range of different backgrounds, abilities and disabilities. "Diversity and difference in classrooms are a reality" (Jobling & Moni, 2004, p. 5). Today's inclusive classroom practices support and benefit all learners. Savolainen, Engelbrecht, Nel, and Malinen (2012) reminded us that

> Including students with diverse educational needs in mainstream schools is now at the heart of education policy and planning through the world and this emphasis on education for all within inclusive schools as served as a catalyst for the transformation of schools. (p. 51)

There is international agreement that access to education is a basic human right and we "need to work towards 'schools for all'—institutions which include everybody, celebrate differences, support learning, and respond to individual needs" (UNESCO, 1994, p. iii). The rights of all learners to access quality learning experiences includes those who are marginalized within general education systems such as those with special educational needs. As such, how are teachers being prepared to meet the learning needs of all students?

Inclusive education is the "merger of special and regular education into a unified system required adaptive instruction, consultation, and collaboration to address the special needs of students" (Andrews, Drefs, Lupart, & Loreman, 2015, p. 25). A broad view of inclusion focuses on active participation in education by all and provides opportunities to reduce the marginalization of learners with irrespective of gender, sexuality, language, class, poverty, and medical needs as well as those identified under a traditional special needs view of education (Ainscow & Booth, 1998). As noted by Andrews et al. (2015) it is not adequate for teachers to know of the various diagnoses or labels for learners and how to target instructional strategies to accommodate such needs. Rather, they argued "teachers also need to be able to understand all types of student variance (e.g., gender, religion, social class, race, and ethnicity) and provide appropriate instruction to address all their students' individual and collective needs" (p. 26). This means that each student in each classroom has a unique set of educational demands.

Preservice Teacher Concerns

PSTs are commonly daunted by the challenges of including students with special educational needs into general classroom settings. Teacher education programs "produce teachers bound for professional placements feeling unprepared and inexperienced" (Hamilton-Jones & Vail, 2013, p. 58). Having said that, research undertaken by Costello and Boyle (2013) indicated that preservice teachers had a positive attitude toward inclusion. They also contended that competency influenced preservice teachers' attitudes. The challenge is how to help prepare preservice teachers to develop an understanding of diversity and how to be responsive in meeting the needs of all students in an inclusive classroom.

Context

The PST participants were enrolled in a secondary curriculum and pedagogy course in their second year of a four-year teacher education program or in the first semester of a one-year graduate diploma in teaching and learning. The course introduced a range of curriculum and pedagogy issues (such as inclusion, cyberbullying, indigenous perspectives and cultural diversity) and occurred prior to them completing a compulsory inclusive education course.

As part of the course, PSTs engaged in a six-week online international project focused on diversity and inclusivity. Students progressed through the following four stages of the project:

1. Community building—PSTs introduced themselves to others and began to develop a social presence online.
2. Learning from a shared experience—To begin, each PSTs read one of four stimulus novels. They were to review the novel, note pedagogical and curriculum linkages and create inquiry questions that would spark conversation. A number of these questions were used to begin the online dialogue facilitated by the teacher educator.
3. Learning from peers and teachers as experts—The teacher educator selected pedagogical questions gathered from Stage 2 to open up a two-week peer to peer discussion about inclusion. After those discussions, in-service teachers and other teacher educators in the role of experts joined the online conversation for 2 weeks. These experts were from Canada and Australia. To complement the asynchronous online discussion, synchronous discussions entitled Café Conversations. In these 1-hour synchronous sessions, an expert joined with the PSTs in talking about a particular scenario that pro-

vided the foundation for thinking about strategies, resources, and professional development need to support the required pedagogical practice for the classroom.
4. Critical reflection—During the final week, PSTs were asked to reflect on their experience working both in terms of the process and content. They were also required to respond to one of five different scenarios. The reflections and scenario responses were shared with colleagues in the online environment (Lock & Redmond, 2011; Redmond & Lock, 2009).

In relation to this book chapter, the data for this chapter came from this international online project, where PSTs investigated the topic of inclusion in relation to learners with special educational needs. In Stage 2, the preservice teachers were required to read the stimulus novel *The Curious Incident of the Dog In The Night Time* (Hadden, 2002). The novel set the stage for the preservice teachers' inquiry into special education and inclusion. For Stage 3, preservice teachers were joined by teachers and teacher educators who were experts in teaching students with special education needs. PSTs brought to the discussion ideas and questions from the stimulus novel, their textbook, other literature, their own childhood, perspectives as a parent, and previous relevant job experience. Within the online discussion forums, they responded to initial inquiry questions that led to further peer discussion and debate and then expanded their understanding of inclusion through discussion with the experts.

Research Design

The purpose of the study was to explore the concerns and knowledge of secondary preservice teachers regarding the inclusion of students with special educational needs in their discipline specialist classrooms. The research question which guided the work was: What is the nature of secondary preservice teachers concerns about teaching students with special educational needs?

The research was conducted under a naturalistic paradigm (Lincoln & Guba, 1985; Stake, 1995) using the real world as the research setting, without any control or manipulation. A single case study methodology was used to examine preservice teachers' perceptions of inclusive education.

Ethics approval was received from the host university. Data were collected within archived online discussion forums. The archived online postings were de-identified by a research assistant prior to analysis. The PST participated in this learning experience as part of their assessment and they were expected to post three to five times each week during the

2-week period. However, it was found that seven was the average number of posts per participant as there were 343 posts by 44 preservice teachers and 6 expert participants.

Using a qualitative analysis of the online posts, the researchers used a constant comparative approach (Wellington, 2000). As noted by Creswell (2002), this process has the researchers "constantly comparing indicators to indicators, codes to codes, and categories to categories" (p. 451). Through this process, the researchers identified patterns and themes in the data while also looking for contrasts or irregularities.

Discussion of Findings

Figure 3.1 summarizes six key themes derived from an analysis of the content of the preservice teachers' online discussion posts.

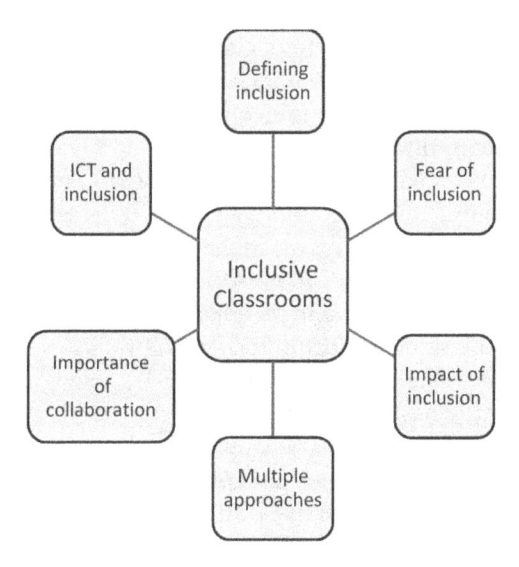

Figure 3.1. Broad themes from preservice teachers' online discussion posts.

Defining inclusion. In literature and in practice, there is no clear or common definition of inclusion. Many definitions in the literature include terms such as integration or mainstreaming (Hausstätter, 2013; Ryndak, Jackson, & Billingsley, 2000) of students with specific educational needs. The concepts of equality, fairness, social justice, or treating some learners unequally to gain equality are key to the construct (OECD, 2011). It could be said that the term inclusion is about the right for all children "to participate and benefit from education" (Hausstätter, 2013, p. 1).

In the online discussion, PSTs debated concepts of tolerance, acceptance and embracing difference when referring to inclusion. As reported by PST-B, "inclusion is more about everyone belonging (being included) in the school and not limited to disability, race, politics religion, ideals etc." This was supported by PST-E who acknowledged that "it is important that we view every child regardless of race, religion, ability, and disability etc. as having the equal right to be educated and to have an education." Whereas PST-F noted that, "The act of inclusion means fighting against exclusion.... Fighting for inclusion also involves assuring that all support systems are available to those who need such support. Providing and maintaining support system is a civic responsibility, not a favour." What the preservice teachers were discussing parallels the research conducted by Hughes and De George-Walker (2010) who also found that values such as "tolerance, empathy and respect" (p. 114) were key concepts of importance for effective inclusive education.

PSTs made reference to inclusion as an intentional act. For example, PST-R revealed that a student with special needs at her professional experience placement "was meaningfully included in all activities and the other students learned acceptance, patience and compassion." Through their practicum placements in schools, they observed how teachers intentionally designed and supported inclusive practices; they witnessed inclusive theory put into everyday practice.

The concept of equity within an inclusive classroom was discussed in depth by both the experts and the preservice teachers. PST-K argued that "[d]ifferent people have different needs and therefore inclusion means giving everyone the same opportunities even if that means more support for one student than another!" In contrast PST-J believed that equity was about "treating students the same as opposed to responding to individual's needs." Through their discussion of equity, they developed a deeper appreciation and understanding of the concept.

Experts shared their perspectives which supported and/or conflicted with the PSTs ideas. For example, Expert-O shared the following account in terms of how every student is different: "Each one is unique. So treating everyone equally becomes a contestable ideal. Practically, we need to identify barriers to access and participation in curriculum." As the experts engaged in the discussion, they acknowledged the various key words that are used in defining or describing such as "inclusion, equality, equitable, fair, and same" (Expert-K). Yet, how it is defined is grounded on a values systems. Expert-L proposed that such a term is "based on value systems that are deeply rooted in culture, sub-culture and personal experience." To help the PSTs explore their own personal definition, Expert-M commented: "Treating disadvantaged people equally can lead to them remaining disadvantaged, because they may never be able to take advantage of or have access to the resources that others have in the same context."

With the support of the online experts, preservice teachers began to explore the concept of inclusion as a way of thinking, acting, valuing, and being. As they grappled with defining the term, many of the posts revealed their fears of inclusion.

Fear of inclusion. PSTs are often fearful of the inclusion of students with special education needs in their classrooms (Jobling & Moni, 2004). Research by Savolainen et al. (2012) proposed that "teachers fears are pragmatic and that their 'teachers' attitudes toward inclusion are often not based on ideological arguments, but rather on practice concerns about how inclusive education can be implemented" (p. 32).

From the analysis of the data, the following four key fears were identified: (1) time to be pedagogically inclusive; (2) their own capabilities; (3) constant change; and (4) the unknown. PST-I questioned, "How teachers can treat all students equally and fairly if some children require more attention, planning and accommodations than other … trying to address different learning needs requires varying amounts of time and effort." PST-A and PST-R reinforced the fact that time was a fear given some students may need more of the teachers' time and attention. This was supported by PST-M who acknowledged this concern as a teacher,

> my time will absolutely Run Out … no matter what I do, I will leave most children well under their potential, so knowing and being happy to "move on" to the next student, and leave a student in the knowledge that they haven't quite got a full understanding, will be very difficult!

The participants also expressed concern that the support in schools may not be adequate for the high incidence exceptional children therefore, placing more strain on the classroom teacher. They went on to acknowledge that such fears maybe dependent on the school, personal knowledge, special needs assistants, and the administration. PST-B carefully articulated questions that highlighted common anxiety experienced by PSTs: "Will I be adequately resourced to be able to effectively teach the class with a wider student needs? Will there be a teacher aide? Are the physical characteristics of the classroom able to cope? Are the materials that we are using able to be adapted for all students?"

Another common fear was not being capable or competent in their ability to fulfil the demands of all students. PST-W argued that, "When teachers fear practicing inclusion, it is about THEIR fear—their fear of failing and looking 'stupid.' They need to realize that fear helps them to learn and succeed." They went on to say "face the fear monster; stare it down. Name it, move on, and reap the benefits." PST-L mentioned,

I quake in my boots at the thought of having a class with an Indigenous student, a gifted student, a special needs student, a new Australian with ESL and a behavioural problem student. But this is actually a very likely situation!

The situation may push a teacher or PST beyond his/her comfort zone. As noted by PST-J when she reflected on her mentor teachers, "Some seem to take it in their stride, but some really struggle as they are not equipped to do what is expected of them."

The PSTs also noted that the fear of change is common in the teaching profession. In terms of teaching in an inclusive classroom, PST-V suggested that teachers fear "changing the way they do things e.g. needing to write a special program." PST-W believed that teachers may fear inclusion because it means a "[c]hange to their style, experiences, planning, behaviour management and commitment to their profession … it is often difficult to maintain this goal without constant reflection, re-design and professional training in inclusive methods."

PST-Q believed a major fear for teachers with regard to inclusion is "what is the unknown. Not only what the teacher doesn't know about the children but also what the children don't know about each other." Jobling and Moni (2004) elicited that "pre-service teacher education programs [should] take some responsibility for preventing the development of negative attitudes towards students with special needs as well as challenging non-inclusive practice" (p. 6).

Participants in this study mirrored those PST within Jobling and Moni's (2004) synthesis from other studies. They noted that teachers can develop "negative attitudes toward inclusion and had doubts about their abilities to teach students with disabilities … express their concerns about a general lack of preparation and confidence in providing for students who have disabilities" (p. 6).

PSTs revealed that they had number of fears about teaching within an inclusive classroom. They were uncomfortable about their limited knowledge, skills and experience to plan and implement effective teaching and learning for students with special needs. This fear may exacerbate their perspectives of the impact of inclusion.

Impact of inclusion. The implementation of an inclusive pedagogy has an impact on students with special education needs in the class as well as the teachers, parents and other students in addition to the resource distribution in the school or classroom. Although, the PSTs referred to the impact on parents and other students they particularly identified the impact with reference to economic cost and levels of responsibility.

The concept of the cost of inclusion was articulated by a number of pre-service teachers. For example, PST-I shared, "I love the idea of inclusion, but wonder what cost it comes at. I would never advocate bringing back special schools, but I do wonder how it is the government can continue not funding what is so desperately needed." This was supported by PST-P who proffered, "I don't want to sound like an economic rationalist, the argument goes that it is cost effective to provide services in one place rather than in every classroom." Through these PSTs' discussion, they were grappling with the question: Can a price be put on inclusion?

Through moral, ethical, and pedagogical lenses, the PSTs wrestled with the economic impact of creating and supporting inclusive mainstream classrooms. PST-H remarked that the

> problem lies not just for our teachers having to deal with a lack of resources but making them expel more energy in having to develop and/or customise teaching and also learning and behavioural strategies within the constraints that already exist.

The embodiment of inclusion in today's education is a responsibility at all levels: school, district, and national. All stakeholders (e.g., teachers, administrators, politicians, parents) must work together to ensure resources and supports are in place to foster and nurture inclusive learning environments. This also means that PST have a responsibility in preparing themselves to accept their role in creating inclusive environments for all children in their classrooms.

Through their online discussions the PSTs expressed the belief that establishing inclusive classrooms impacts on others at a range of levels as well as having a financial impact. Interestingly, although mentioned in passing, the PST focus on impact did not extend to the impacts that are revealed by other studies. For example, Salend and Duhaney (1999) suggested that there are academic and social impacts when placing students with special education needs in a mainstream classroom to create an inclusive setting. The following section describes the next theme from the data which is the multiple approaches which may be implemented to create an inclusive classroom.

Multiple approaches. The PST noted that they had observed a number of different approaches for inclusion within secondary schools. There was an acknowledgment from the participants that different educational needs often require different approaches from a school and classroom level. There was also an agreement that overtime approaches to inclusion have changed, especially for students with identified special educational needs.

The PSTs provided the following examples of different approaches for students with special education needs: separate schools, separate classes, pull out programs, drop in programs, socializations programs, and the use of teacher aides as one-on-one or small group support. Rosenberg, Westling, and McLeskey (2011) indicated that dependant on the severity of the educational need students may be involved in any of the approaches above or even in a mixture of approaches. When investigating the range of approaches PST-A maintained that

> Sometimes pull-out programs are most helpful, sometimes full inclusive classrooms are best but in order to determine which program to implement, I think conversations with the student, their parents, the teachers involved, school administrators and support staff needs to take place.... Doing what is best for the student and their learning is most important.

During the discussions, PSTs reflected on what they had observed at their professional experience placements. PST-C shared a different perspective based on a very inclusive experience: "The school also has a very special culture around acceptance of these students. It results in a largely unconscious acceptance by students of those members of the class with special needs."

Over several decades, different approaches have been used to educate children with special needs. There has been a move from separate special education schools to special education centres in mainstream schools and the integration of students with special educational needs into mainstream classrooms. As part of the evolutionary progress from segregation, integration, mainstreaming to inclusion, Andrews et al. (2015) argued that the "predominant and developing educational trend in diversity education is personalized instruction" (p. 29). They suggested that

> personalized instruction takes into account and considers education with the broader contexts of community, school and home environments and tailors the curriculum and instruction to the unique experiences, abilities, needs, and self-identify of each student to ensure engagement in meaningful, relevant, and appropriate work. (p. 29)

The research of Andrews et al. (2015) aligned with the views expressed by the participants in this study that one size does not fit all. PST-V reminded others that the uniqueness of every student requires multiple and integrated approaches and teachers should be "[d]oing what is best for the student." When exploring the different approaches to inclusivity the concept of collaborative approaches was raised.

Importance of collaboration. There was common agreement between the PSTs around the concept, "it takes a village to raise a child." They appreciated that no one individual teacher would be responsible for positive educational outcomes for students with special educational needs. There was an acknowledgment of the importance of professional networking and the need for a whole school approach for inclusion. A belief of PST-X was that "[e]ssentially a difficult task is made near impossible when support networks are removed and teachers are left to fend for themselves." In this discussion, preservice teachers talked about the importance of communication, especially between the school and parents, but also with the team of professionals who are supporting the student. PST-Z's comment highlighted the importance of communication, "Conversations —ongoing ones—need to occur between parents, teachers and other staff members to ensure we are providing a true inclusive environment."

The PSTs saw themselves as a member of a collaborative team. Yet there seemed to be a disconnection in terms of practice. The following two quotes capture this disconnect. PST-V believed that every "student was the school's responsibility, not just one specific teacher's concern." In contrast PST-U, claimed that

> "Teachers are alone"... With the right support from management, specialist teachers and other resources ... or within the community, you can access a range of individuals with a range of skills. Perhaps the best way to overcome this feeling of isolation is to have a good knowledge of the roles and skills these individuals can offer.

When discussing the lack of support and ability of teachers to cope PST-U shared that "I've always found there are people ready to help and support you when you ask them." Rosenberg et al. (2011) suggested there is a range of sources for teachers including the following: (1) more experienced teaching colleagues; (2) attendance at professional development; and (3) advice from other professionals and paraprofessions (e.g., advisory visiting teachers, guidance officers, special education teacher/expert; teacher aide, and occupational therapist). Expert-C proposed, "When our administrators (school district, principal, consultants) support the teachers by providing the necessary resources (extra time, professional development, teaching assistants, etc.) then inclusive education will be easier and these nay-sayers will more likely jump on board."

One type of support is that of a team. "Teams comprising of parents, executive staff, general and special education teachers, therapists and other professions or community members can work together to guide the child's learning plan" (Pearce & Forlin, 2005, p. 101). This view of a collaborative approach was shared by the PSTs and is encapsulated in the post by PST-T who stated, "when we are educating the whole child, we are actually part of a team. This team ... should include the parents, the school administration, school staff and specialists."

Having a team approach in the school, as well as, networks beyond the school were commonly mentioned in posts. PST-P revealed, "I certainly want to create a network of professionals in the education field that I can go to for support, and in turn maybe offer my support to them? I like the idea of being part of an 'educational team.' " Whereas, PST-W observed that "a lot of the time the support and resources come from community organisations and this can act as an integration tool."

The view of inclusion being a collaborative effort is supported by Pearce and Forlin (2005). They proposed that "[o]ne of the primary means of achieving inclusion is for teachers with general and special education training to work together collaboratively in one inclusive educational system" (p. 101). They suggested that teachers' ongoing training and support can be sourced through working with colleagues, co-teaching, and mentoring.

The participants reported that collaboration with others is an important aspect of successful inclusion. The findings in this study indicated that the participants' views aligned with the research and expected practice of teachers. They are aware that they do not need to go it alone and that there is a range of support available and a collaborative approach is likely to gain a more effective inclusive outcome. Many of the preservice teachers admitted that it would be important for them to seek assistance from others, particularly when using ICTs in an inclusive classroom.

ICT and inclusion. Towards the end of the two-week period in the online discussion with the experts, one of the preservice teachers commented that they were surprised they had yet to discuss the effect of information and communication technologies (ICTs) in supporting students with special needs. For students with special educational needs, ICTs have a key role in expanding curriculum learning opportunities.

The participants began to question if ICTs would in fact assist learning or lead to other issues that may impede learning. PST-G asked the following questions of the online experts and their peers: "I am presuming that ICT's complicate things, but can this be used to assist in the teachings of inclusivity or does it only impede? Or does the internet present a whole different kind of inclusivity into society?" These questions align with the opinion of Brodin and Lindstrand (2003) who suggested that educators views on the use of ICTs have "become more balanced and a more realistic and critical attitude to ICT is discernible" (p. 72).

From their observations and reading of the literature, the PSTs identified various issues when using technology. PST-A responded that "[m]y observation is that the school and teachers struggle with knowing how to best use them [technology] for educational purposes—that promote good outcomes, are safe, accessible and relevant." This idea was further explored by PST-D who argued that the problem of using ICT may

> lead to an over-reliance on IT to communicate to others. There have already been studies that show that online social networking can lead to a decrease in physical social skills, as people become dependent on ICT and avoid personal interaction.

Expert B acknowledged the "delicate dance" with ICT in inclusive classrooms. With the use of technology, also comes a responsibility for the preservice teacher to learn when and how to use it to appropriately support student learning. Lock and Friesen (2015) argued that networked digital technologies are part of the contemporary classroom. It is in the design of the learning with the purposeful integration of technology that will generate a more positive learning outcome. "The inclusive, accessible classroom is one in which all children are provided with multiple and flexible means of representation, expression, and engagement" (Lock & Friesen, 2015, p. 97). ICTs provide the teacher with multiple opportunities to represent information for the students and it also provides the student with different tools to demonstrate their knowledge.

Within this study, there was some apprehension for PSTs when dealing with specialised technologies for students identified with high special educational needs. Assistive technologies can assist learners with some special educational needs participate in education and can be particularly beneficial in facilitating writing, communication and play (Brodin & Lindstrand, 2003). They go on to comment that the "use of technology should be educationally led, rather than led by the technology itself" (p. 72). As argued by Dell, Newton, and Petroff (2012) there is a "gap between the *possibilities* of assistive technology and the actual implementation of it in our school" (p. 305). Within the discussion, the PSTs were beginning to examine this gap and what they need to learn to be prepared to support student learning with assistive technologies.

Implications

Data from the online discussions suggest four implications for PSTs and for teacher education programs. The goal of the learning experience was to introduce the concept of inclusion and open preservice teachers' eyes to the reality of inclusion in today's mainstream secondary classrooms. During this online learning experience, PSTs' discussions indicated that they achieved a broader awareness of inclusion, they shared strategies for an inclusive classroom, and also reflected on their professional experience placements. Implications of the findings from this study are discussed below.

First, PSTs need a positive attitude towards inclusion. They need to approach it with an open mind. The data indicated a wide variety of knowledge, experience and perspectives connected to inclusive classrooms and teaching students with special education needs. As part of the teacher education training, PSTs require experiences where they can realize that their personal experience with inclusion may not be that which is promoted through policy or true inclusive pedagogical practices in today's classrooms. Learning experiences should challenge PSTs' perception and develop an openness to employing various strategies and approaches in creating and supporting an inclusive learning environment. It is about creating conditions to foster the development of a disposition of inclusivity.

Second, PSTs' personal knowledge of inclusive practices are not strong. Many of them have doubts about their ability to teach students with special education needs due to the lack of preparation and limited confidence. It was evident from the data that they had minimal knowledge given limited or no reference to such items as legislation, curriculum and/or instruction. This gap should be observed as part of a continuum of practice. As the PSTs enhance their knowledge and skills through their academic program and professional experience placements their confidence and competence of inclusive practices and specific strategies will continue to develop. For teacher education, the concept of inclusion should not be a one-off effort with a single standalone course focused on inclusion. Rather, there should be multiple touch points where inclusive practice can be integrated into various courses (e.g., curriculum) so that PSTs are continually thinking about how to design and facilitate learning for all students.

Third, it is important for PSTs and teacher education programs to recognise that different approaches and working in collaboration are common in inclusive education. There is no "one size fits all" approach. Approaches may differ depending on the severity of the educational need of the learner and the resources available within the school. One teacher cannot do it all, nor will they know it all. It is important for secondary PSTs as a discipline specialist to be encouraged work with other relevant stakeholders such as the administration, other teachers who specialize in special education, and parents and caregivers to promote an effective learning outcome for students. Within their practicum placements, partner teachers play a critical role. Partner teachers in the role of mentors should share their practice, address questions, as well as guide the PSTs' practice in becoming an inclusive educator.

Fourth, there are some broad implications for initial teacher education programs. Teacher education programs need to have explicit teaching of knowledge and skills to support a range of students with special educational needs, including the use of assistive technologies. Also where possible, they should provide opportunities for targeted professional experience to work either in inclusive learning environments, a special needs school, in a special education centre within a secondary school, or to be mentored by a special education/inclusive teacher within mainstream classes. PSTs will require multiple opportunities to develop knowledge and skills in inclusion. At the macrolevel, teacher education programs need to plan for such experiences across secondary programs. Intentionality in creating opportunities across a program is required for PSTs to experience and to develop knowledge and skills with regard to special education practices.

This online learning experience provided PSTs with the opportunity to discuss strategies for inclusive secondary classroom with experts in the field. Rayner and Allen (2013) suggested that PST placed a higher value on the expertise of practitioners when compared to academics, and like their study, the PSTs in this learning experience embraced the teachers as experts as an integral part of the learning process.

Utilizing online discussions with teacher experts as well as PSTs located in range of geographical locations facilitated the ability of learning about inclusive practices in different contexts, sharing a range of different approaches, and the ability to learn *from* and *with* others. Varcoe and Boyle (2014) identified that a "single approach to training pre-service teachers inclusive education is not sufficient" (p. 335). This learning experience was an introduction to the concept of inclusion for the secondary PSTs. Their teacher education program builds on these concepts in other curriculum and diversity courses providing them with multiple opportunities and different approaches to gain an understanding on how they might differentiate teaching to meet the specific learning needs of all students in inclusive classrooms.

Limitations and Directions for Future Research

This single case study has limitations in that the results come from an analysis of a course that occurred in one semester at a regional university. The findings may not be generalizable to other PST contexts. However, there is currently limited research in the area of inclusion in mainstream secondary classrooms. Future research needs to investigate specific strategies to support rich inclusive practice for secondary PSTs education or explore if there is discipline differentiation of inclusion in secondary schools.

This two prong approach may be considered for future research. At the academic level, research needs to occur investigating the pragmatic elements. That is, studying what is occurring in classroom in relation to strategies and layering of pragmatic approaches in schools. Further, research needs to continue examine the impact of policies that support and facilitate inclusion and inclusive practices in schools. At the PST level when they become teachers, they should be encouraged to engage in studying their teaching using a participatory research approach. Using action research, participatory action research, and/or design-based research methodologies, they will be able to interrogate and critically reflect on their practice. It provides a means for them to link theory to practice and practice to theory in terms of how to design and support inclusive education in their classrooms and schools. Special education and inclusion knowledge mobilization will continue to be advanced if both academics and teachers (former PSTs) engage in research.

Conclusion

The PSTs in the study explored through questions and discussion with experts their issues and concerns with regard to inclusion in secondary educational settings. The PSTs had an opportunity to openly interrogate the topic in a safe learning environment. They were able to assess what they know and believe, as well as, to begin to identify what more they need to learn about inclusion and inclusive practice. This online experience gave them the opportunity to determine the next steps in their professional learning to inform their knowledge and practice with regard to inclusion and inclusive education.

Within teacher education programs, conditions need to be created that foster the purposeful integration inclusion across the program. A standalone course offered in a program is not adequate in providing the necessary knowledge and skills for today's diverse classrooms. Rather, PSTs need to be continually learning about special education practices and strategies and given opportunities to apply theory to practice. Opportunities to engage in conversation with various stakeholders and to observe their practices will help them to develop their knowledge and skills. Through teacher education, we need to be helping PSTs to develop a disposition of inclusivity that impacts their day-to-day practice with students.

REFERENCES

Ainscow, M., & Booth, T. (1998). *From them to us: An international study of inclusion in education*. London, England: Routledge.

Andrews, J. W., Drefs, M. A., Lupart, J., & Loreman, T. (2015). Foundations, principles, and student diversity. In J. W. Andrews & J. Lupart (Eds.), *Diversity education: understanding and addressing student diversity* (pp. 24–73). Toronto, ON: Nelson Education.

Brodin, J., & Lindstrand, P. (2003). What about ICT in special education? Special educators evaluate information and communication technology as a learning tool. *European Journal of Special Needs Education, 18*(1), 71–87. doi:10.1080/0885625032000042320

Costello, S., & Boyle, C. (2013). Pre-service secondary teachers' attitudes towards inclusive education. *Australian Journal of Teacher Education, 38*(4), 129–143.

Creswell, J. W. (2002). *Educational research: Planning, conducting, and evaluating quantitative and qualitative research*. Upper Saddle River, NJ: Pearson.

Dell, A. G., Newton, D. A., & Petroff, J. G. (2012). *Assistive technology in the classroom: enhancing the school experiences of students with disabiites* (2nd ed.). Boston, MA: Pearson.

Hadden, M. (2002). *The curious incident of the dog in the night-time*. Toronto, ON: Doubleday

Hamilton-Jones, B., & Vail, C. O. (2013). Preparing special educators for collaboration in the classroom: pre-service teachers' beliefs and perspectives. *International Journal of Special Education, 28*(1), 56–68.

Hausstätter, R. S. (2013). In support of unfinished inclusion. *Scandinavian Journal of Educational Research, 57*(1), 1–11. doi:10.1080/00313831.2013.773553

Hughes, S., & De George-Walker, L. D. (2010). Connecting to community: what do we want in our special education graduates? *Australasian Journal of Special Education, 34*(02), 109–118. doi:10.1375/ajse.34.2.109

Jobling, A., & Moni, K. (2004). 'I never imagined I'd have to teach these children': providing authentic learning experiences for secondary pre-service teachers in teaching students with special needs. *Asia-Pacific Journal of Teacher Education, 32*(1), 5–22. doi:10.1080/1359866042000206026

Lincoln, Y. S., & Guba, E. G. (1985). *Naturalistic inquiry*. Newbury Park, CA: SAGE.

Lock, J., & Friesen, S. (2015). Twenty-first-century learning and student diversity. In J. W. Andrews & J. Lupart (Eds.), *Diversity education: Understanding and adressing student diversity* (pp. 74–102). Toronto, ON: Nelson Education.

Lock, J., & Redmond, P. (2011) International online collaboration: giving voice to the study of diversity. *One World in Dialogue, 1*(1), 19–25.

OECD. (2011). *Building a high-quality teaching profession: Lessons from around the world*. Retrieved from http://www.qct.edu.au/Publications/Retention_Research_Report_RP01.pdf

Pearce, M., & Forlin, C. (2005). Challenges and potential solutions for enabling inclusion in secondary schools. *Australasian Journal of Special Education, 29*(2), 93–105. doi:10.1080/1030011050290202

Rayner, C., & Allen, J. M. (2013). Using online video-recorded interviews to connect the theory and practice of inclusive education in a course for student teachers. *Australasian Journal of Special Education, 37*(2), 107–124. doi:10.1017/jse.2013.14

Redmond, P. & Lock, J.V. (2009). Authentic learning across international borders: Across institutional online project for pre-service teachers. In C. Maddux (Ed.), *Research Highlights in Technology and Teacher Education 2009* (pp. 265–273). Chesapeake, VA: Society for Information Technology and Teacher Education (SITE).

Rose, D., Meyer, A., & Hitchcock, C. (2005). *The universally designed classroom: Accessible curriculum and digital technologies*. Cambridge, MA: Harvard University Press.

Rosenberg, M. S., Westling, D. L., & McLeskey, J. (2011). *Special education for today's teachers: An introduction* (2nd ed.). Upper Saddle River, NJ: Pearson Education.

Ryndak, D. L., Jackson, L., & Billingsley, F. (2000). Defining school inclusion for students with moderate to severe disabilities: What do experts say? *Exceptionality, 8*(2), 101–116. doi:10.1207/S15327035EX0802_2

Salend, S. J., & Duhaney, L. M. G. (1999). The impact of inclusion on students with and without disabilities and their educators. *Remedial and special education, 20*(2), 114–126. doi:10.1177/074193259902000209

Savolainen, H., Engelbrecht, P., Nel, M., & Malinen, O. (2012). Understanding teachers' attitudes and self-efficacy in inclusive education: implications for pre-service and inservice teacher education. *European Journal of Special Needs Education, 27*(1), 51–68. doi:10.1080/08856257.2011.613603

Stake, R. (1995). *The art of case study research*. Thousand Oaks, CA: SAGE.

Subban, P., & Mahlo, D. (2016). 'My attitude, my responsibility' Investigating the attitudes and intentions of pre-service teachers toward inclusive education between teacher preparation cohorts in Melbourne and Pretoria. *International Journal of Inclusive Education, 21*(4), 441–461.

UNESCO. (1994). *The Salamanca Statement and framework for action on special needs education*. Retrieved from http://www.unesco.org/education/pdf/SALAMA_E.PDF

Varcoe, L., & Boyle, C. (2014). Pre-service primary teachers' attitudes towards inclusive Education. *Educational Psychology, 34*(3), 323–337. doi:10.1080/01443410.2013.785061

Wellington, J. (2000). *Educational research: Contemporary issues and practical approaches*. London, England: Continuum.

CHAPTER 4

INTEGRATING LEARNING SPACES

Understanding Conditions That Enable Transformational Shifts in Teacher Education Programs and Practices

Lisa J. Starr and Kathy Sanford

Introduction

Educational researchers such as Cochran-Smith, Ell, Ludlow, and Aitken (2014), Darling-Hammond (2006), and Russell, McPherson and Martin (2001) have argued for teacher education programs to acknowledge and more importantly respond to the complex and diverse needs of the profession. As teacher educators, we are most concerned with helping preservice teachers (PSTs) understand the conditions that best enable learning in order to become and evolve as teachers (Korthagen, Loughran, & Russell, 2006; Munby, Russell, & Martin, 2001). And while contextual variables demand flexibility and adaptability in programming, core elements of innovative and effective teacher education programs exist that enable teachers to thrive in ever-changing environments. Examinations of teacher

---

Transformative Pedagogies for Teacher Education:
Critical Action, Agency, and Dialogue in Teaching and Learning Contexts, pp. 55–67
Copyright © 2019 by Information Age Publishing
All rights of reproduction in any form reserved.

education have identified several persistent challenges that PSTs often face in the intersections between field and coursework, such as: (1) articulation of professional identity; (2) disconnect between theoretical and practice-based understandings; (3) fragmentation of courses/experiences; (4) the need for professional learning communities to prepare for change within universities as well as in schools; and (5) the need for recognizing the importance of relational understandings and relationship building, with peers, mentors, students, families, the public, self, and knowledge (Darling-Hammond, 2006; Korthagen et al., 2006; Russell et al., 2001). A challenge we have found especially problematic is that PSTs frequently view their campus-based courses as extraneous to learning to teach, instead placing greater value on their field-based placements as "real" sites for becoming a teacher. While we disagree with the disproportionate value PSTs place on field based learning, we acknowledge that the critique is fair when professors do not recognize or realize in their practice the need for intimate connections between theoretical understandings and the realities of today's classrooms and schools (Korthagen et al., 2006; Segall, 2002). As Russell (2012) commented, "teacher educators themselves need to make paradigmatic changes before expecting pre-service teachers to do the same" (p. 3). Creating confident and capable professionals who will be able to contribute to a transformation of education requires close examination of the learning that is needed in professional teacher education programs in order to prepare PSTs to meaningfully move educational spaces in schools and classrooms into the 21st century. Based on such an examination, we have developed an alternative approach, *Transforming UVic (TRUVic) teacher education program*, to preparing preservice teachers and supporting in-service teachers to embrace the innovative and responsive pedagogies that shift their teaching frames from how they were taught to how they need to teach in increasingly diverse schools and classroom contexts.

The TRUVic program is a structured response to the challenges previously articulated that grew out of a desire to better integrate two conventional learning spaces in teacher education programs—the university and the school. This program includes several key features that enable our students to begin addressing the challenges identified above. In the first term of a four-term program (16 months), PSTs in interdisciplinary cohorts engage one day a week in a local school where they are able to observe, engage with adolescents and teachers, question existing practices, and have practices modeled for them by a range of practitioners. Additionally, this observational day is bookended (7:30–8:30 A.M. and 3:30–5:30 P.M.) by a university seminar course taught by a university instructor who is also an active teacher in the school. Working with school-based teachers offers access to a rich examination of the school context otherwise absent from early experiences in teacher education programs. Further, the bookended seminar structure enables relationship-building with teachers who can answer the PSTs' questions—sometimes challenging—to provide insights, and have strong educational practice modeled. Throughout the 10 school visits in the first term, strong relationships are formed between PSTs and teachers, enabling authentic mentorship and future practicum opportunities during the remainder of their program. In the interdisciplinary first term, the PSTs identify and develop an inquiry project, delving into an aspect of education of personal and professional interest. Throughout the term they read research, hone their inquiry question, observe, and engage with teachers and students to develop a final project that is presented at the Gallery Walk at the end of the term. This event is a consolidation of their professional learning throughout the term, shared in a public forum with each other and invited guests, including school educators and administrators, superintendents, Ministry of Education personnel, faculty members, and other colleagues and friends.

In addition to the seminar course and weekly school-based observations, the PSTs are also engaged in classes related to disciplinary and cross-disciplinary pedagogy, learning theories, and educational technology. The instructors work collaboratively to interweave knowledge of each of the courses together in supportive and reinforcing ways, modeling effective pedagogies and critical engagement, continually drawing from the school-based experiences to inform their campus-based courses. Finally, the program derives its focus from Indigenous principles learned from our colleague Lorna Williams, including

- *The importance of focusing on the **learning of our colleagues** before our own learning, enabling learning opportunities that are exponentially greater than if we focus only on our own learning*
- *Consideration of how our work will **benefit the next seven generations to come;** our class work will influence future generations of students and teachers*
- ***Finding our passion** and then investing this passion in our work to energize the community and inspire the learning of others.*

This approach to teacher education, we feel, better integrates embodied understandings of curriculum, pedagogy and identity with the principles of 21st century teaching and learning. Developed and continually refined in response to feedback from many secondary teacher education students over the past several years, as well as our own experiences, successes and frustrations as teacher educators, we have sought to redefine PSTs' conceptions of education, teaching, learning and what it means to contribute to a learning community. In our program development we have drawn on the formally articulated experiences of over 40 students and 5 instructors continuously over the course of five years, informal feedback from many more PSTs and teachers, as well as our own observations throughout that time.

Our rationale for this chapter is to address what we see as an ethical imperative in teacher education. As education becomes increasingly complex and demanding, we believe teacher education programs must provide opportunities for prospective teachers to be as prepared as possible to take up their role as professionals. With this in mind, the teacher education program we are describing has shifted in structure and intention in order to better address the needs of our preservice teachers and to respond to changes to educational changes within the K-graduation school system. Developed with significant input from a group of secondary education students, we have sought to redefine their conceptions of education, teaching, and learning; to make connections between theories of learning/education and practice; to learn from experienced teachers in schools and university; and to gain greater perspective on the needs, interests, and expectations of today's youth. In the TRUVic program model, the courses in their first term of the teacher education program are organized collaboratively and holistically. Further, the course content commits to engagement in a high school. Specifically, students in their cohorts engage meaningfully with practicing teachers and adolescents during their one day a week visits.

Our experiences as teacher educators have led us to the following questions: When we think of innovative practice in teacher education we wonder what conditions enable transformational shifts to teacher education programs and practices for pre- and in-service teachers? How can these transformations be developed, implemented, continually assessed and sustained in relation to the challenges of the 21st century? What are the critical conceptual understandings of learning in professional programs that need to be embedded into teacher education programs? What is the role of experiential learning in providing "reflective spaces" that embrace both theoretical and practical understandings of becoming a teacher/professional? We have examined these questions in light of our current teacher education programs and needs for future development.

Problematizing the Nature of Learning in Teacher Education

The desire to transform education is premised on the belief that contemporary educational structures and approaches require change so as to better address the needs and interests of today's diverse and multifaceted learners and our increasingly complex society. Our belief stems from our questioning the nature of learning in teacher education and the need to prepare well-rounded professionals for a future that we cannot yet envision (Conroy,

Hulme, & Menter, 2013; Darling-Hammond & Lieberman, 2012; Sanford, Hopper, & Starr, 2015). We need, then, to focus on a competency-based rather than content-based curriculum and appropriately aligned assessment practices, shifting to integrated, meaningful learning experiences that actively engage the learners. Education has long been located in a technical-scientific-industrial worldview (O'Sullivan, Morrell, & O'Connor 2002). Despite calls for transformation of education like the one motivating this chapter, the educational climate has continued to emphasize a standards-based accountability climate reflective of the movement towards efficiency rather than the unwieldy business of learning. As learners and teachers, we are expected to adopt an impossibly impenetrable persona that is capable, competent, effective and able to meet curricular mandates and expectations; lesson plans must be detailed, unit plans equally so, assessment must line up with learning outcomes. These expectations are not inappropriate but are extremely limited and aligned with an industrial and fragmented model of education that encourages competition, rote memorization, and compliance. This mechanistic structure frequently informs teacher education and in large part goes unquestioned by preservice teachers, not from a lack of concern or recognition but rather from a lack of genuine opportunity to consider the real purposes of education and their role as educators.

In Canada, several provinces have begun to consider reform that places more complex and diverse needs of 21st century learners at the center of curricular reform. In British Columbia, the Ministry of Education unveiled a reformed elementary curriculum to address the needs of 21st century learners; the secondary curriculum is due to be implemented in 2019. Such reforms require that Faculties of Education responsible for teacher education take steps to incorporate 21st century learning and pedagogy into their teacher education programs in order to adequately prepare PSTs to succeed in classrooms where educational reform, reflective of 21st century learning, has become a driving force. Twenty-first century curricular reform theoretically provides an educational model that transcends the industrial and information models and that places significantly greater emphasis on the transfer of knowledge to real world contexts and problem solving that is interdisciplinary, creative and innovative (Friesen & Jardine, 2009; Partnership for 21st Century Learning, n.d.). If one believes a paradigmatic shift that emphasizes creative, innovative and interdisciplinary problem solving is both worthwhile and necessary as we do, engaging in those skills as part of teacher education is paramount. Our programs must move beyond seeking "right answers," instead teaching "how to ask the right questions, evaluate information critically, and communicate effectively" (Action Canada, 2013, p. 4). C21 Canada (2012), a national nonprofit organization that advocates for 21st century models of learning in education, called for immediate action by Faculties of Education to instruct and model "modern instructional practices, including the teaching of 21st Century competencies" (p. 17) as well as "offer learners interconnected learning experiences, choices, and opportunities" (p. 17). This demand has driven our thinking and action through the question, how do PSTs learn to integrate 21st century learning when their own schooling experiences, as well of those of the teacher educators working with them, have been rooted in a traditional instructional model?

Complexity and Relationality as Underlying Conditions for Transformation

Senge, Cambron-McCabe, Lucas, Smith, Dutton, and Kleiner (2000) posited that learning is less about amassing facts and figures or even constructing knowledge and more about transformation of spirit and mind. Based on Senge et al.'s idea, in the TRUVic program traditional notions of knowledge construction, predominantly cognitive in nature, are expanded to include emotions, feelings, critical and creative ideas (Li, 2002). From the outset in the TRUVic program, preservice teachers engage with school-based teacher educators and even more importantly, with adolescent learners. They also have opportunities to meaningfully engage with their peers and with themselves, examining and challenging their deep-seated assumptions, their fears, biases and misconceptions in safe and supportive learning environments. This type of learning is synonymous with the capacity for change "when new skills and capabilities, new awareness and sensibilities, and new attitudes and beliefs reinforce each other" (Li, 2002, p. 402). Regular ongoing interactions in schools, working with youth and school partners, allows for new awareness of ways in which education is changing. Clark (1993) believed that a critical feature of transformational learning also changes how individuals see themselves and their world and in relation to others. Kegan (2000) added that through the process of engaging in transformative learning we move beyond simply adding to what we already know to profoundly alter *how* we know. By engaging with youth, developing an understanding of their interests and needs, creating learning opportunities for them, PSTs come to reimagine their role and develop meaningful relationships with others. The capacity for personal change is significant in our work with our preservice teachers as they grapple with who they are becoming as teachers; we want to empower them with the capacity for and belief in change as fundamental to their practice as teachers. Knowing this, the paradigmatic shift we have advocated for and attempted to embody is underpinned by complexity and features the experience of *be(come)ing*. Deleuze and Parnet (1987) suggested be(come) ing is represented by multiplicities that are "neither unities nor totalities" (p. vii). The relations formed therein cannot be reduced to the sum of parts. In our view, education is a relational endeavor that is both product and process akin to what Semetsky (2006) described as a holistic multiplicity. The interconnection of courses with field experiences, sharing assignments across courses, and regular interactions between instructors and preservice teachers enables all partners to gain a more holistic understanding of the complexity of school and ways in which they need to work together.

As complex systems, the structure of schools, the nature of the learning and the populations that are served within them are an interconnected and tangled mass (Sanford, Hopper, & Starr, 2015). Wheatley (2006) viewed education as an enterprise that co-evolves through the interactions of individuals. Such complexity requires us to abandon the antiquated teacher-training model to create space for embracing a collaboratively educative process. The TRUVic experience enables collegial interactions among instructors and students, encouraging authentic engagement with each other and with new ideas. Within education, we must embrace a process orientation that promotes understanding and valuing the relationships that are created through engagement. Education and schools will continue to be built upon relationships; the quality of those relationships and the primacy of them are what require greater attention. Senge, Scharmer, Jaworski, and Flowers (2005) offered *sensing*, *presencing*, and *realizing* as skills or actions necessary for educators to engage in complex systems. Sensing is about inner knowing where "the person's more informed, cognisant, attentive, and vigilant awareness enables the production of a unique and comprehensive, but intrinsic, perspective of the whole situation" (Branson, 2009, p. 121). Presencing is similar to mindfulness in that it requires the educator to suspend and redirect attention so that perception emerges from within the wholeness of the living system. In other words, it requires the educator to let inner knowing emerge and recognize that knowing as valid (Senge et al., 2005). TRUVic preservice teachers, throughout their first term, come to let go of preconceptions of educational "success," learning to pay attention to their intuitive senses as well as the environment around them. Realizing the dynamic process of co-creation of meaning enables educators to "adapt, create, and progress" (Branson, 2009, p. 120). Through realizing, educators, including PSTs and teacher educators, are better able to "see new possibilities, envisage new ways, or adopt new expectations" (p. 120). The vision of Senge et al. aligns with the view of schools as complex and learning as rhizomatic and in keeping with Reigeluth's (2004) belief that educators must be able to "constantly adjust and adapt the process to the emerging, ever-changing reality" (p. 8).

Because we see education as a complex, relational endeavor, we work actively against breaking down the process of teaching and learning into fractured parts. Yet, we acknowledge this can be a challenge. Too often, our schools and teacher education programs continue to compartmentalize subjects and even the time when those subjects are taught, favoring mechanism over fostering the interconnectedness featured in relational pedagogy. The type of connection forged of a relational pedagogy needs to guide the development of our preservice teachers is a more profound way.

Creating More Appropriate and Sustaining Ways of Supporting Growth in New Teachers

TRUVic is unique in its holistic, collaborative and creative approach to interconnected learning. Shaping the first term of our teacher education program to engage preservice teachers responsibly in their own learning and make them relationally accountable, we have enabled our PSTs to take responsibility for their own learning, recognizing and adopting indigenous learning principles (Sanford, Williams, Hopper, & McGregor, 2012; Wilson, 2008) identified earlier. The premise in this approach is that in order to be responsible for the other, preservice teachers need to recognize themselves as learners and relational beings. Greene (1977) encouraged teacher educators to enable "individuals to reflect upon their lived lives and the lives they lead in common with one another, not merely professionals-to-be, but as human beings participating in a shared reality" (pp. 54–55). Grumet (1989) suggested that curriculum theory "seeks to restore the contemplative moment in which we interrupt our taken-for-granted understandings of our work and ask again the basic questions that practical activity silences" (p. 13) and offers "places where individual theories about education may be contradicted by the specificity of experience" (p. 13).

To embed the importance of understanding the intersections of personal and professional identities in the process of be(come)ing, we invited our preservice teachers to narrate their experiences through autobiographical or autoethnographic explorations into their own lives. Through narrative, they have explored their assumptions and the uniqueness of their own powerful teacher becoming stories, then shared these with their cohort to foster a sense of community that can support them all to become reflexive in their ongoing practice. Preservice teachers' autobiographical writing "invites those who would teach to recover the world within which they came to be knowing subjects; it invites them to recover their own intentionality, and requires them to articulate and make explicit the relations which all take for granted" (Grumet, 1989, p. 15). One of the early assignments in our program tasks the PSTs with creating 90 second "Who am I?" videos, enabling them to explore—for themselves and their peers—their background experiences, to begin to consider their professional identity, and to recognize that prior knowledge is of importance to their future learning. These videos are collated and shared with their cohort peers, enabling them to create a community of both shared and diverse experiences, values, and knowledge; they provide authentic feedback to each other which also begins to open the conversation about meaningful approaches to assessment for diverse learners.

The TRUVic program offers coursework integrally linked with school-based experience, courses meld into one holistic experience that has seen instructors work collaboratively across spaces and places within both the university and local secondary schools. These approaches have allowed us to interweave curricular, identity and pedagogical understandings in embodied ways. Through the integration of these new learning spaces, that is, not in school, not in university classrooms, but in dialogic relational spaces in-between, preservice teachers and instructors have connected with students through conversations, observations, reflections, and collaborations that have led to more complex understandings of the needs of learners. Another assignment in the program is the development of a case study of a particular student (one who is unlike them) that they have encountered during their weekly school visits. This assignment builds on their "Who am I?" video and encourages them to consider their own positionality as they consider the needs and interests of this student and ways in which they could appropriately engage with this student.

Participated in weekly opportunities to immerse themselves into school/classroom life, PSTs are mentored by experienced teachers, and work alongside a range of educators working in variety of education contexts. In doing so, they are exposed to diverse pedagogical approaches, including the innovative use of technology, assessment practices, and collaborative/constructivist approaches to learning and teaching. A further expectation of the program is that, during their weekly school visits, they find opportunities to begin exploring their "teacher" roles, engaging with students as teachers. A discussion of the role of "teacher" ensues, as teaching encounters include many forms, from one-on-one support, small group engagement, peer- and team-teaching opportunities. They write reflections on what they have learned about "teaching" through these encounters, which activates not only their cognitive knowledge and skills, but also connects to the emotional aspects of these encounters, enabling them to "feel" what it is like to be a teacher.

As prospective teachers, they also engage with curriculum documents and have visited a range of teaching and learning contexts. Working in interdisciplinary teams, they create thematic units of study, broadening their conception of ways to approach pedagogy through issues and problem-based engagement rather than through didactic imparting of facts. This approach has provided an essential window into thinking about how to integrate curricula with a depth of understanding about learning, meeting diverse needs, and student engagement as well as to recognize and explore the tensions and contradictions they observe within school, between school and their university courses, as well as with the broader community. They have been supported in reflecting authentically on their learning experiences, both on campus and in the school, having storied their complex experiences and sharing with others.

Modeling a team-teaching approach, TRUVic instructors have connected regularly about next steps, directions, and outcomes. Community meetings with the students have been held regularly to gather feedback and input into what was working for students and what was not. Where possible in their schedules, instructors have attended each other's classes in order to support and inform how future classes are designed, building on theoretical discussions, practical queries and extensive observations.

TRUVic's cohort model has also enabled authentic learning relationships among the students, having supported them in discovering that they can be each other's best resources and to let go of their initial desire for their teacher education program to provide them with a blueprint guide to becoming a teacher. A community of learners that has supported each other in authentic ways will occur only when its members are not competing with each other for grades and recognition. As a result, an alternative form of assessment, contract grading, has been used in order to mitigate students' concerns about taking risks, and to eliminate the need to hierarchically rank the students. Through contract grading, TRUVic students have committed to developing as professionals in their teacher education program as opposed to being students focused on grades. All students achieved a B+ level for completing the formal requirements of the courses. Those who wish to attain a higher grade have negotiated further projects that (in keeping with the Indigenous principles underpinning the TRUVic approach) have enhanced the learning of the cohort as well as their own. These have often taken the form of creating further resources, developing handbooks of potential fieldtrips, and leading workshops for peers. Such re-framing of conventional notions of assessment and evaluation has enabled TRUVic students to share ideas, give each other feedback, and work together on projects, aware that they were not judged against each other or ranked in the class. Doing so has engaged them in a collaborative learning system, rather than a sorting system.

In reconceptualizing location, purpose, relationality, and assessment in our teacher education program, multiple spaces have been provided for thinking about teacher education and the preservice teachers' place in both the global and local contexts. As Doyle and Carter (2003) commented, "as teacher educators we try to inculcate too much too early" (p. 135). We have used dialogic relational pedagogies to enable narratives to emerge, to give language to experiences, and to explore fundamental educational dilemmas they regularly encounter. We have created a new institutional form in an effort to interweave storied curriculum in time and space that has been juxtaposed with frenetic classroom life so as to enable deep thinking and meaning-making.

Concluding Thoughts

As mentioned at the outset of this paper, much has been written about the need for transformation of teacher education practices. Our effort here is one contribution to the discourse based on the success of a model that we believe walks the talk of transformation in teacher education. We have attempted to build a course of action that we believe benefits PSTs as well as teacher education more broadly. TRUVic is one of many initiatives undertaken by teacher educators like ourselves that attempts to move teacher education beyond the techno-rational into a space that is more authentic, realistic and reflective of the needs of today's learners. We have taken the criticisms of teacher education and created a program that is a humble attempt at the antithesis of those criticisms. TRUVic offers PSTs opportunities to delve deeply into the formation of their professional identity and the implications of that identity on their pedagogical choices. Theory and practice are intertwined and are simultaneously examined in the field with the practicing teachers responsible for the seminar classes. The holistic approach to courses in the fall term allows the natural overlaps to strengthen PSTs' understanding of the complexity of education rather than asking them to try to neatly package the process of learning to teach into unrealistic, disingenuous little boxes stacked on top of one another. Legitimate professional learning communities emerge and are nurtured because of collegial membership of PSTs' practicing teachers, university faculty and community organizers. And perhaps most importantly, the view of education as relational has become less about rhetoric and more about the real world connections between people, place, and idea. Our efforts and actions demonstrate Russell's (2012) suggestion that teacher educators must shift their own paradigmatic stances in order for PSTs and the field of education they enter into to do the same. This chapter is one of many calls to action that we hope will support our colleagues and peers in their attempts to engage in the valuable process of transforming teacher education.

REFERENCES

Action Canada. (2013). *Future tense: Adapting Canadian education systems for the 21st century*. Retrieved from http://www.actioncanada.ca/wp-content/uploads/2014/04/TF2-Report_Future-Tense_EN.pdf

Branson, C. M. (2009). *Leadership for an age of wisdom*. Dordrecht, Netherlands: Springer Educational.
Canadians for 21st Century Learning and Innovation (C21). (2012). *Shifting minds: A 21st century vision for public education in Canada*. Retrieved from http://www.c21canada.org/wp-content/uploads/2012/11/Shifting-Minds-Revised.pdf
Clark, M. C. (1993). *Transformational learning*. Paper presented at the An Update on Learning Theory: New Directions for Adult and Continuing Education, San Francisco, CA.
Cochran-Smith, M., Ell, F., Ludlow, L., & Aitken, G. (2014). The challenge and promise of complexity theory for teacher education research. *Teachers College Record, 116*(5), 1–38.
Conroy, J., Hulme, M., & Menter, I. (2013). Developing a "clinical" model for teacher education. *Journal of Education for Teaching, 39*(5), 557–573. doi:10.1080/02607476.2013.836339
Darling-Hammond, L., & Lieberman, A. (2012). *Teacher education around the world: Changing policies and practices*. London, England: Routledge.
Darling-Hammond, L. (2006). Constructing 21st-century teacher education. *Journal of Teacher Education, 57*(3), 300–314. doi:10.1177/002248710528596
Deleuze, G., & Parnet, C. (1987). *Dialogues* (H. Tomlinson & B. Habberjam, Trans.). Minneapolis, MN: Minnesota University Press.
Doyle, W., & Carter, K. (2003). Narrative and learning to teach: Implications for teacher-education curriculum. *Journal of Curriculum Studies, 35*(2). 129–137.
Friesen, S., & Jardine, D. (2009). *21st century learning and learners*. Prepared for Western and Northern Canadian Curriculum Protocol by Galileo Educational Network.
Greene, M. (1977). Towards wide-awakeness: An argument for the arts and humanities in education. *Teachers College Record, 79*(1), 119–124.
Grumet, M. (1989). Generations: Reconceptualist curriculum theory and teacher education. *Journal of Teacher Education, 40*(1), 13–17.
Kegan, R. (2000). What 'form' transforms?: A constructive-developmental perspective on transformational learning. In J. Mezirow (Ed.), *Learning as transformation: Critical perspectives on a theory in progress* (pp. 35–69). San Francisco, CA: Jossey-Bass.
Korthagen, F., Loughran, J., & Russell, T. (2006). Developing fundamental principles for teacher education programs and practices. *Teaching and Teacher Education, 22*, 1020–1041.
Li, M. (2002). Fostering design culture through cultivating the user-designers design thinking and systems thinking. *Systemic Practice and Action research, 15*(5), 385–410.
Munby, H., Russell, T., & Martin, A. K. (2001). Teachers' knowledge and how it develops. In V. Richardson (Ed.), *Handbook of research on teaching* (4th ed., pp. 877–904). Washington, DC: American Educational Research Association.
O'Sullivan, E. V., Morrell, A., & O'Connor, M. A. (2002). *Expanding the boundaries and transformative learning: Essays on theory and praxis*. New York, NY: Palgrave.
Partnership for 21st century learning. (n.d.). *The intellectual and policy foundations of the 21st Century Skills Framework*. Washington DC: Author. Retrieved

from http://www.p21.org/storage/documents/docs/Intellectual_and_Policy_Foundations.pdf

Reigeluth, C. (2004). Chaos theory and the sciences of complexity: Foundations for transforming education. Retrieved from http://www.indiana.edu/~syschang/decatur/documents/chaos_reigeluth_s2004.pdf

Russell, T. (2012). Paradigmatic changes in teacher education: The perils, pitfalls and unrealized promise of the reflective practitioner. *Journal of the Theory and History of Education International Research Group, 13*, 71–91. Retrieved from https://queens.scholarsportal.info/ojs-archive/index.php/encounters/article/view/4426/4517

Russell, T., McPherson, S., & Martin, A. (2001). Coherence and collaboration in teacher education reform. *Canadian Journal of Education, 26*(1), 37–55. Retrieved from http://journals.sfu.ca/cje/index.php/cje-rce/article/view/2793/2094

Sanford, K., Hopper, T. H., & Starr, L. J. (2015). Transforming teacher education thinking: Complexity and relational ways of knowing. *Complicity: An International Journal of Complexity and Education, 12*(2), 26–48. Retrieved from http://ejournals.library.ualberta.ca/index.php/complicity/article/view/23817/19184

Sanford, K., Williams, L., Hopper, T., & McGregor, C. (2012). Decolonizing teacher education: Indigenous principles informing teacher education. *In Education, 18*(2). Retrieved from http://www.ineducation.ca/ .

Segall, A. (2002). *Disturbing practice: Reading teacher education as text.* New York, NY: Peter Lang.

Semetsky, I. (2006). *Delueze, education and becoming.* Rotterdam, Netherlands: Sense.

Senge, P., Cambron-McCabe, N., Lucas, T., Smith, B., Dutton, J., & Kleiner, A. (2000). *Schools that learn: A fifth discipline fieldbook for educators, parents, and everyone who cares about education.* New York, NY: Currency.

Senge, P., Scharmer, C.O., Jaworski, J., & Flowers, B.S. (2005). *Presence: Exploring profound change in people, organization and society.* London, England: Nicholas Brealey.

Wheatley, M. J. (2006). *Leadership and the new science: Discovering order in a chaotic world* (3rd ed.). San Francisco, CA: Berrett-Koehler.

Wilson, S. (2008). *Research is ceremony: Indigenous research methods.* Black Point, Nova Scotia: Fernwood.

CHAPTER 5

RETHINKING THE INTERSECTIONALITY OF THE ZONE OF PROXIMAL DEVELOPMENT

The Challenges of Disruptive and Transformative Change to Improve Instruction

Enrique A. Puig

Introduction

If good instruction has the potential to lead development (Vygotsky, 1978), then school systems, practitioner-scholars, and university-scholars have the transformational challenge of assessing and inventorying the intersectionality of students' Zones of Distal Development (Spear-Ellinwood, 2011), Zones of Proximal Development (Vygotsky, 1978) and Zones of Mesial Development to improve instruction. Consequently, the challenges of transformative change to improve instruction have to be realigned with

Transformative Pedagogies for Teacher Education:
Critical Action, Agency, and Dialogue in Teaching and Learning Contexts, pp. 69–85
Copyright © 2019 by Information Age Publishing
All rights of reproduction in any form reserved.

a growth mindset (Dweck, 2012) where the focus is not on how educators teach, but rather on how students learn. An issue that may be plaguing instruction is a lot of attention has been given to understanding the students' Zones of Proximal Development (Vygotsky, 1978) with little to no attention given to what students can and cannot accomplish independently.

The purpose of this chapter is to disrupt and problematize the practice of assuming that identifying a student's Zone of Proximal Development (Vygotsky, 1978) is sufficient to employ effective instructional practices informed by assessment. The chapter addresses both problematic and productive sides of current professional learning opportunities, instructional practices, and assessment. The author addresses these topics on the basis of a micro-ethnography through qualitative interviews, classroom observations, and student data with Foucault (1977) as a theoretical tool and lens. A goal of the chapter is to illustrate how it can contribute to the discourse of both productive sides and issues with assessment in literacy acquisition and instruction; regardless of core content area (e.g., English language arts, mathematics, science, and social studies) and its impact on professional learning.

Contemporary political and pedagogical agendas are briefly discussed as a way of establishing relevancy. Existing assessment literature and Foucault's (1977) theories encompassing power, disciplining technologies, discourse and panopticism are used as an analytical framework in order to demonstrate and enable an understanding of transformative challenges and potentials concerning literacy acquisition, assessment, instruction, and professional learning opportunities.

Adaptive Challenge

Heifetz and Linsky (2002), argue that adaptive challenges demand a transformation in beliefs and approaches that can take a long time to unravel and implement. The challenges of transformative change to improve instruction are adaptive challenges that necessitates disrupting and problematizing an issue in numerous spaces (i.e., classrooms, schools, districts) and across organizational borders (i.e., universities, school systems, state departments). The adaptive challenge and issue addressed in this chapter is the practice of assuming that identifying a student's Zone of Proximal Development (Vygotsky, 1978) is sufficient to employ effective instructional practices informed by assessment.

International, national, and state data are showing low progress in student learning and literacy acquisition over time; although certain studies illustrate students are currently reading and writing far more than the previous generation. Additionally, district administrators and classroom teachers are expressing that students are not making the accelerated progress demanded by national and state standards.

In the United States, in an attempt to improve literacy acquisition and instruction many states and districts to ensure funding are required to employ high stakes static assessments that highlight student deficits as a solution to improve instruction and over time have become a systematic impediment to literacy acquisition, instruction, and professional learning. Consequently, static assessments such as state standardized assessments and end of course exams have become a "technology of domination" (Foucault, 1977) over teachers and students used to engineer a conceptual panopticon to monitor school and classroom activities under a mantle of systematic and explicit instruction void of intention or thought and coherence. Along with punitive evaluations and school grading, years of leaving no child behind and racing to the top has shown that a strong focus on high stakes testing is not the answer to improving either instruction, students' literacy acquisition, or practitioner-scholars' professional learning.

Part of the concern with employing technologies of domination to control curriculum is narrowing definitions to increase control. Experienced educators understand that narrow definitions of instructional practices will not engage all learners (Clay, 2015). Currently, one term in particular is used extensively in the hopes of improving instruction—Vygotsky's Zone of Proximal Development (ZPD) (1978). The zone where learners can learn with the support of a more knowledgeable other or some other external mediator to learning such as electronic devices. At present, quite a few schools and parents are receiving misnamed diagnostic reports that equate students' ZPD to a grade equivalent (e.g., 2.4–3.4) based on a computer administered reading test without taking into account what students can do and cannot do; much less, how are they processing information or a practitioner-scholars professional opinion grounded in day-to-day interactions with students. Figure 5.1, is an actual example of part of a diagnostic report teachers and parents receive equating the Zone of Proximal Development to a grade equivalent.

This report presents diagnostic information about the student's general reading skills, based on the student's performance on a ▓▓▓ Reading test.

SS	GE	PR	PR Range	Below Average	Average 50	Above Average	NCE	IRL	ZPD
306	2.6	18	12-25	◆			30.7	2.6	2.4-3.4

Figure 5.1. Diagnostic report.

Without accounting for students' funds of knowledge (what they know and/or can do) and what is completely out of their reach, identifying a student's ZPD in the hopes of guiding instruction effectively and responsively may be misleading and misinforming practitioner-scholars and parents on how to support their children's literacy acquisition. Furthermore, to add to the confusion of understanding the Zone of Proximal Development, Figure 5.2 shows that the same diagnostic report mentioned above associates the ZPD with what a student can do independently. This is a blatant and confusing contradiction in terms. The ZPD does not define independent learning but does take into account what a student can do with the support of a more knowledgeable other (Vygotsky, 1978). How "proximal" is being defined may be the issue.

This student's Zone of Proximal Development (ZPD) for independent fiction is 2.4 - 3.4.

Figure 5.2. Diagnostic report associating the ZPD with what a student can do independently.

These "diagnostic" reports, distributed at a national level, caused the researcher to investigate practitioner-scholars concepts of not only of the ZPD, but what their understandings of what can students do or not independently. The following questions guided the work:

1. What are practitioner-scholars' understanding of the Zone of Proximal Development?
2. What are practitioners'-scholars' understanding of how students process information to identify students' strengths and needs to inform instruction?
3. What are practitioner-scholars' understanding of the Zone of Distal Development?

Methods

The concept of a formative experiment framed this investigation. A benefit of using classroom research from a formative experiment perspective is that the effects of instruction are recognized to be the product of a network interacting variables within the school and the classroom environment. Formative experiments explore how potentially positive practices can be applied to attain highly regarded pedagogical objectives that are often disruptive or transformative (Reinking & Bradley, 2008). Formative experiments aim to align theory, research, and practice by designing instructional practices in realistic contexts.

A formative experiment is one among many methodological approaches that are within a more comprehensive classification usually referred to as design-based research (van den Akker, Gravemeijer, McKenny, & Nieveen, 2006) or design experiments (Brown, 1992). Design-based research, and subsequently formative experiments, see education research as similar to engineering where theories are put into practice, testing and refining those theories systematically through the methodical design of practical solutions to achieve precise objectives (Sloan & Gorard, 2003). Formative experiments have developed as an alternative to conventional experimental or naturalistic methodological approaches that have not satisfactorily linked the gap between research and practice (Bradley & Reinking, 2010; Reinking & Bradley, 2008).

In a formative experiment, systematic data collection highlights features that augment or hinder the effectiveness of the instructional practice in accomplishing the objective and that data informs ongoing adaptations of the instructional practice. Although design-based research, including formative experiments, often involves mixed methods of data collection, the present study employed a micro-ethnography approach to accumulate and examine data. The present study, was also informed by Reinking and Bradley's (2008) guiding questions for creating, facilitating, and reporting a formative experiment, which follows:

1. What is the pedagogical goal of the experiment and what pedagogical theory establishes its value?
2. What is an instructional intervention that has potential to achieve the identified pedagogical goal?
3. As the instructional practice is implemented, what factors enhance or inhibit its effectiveness in achieving the pedagogical goal?
4. How can the instructional practice and its implementation be modified to achieve more effectively the pedagogical goal?
5. What unanticipated positive or negative outcomes does the instructional practice produce?
6. Has the learning environment changed as a result of the instructional practice?

Using a hybrid of traditional ethnographic approaches of triangulating participant observations, nonparticipant observations and artifacts, the researcher employed a mixed method design of qualitative and quantitative assessments. Data was collected during all phases of the study to provide and obtain timely formative feedback. Constant comparative analysis (Glaser & Strauss, 1967; Strauss, 1987; Strauss & Corbin, 1990) was used to analyze the data. Although it may appear that grounded theory was at the forefront of the study to generate and ground theoretical understandings, the author's primary purpose was to bring particular perspectives to the analysis based on current assessments provided to practitioner-scholars to inform instruction. In addition to student assessments, data collection methods included field notes and a schedule of observation dates. These methods coupled with observations, and semi-structured focus group conversations helped the researcher develop a holistic perspective, and a better understanding of the phenomena assessed. On the surface, the study and analyses comes across as linear. As most micro-ethnography, it was cluttered, recursive, at times random, and dialogical.

The study is confidential: although the researcher will know the identity of subjects but will not divulge identity or private information to others without permission as agreed upon when information was given. The participant and nonparticipant field notes from classroom observation do not identify students or teachers by name. Field notes were coded with a T for teacher discourse and S1, S2, S3, and so forth, was used to distinguish student responses. No sensitive information on either teachers or students was collected in this study to identify individuals.

Theoretical Perspective: Triadic Zones of Development Theory

When we define literacy as the ability to characterize, confirm, comprehend, clarify, create, calculate, interpret, critique, and convey information by whatever sources and resources available for individuals to thrive in a given society and culture; all assessment and evaluation of literate behaviors is dependent on language and theory. This broad definition of literacy serves as a guiding force to investigate instructional practices that take into account students' strengths as well as their needs. The proposed triadic model of dynamic learning and teaching is grounded on funds of knowledge theory from a sociocultural and historical perspective. It introduces a framework for thinking about assessment and instruction that disrupts and problematizes instruction in Vygotsky's Zone of Proximal Development (ZPD) (1978) and accounts for independent learning behaviors as well as learning behaviors associated with learners' ability to recognize the unknown.

As explained by Vygotsky (1978), learning opportunities occur in the ZPD with the support of a more knowledgeable other or other forms of external mediators. As language and knowledge is acquired and consistently employed, it becomes "fossilized" in what the researcher/author terms the Zone of Mesial Development (ZMD) fostering agentic autodidactic behavior through self-regulation, self-monitoring, and self-directing. Borrowing from the medical field, the term "mesial" illustrates the opposite of distal. It is used in this chapter to describe another conceptual space where learners accumulate and store funds of knowledge (Moll, Amanti, Neffe, & González, 1992) and become critical autodidactic learners taking on responsibilities for their own acquisition of knowledge and physical abilities. I use the term "mesial" to define a core zone or foundation of knowledge and abilities situated in a conceptual center.

Simultaneously, proficient learners recognize that there is more to learn that they do not know or cannot do alone. This acknowledgement of the unknown occurs in the Zone of Distal Development (ZDD) (Moll, 2014; Spear-Ellinwood, 2011) and nurtures curiosity, wonder, goal setting, and potentially motivation to sustain learning over time. The term ZDD (Spear-Ellinwood, 2011) describes another conceptual third space in a triadic model where learners cannot construct any new learning or accomplish any new task even with the support of a more knowledgeable other or any external mediators but may serve as a springboard for motivation or feedforward mechanism in a learning environment primed for learning.

Within each identified "zone" there is a subtext, text, and hypertext. From a learner's perspective subtexts are inferences constructed from lived experiences in the learning environment and usually are accompanied by an emotional response; texts can be conceptual or concrete but either are content for dissection and discussion; and hypertexts are the genuine questions prompted by engagement with either the texts or subtexts. The aforementioned learning environment can be either in a traditional school setting or outside of the traditional school setting. From an instructional perspective, if subtexts, texts, and hypertexts are to inform instruction they have to be assessed dynamically and statically. In this case, the subtexts are the inferences or conclusions an observant practitioner-scholar makes, while the texts are usually observable and evident. Hypertexts in this theoretical construct are the unanswered questions raised by observant educators. Effective educators triangulate all three types of texts seamlessly to ground instruction on students' strengths before determining needs. Unfortunately, many practitioner-scholars jump quickly to addressing student needs without accounting for their strengths. In many cases, we have observed misinterpretation of assessments translate into what Paolo Freire (1970) termed a "banking" model of instruction where item knowledge is continuously "deposited" into the learners' head. When this occurs, valuable instructional time is wasted and acceleration in learning is delayed or hindered. Note that the term texts in this context are not restricted to print.

Under the proposed triadic model of learning, all three "zones" of a learner needs to be taken into account for instruction to be effective and efficient to support the development of a self-extending system for learning (Clay, 2005) and a growth mindset for instruction (Dweck, 2012; Johnston, 2012). Figure 5.3 provides a graphic representation of the concept. The author proposes that effective informed instruction occurs when practitioner-scholars recognize students' strengths and needs and the intersectionality of the ZMD, ZPD, and ZDD.

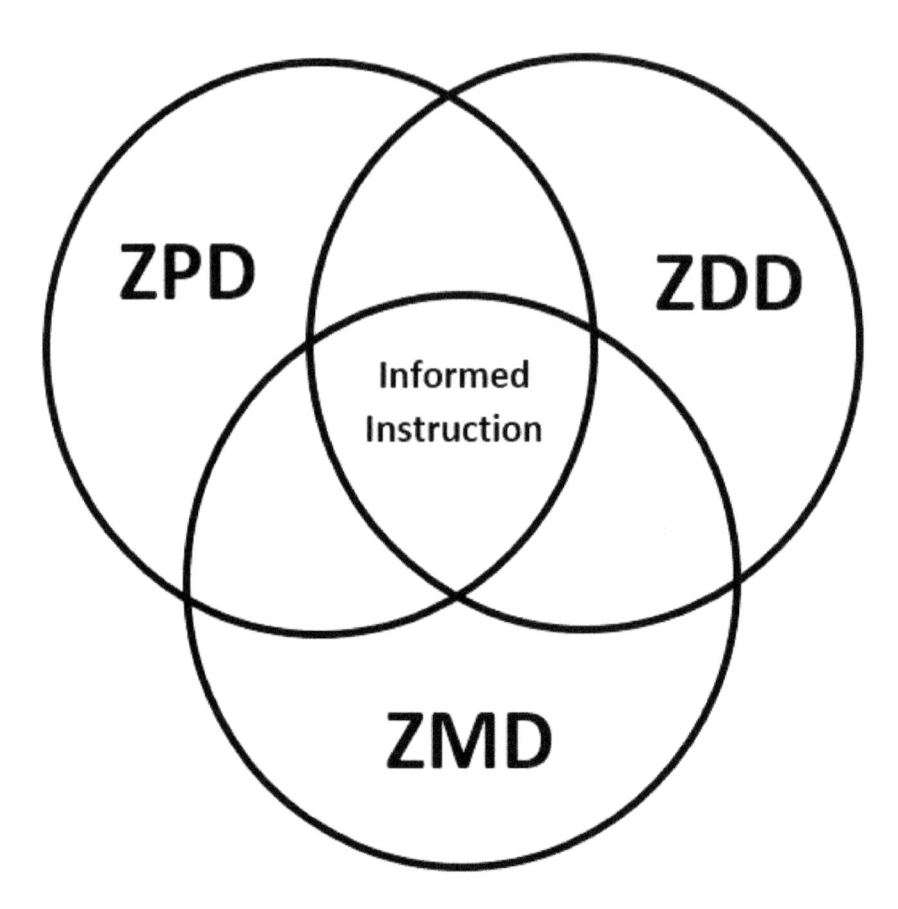

Figure 5.3. Triadic model of learning.

Assessments that document and report students' deficits are counterproductive to developing a growth mindset. Identifying and capitalizing on all three zones can bolster positive change in students' education. If learners grow into the intellectual environment they are in (Vygotsky, 1978), focusing instruction in one zone without assessing, evaluating, and considering the others has the potential to disable learners by the conditions of learning that are engineered into the environmental design of a classroom (Clay, 1987). Consequently, all three zones are dependent on the Conditions of Learning (Cambourne, 1995) that are in place. Cambourne's

Conditions of Learning is explained further under the section for implications for instruction and professional learning.

On the other hand, if extensive or ongoing instruction focuses solely on a learner's ZPD, learners may become dependent with the dependence potentially manifesting itself as a labeled disability of environmental nature. However, if extensive or ongoing instruction focuses solely on a learner's ZMD learning may become stagnant and limiting; and if extensive ongoing instruction focuses solely on the ZDD learners will be frustrated and develop a sense of helplessness over time with diminishing interest and motivation.

Relying solely on static assessments such as state standardized assessments has provided a skewed understanding of where instruction needs to be. Currently and erroneously, high-stakes and static assessments are used to determine a student's Zones of Proximal Development void of the professional opinion of the practitioner-scholar supported by dynamic assessments. Determining a student's "next" zone of development or ZPD requires engaging with students and employing dynamic assessments by an observant knowledgeable educator. Utilizing an observant and knowledgeable educator, data can then be used to make informed decisions about appropriate effective and efficient instruction based on students' strengths and needs.

Generally, static assessments potentially identify a learner's ZDD. To provide data-informed instruction, educators need to become familiar with various dynamic assessments and static assessments; and triangulate conclusions that bring to the forefront the learner's ZDD, ZPD, and ZMD. The plural "zones" is used intentionally throughout this chapter since each academic and social context creates a variety of zones with all learners. In other words, proficient learners have many Zones of Mesial Development, many Zones of Proximal Development, and many Zones of Distal Development that are dependent on the context and the content in which learning takes place and the learning environment for the learning to take place.

Zones of Distal Development (ZDD)

As educators and learners assess and inventory Zones of Proximal Development, we must be conscious of the Zones of Distal Development (ZDD) when teaching towards students' next zone of development. The ZDD is the conceptual zone of learning originating at the outer limits of what the learner can learn in cooperation with a more knowledgeable other or external mediator/s and extending beyond what is completely out of reach or unattainable, even with the support of a more knowledgeable other

(Spear-Ellinwood, 2011). Without a working understanding of students' ZDD, determining the ZPD will be challenging.

The ZDD requires the learner to acquire knowledge in the ZPD and potentially develop distal goals with or without assistance. Educators should consider how to organize free-to-take-risks learning environment acknowledging Zones of Distal Development, mindful of the intentional guidance to build on knowledge and practices acquired in successive experiences—the culmination of which brings the distal goal—critical competence—within proximal reach in the final analysis. Ultimately, curiosity, imagination and a cognitive feedforward/feedback mechanism develops in part in the ZDD to enable learners to be able to predict and anticipate, monitor understanding, and search for more information.

Zones of Proximal Development (ZPD)

The Zone of Proximal Development, often abbreviated as ZPD, is the difference between what a learner can do without support and what a learner can do with support. It is a concept proposed, but not fully expanded, by the Russian psychologist Lev Vygotsky (1896–1934) during the last ten years of his life. The Zone of Proximal Development (ZPD) is defined as: "the distance between the actual developmental level as determined by independent problem solving and the level of potential development as determined through problem solving under adult guidance, or in collaboration with more capable peers" (Vygotsky, 1978, p. 86).

Vygotsky regarded interaction with peers as an operative manner of developing executive cognitive function. He suggested that educators use cooperative learning practices where less knowledgeable learners develop scientific or academic concepts and vocabulary with assistance from more knowledgeable others - within the Zone of Proximal Development. With the advent of technology in our lives and educational learning environments, external mediators to learning extend beyond more knowledgeable others.

Vygotsky espoused that when a learner is learning in the ZPD a specific task or concept, providing the appropriate assistance will give the learner enough of an advantage to accomplish the task or grasp the concept more easily. Because of the following statements from Vygotsky's (1986) work, the author defines the term proximal to mean "next." Consequently, the Zone of Proximal Development is defined to mean a learner's next zone of development with the support of a more knowledgeable other or external mediator/s. The following Vygotskian principles guides our thinking into how learning should occur in the ZPD and underscores the concept of a learner's "next" zone of development:

1. What a child can do in cooperation today, he can do alone tomorrow.
2. The only good kind of instruction is that which marches ahead of development and leads it.
3. Instruction must be oriented toward the future, not the past.
4. Instruction does not begin in school.
5. Instruction given in one area can transform and reorganize other areas.

Zones of Mesial Development (ZMD)

The Oxford Dictionary defines mesial as "relating to or directed towards the middle line of a body." In this chapter, I repurpose the word "mesial" to indicate a central or middle space of autodidactic learning and introduce the term Zones of Mesial Development. It may appear that the Zones of Mesial Development has been historically labeled as the independent learning area or third space. Upon a closer inspection, by introducing the term ZMD, the author's goal is to disrupt and further the discourse on the importance of taking into account learners' funds of knowledge as an instrument for self-teaching and development. Since Vygotsky (1978) introduced the concept of the Zone of Proximal Development and Spear-Ellinwood (2011) brought us the Zone of Distal Development, the field was ripe for the introduction of the term Zone of Mesial Development into the discourse. Professional conversations that lack discourse on students' strengths, or funds of knowledge, focuses educators/practitioner-scholars on assessment and instruction from a deficit model that fosters a fixed mindset that has the potential to hinder present and future learning.

In the ZMD, learners develop agentic behaviors that promote self-monitoring, self-regulating, and self-extending behaviors through an increase in language acquisition and experiences. In literate enterprises, the ZMD becomes visible when students self-correct and self-engage in searching behaviors to gather more information to support a defensible interpretation of texts. It is worth noting that as the ZPD expands so does the ZMD and ZDD. Generally, an increase in the ZMD is accompanied by an increase in vocabulary or language which exponentially increases the potential to expand the ZPD and ZDD. The adage, "the more you know the more you don't know" illustrates the synergistic nature and orchestration of all three zones (ZDD, ZPD, & ZMD).

Implications and Potential Impact on Assessment

Assessment and evaluation in education are critical to inform public policy in education, funding, and instruction; but what is not explicitly assessed and evaluated is just as critical in informing public policy in education, funding, and instruction. Coined by the sociologist Daniel Yankelovich (1972), the McNamara fallacy (also known as quantitative fallacy), named for Robert McNamara, the United States Secretary of Defense from 1961 to 1968, describes constructing a conclusion founded exclusively on quantitative assessments and disregarding all others which has the potential to misinform and mislead. The logic assumed is that these other assessments cannot be proven.

Education is not a business endeavor that produces products. Education is in the business of producing complex humans that think critically to become productive and caring citizens in a given culture and society. Experienced and effective educators know that looking at just the "numbers" does not tell the whole story of a complex process that involves broad-spectrum overlapping systems for learning when the goal is to inform instruction; especially when assessing and evaluating the literacy acquisition of students from diverse cultures.

Yankelovich's McNamara's fallacy logic model follows:

- The first step is to measure whatever can be measured easily. Although convenient, it may be misleading. Using Words Correct Per Minute as a sole measurement to report students' reading fluency is one example of something that can be easily measured but misleading. The use of pseudo or nonsense words to measure a young student's phonological knowledge may be another misleading assessment when taken in isolation from real reading and writing.
- The second step is to disregard that which can't be easily measured or to give it an arbitrary quantitative value. For example, using a rubric to document how a student is processing information may be artificial and misleading; especially if we subscribe to the idea that literacy acquisition is a nonlinear and complex process.
- The third step is to presume that what cannot be measured easily really is not important. Comprehension and fluency cannot be truly measured easily, but no one in education will deny their importance. The author acknowledges that some colleagues will argue that comprehension and fluency can be easily measured. Accurate word calling and words correct per minute are not effective measures of deeply comprehending a text.
- The fourth step is to say that what cannot be easily measured really does not exist. In education, this mindset is the antithesis of good instruction.

McNamara's Fallacy is highlighted under implications for assessments in this chapter because a triadic model that accounts for zones of development cannot easily be measured but is critical to inform instruction. The author argues that to genuinely assess and inventory a student's ZDD, ZPD, and ZMD static and dynamic assessments have to be employed by a knowledgeable, observant and mindful educator to improve instruction. Although reliability on static assessments is usually higher than dynamic assessments, it is a broad dipstick to inform instruction. Numbers alone will not tell the whole story of a student's strengths and needs.

Implications and Potential Impact on Professional Learning and Instruction

John Hattie's (2009) synthesis of over 800 meta-analyses on learning, tells us that teacher interaction with students and quality professional learning opportunities for educators has a high impact on student learning. Consequently, Hattie's work should serve as a beacon leading us to the understanding that we have to invest in professional learning opportunities for practitioner scholars.

If we want practitioner-scholars to have a growth mindset and build on students' strengths, responsive and contingent teaching cannot take place unless a teacher has a working knowledge of a student's ZDD, ZPD, and ZMD. By having a working and developing knowledge of a student's ZDD, ZPD, and ZMD, educators can focus on the learner's repertoire of responses, respond without delay with the utmost relevancy, provide provisional support, and modify vital instruction as needed. Armed with the tentative understanding of a student's ZDD, ZPD, and ZMD educators can more likely proceed with immediate intensive instruction to promote acceleration in learning. Marie Clay (2005) tells us that, "It is much easier to learn about the unknown from the very well known" (p. 174). Yet, current static assessment practices focus on what students do not know rather than what is very well known to determine the unknown and perpetuates Freire's (1970) concept of a banking model in education where item knowledge is perpetually deposited into students' heads.

Professional learning and quality instruction go hand in hand. Introducing the ZDD, ZMD, and reviewing the ZPD has complex but manageable implications for creating professional learning opportunities to support practitioner-scholars in becoming keen observers of students' strengths and needs to improve instruction. Guided by the work of Malcom Knowles (1978) on adult learners some key features and questions for consideration are:

1. Professional language needs to be updated to "upgrade" thinking regarding ZDD, ZPD, and ZMD.

2. A powerful and clear focus on understanding literacy learning as a process needs to be developed and repeatedly addressed grounded in the work with students.
    a. What is occurring in the learner's head?
        i. What source/s of information is the student using to predict and anticipate?
        ii. How and what source/s of information are they monitoring to generate a defensible of texts?
        iii. What sources of interpretation do they rely on or neglect to search to comprehend?
        iv. What sources of information do they rely on or neglect to self-correct?
    b. How do I as the teacher, interact with what is occurring?
        1. Is my language as the teacher assisting or assessing the students' performance?
3. Ongoing job-embedded professional learning opportunities that ground theory into practice should be employed.
4. Ongoing professional discourse on the impact of the intersectionality of the ZMD, ZPD, and ZDD to improve instruction.
5. Continuous review of Cambourne's Conditions of Learning in designing multisensory learning environments that take into account.
    a. What demonstrations are being provided for students?
    b. How are students being immersed in content?
    c. What responses are students receiving during the process of learning?
    d. Who is being held responsible for learning?
    e. How are students' approximations addressed in the learning environment?
    f. How are students engaged in the learning environment?
    g. What opportunities are being provided for students to use what they are learning?
    h. How are students' interpreting expectations in the learning environment?

Summary

Disrupting and problematizing instruction using Vygotsky's (1978) Zone of Proximal Development as a springboard through Foucault's (1977) lens of power and education has implications and transformative adaptive challenges for assessment, instruction, and professional learning opportunities for university-scholars, and practitioner-scholars who work with students on a daily basis. Using a formative experiment model, this microethnography included interviews and hours of classroom observations and interactions in both elementary (Grades K–5) and secondary (Grades 11–12) classrooms. It demonstrates that solely using static assessments and looking at the ZPD alone to inform instruction may have limited potential and misleading results in creating dependent learners rather than independent critical thinkers and future citizens. The author found that when practitioner-scholars employed static (e.g., summative assessments, standardized assessments) AND dynamic assessments (e.g., running records, student writing samples) to determine the intersectionality of students' Zones of Distal Development (Spear-Ellinwood, 2011) and Zones of Mesial Development (in addition to the ZPD), it increased the likelihood of more effective and efficient instruction to promote independent critical learners.

Vygotsky (1987) has stated that it is important that theoretical knowledge does not become the end goal, but that the knowledge garnered be targeted at effective and responsible actions toward practical activity. A lot has been written and discussed about a potential "third space" where learners create an identity for learning within classrooms (Cook, 2005; Gutierrez, Baquedano-Lopez, & Tejeda, 2000; Moje et al, 2004). Heeding Vygotsky's (1987) advice, it may be that by shifting the pedagogical discourse to include three broad-spectrum "zones" or third spaces, university-scholars and practitioner-scholars will more readily adopt and adapt a growth mindset to improve the practical activity of instruction over time. This may also have an impact on the professional learning opportunities that teachers are offered to begin focusing on students' strengths as well as needs. Consequently, in an epoch enamored with assessments it may be that future studies on the intersectionality of the ZMD, ZPD, and the ZDD is the next frontier for university-scholars and practitioner-scholars to investigate to improve instruction, assessment and professional learning.

REFERENCES

Bradley, B. A., & Reinking, D. (2010). Enhancing research and practice in early childhood through formative and design experiments. *Early Child Development and Care, 181*(3), 305–319.

Brown, A. L. (1992). Design experiments: Theoretical and methodological challenges in creating complex interventions in classroom settings. *The Journal of Learning Sciences, 2*(2), 141–178.

Cambourne, B. (1995). Toward an educationally relevant theory of literacy learning: Twenty years of inquiry. *The Reading Teacher, 49*(3), 182–190.

Clay, M.M. (1987). Learning to be learning disabled. *New Zealand Journal of Educational Studies*, *22*(2), 155–173.
Clay. M. (2015). *Change over time in children's literacy development*. Portsmouth, NH. Heinemann.
Clay, M.M. (2005). *Literacy lessons designed for individuals: Part two, teaching procedures*. Portsmouth, NH. Heinemann.
Cook, M. (2005). 'A place of their own': Creating a classroom 'third space' to support a continuum of text construction between home and school. *Literacy*, *39*(2), 85–90. UKLA.
Dweck, C. (2012). *Mindset: The new psychology of success* (2nd ed.). New York, NY: Ballantine Books.
Foucault, M. (1977). *Discipline and punish: Birth of the prison*. Toronto, ON: Random House.
Freire, P. (1970). *Pedagogy of the oppressed*. New York, NY: Herder and Herder.
Glaser, B., & Strauss, A. (1967). *The discovery of grounded theory: Strategies for qualitative research*. New York, NY: Aldine.
Gutierrez, K., Baquedano-Lopez, P., & Tejeda, C. (2000). Rethinking diversity: Hybridity and hybrid language practices in the third space. *Mind and Culture and Activity*: *An International Journal*, *6*(4), 286–303.
Hattie, J. (2009). *Visible learning: A synthesis of over 800 meta-analyses relating to achievement*. Routledge/Taylor & Francis Group.
Heifetz, R. A., & Linsky, M. (2002). *Leadership on the line*. Boston, MAL Harvard Business School Press.
Johnston, P. (2012). *Opening minds: Using language to change minds*. Portland, ME: Stenhouse.
Knowles, M. S. (1978). *The adult learner: A neglected species*. Houston, TX: Gulf.
Moll, L. C., Amanti, C., Neff, D., & González, N. (1992). Funds of knowledge for teaching: A qualitative approach to connect households and classrooms. *Theory Into Practice*, *31*(2), 132–141.
Moll, L. C. (2014). *L.S. Vygotsky and education*. Abington, England: Routledge/Taylor & Francis Group.
Moje, E. B., Ciechanowski, K.M., Kramer, K., Ellis, L., Carrillo, R., & Collazo,T. (2004). Working toward third space in content area literacy: An examination of everyday funds of knowledge and discourse. *Reading Research Quarterly*, *39*(1), 38–70.
Reinking, D., & Bradley, B.A. (2008). *Formative and design experiments: Approaches to language and literacy research*. New York, NY: Teachers College Press.
Sloan, F.C., & Gorard, S. (2003). Exploring modeling aspects of design experiments. *Educational Researcher*, *32*(1), 29–31.
Spear-Ellinwood, K. (2011). *Re-conceptualizing the organizing circumstance of learning* (Unpublished doctoral dissertation). College of Education, University of Arizona, Tucson, Arizona.
Strauss, A. (1987). *Qualitative analysis for social scientists*. Cambridge, England: Cambridge University Press.
Strauss, A., & Corbin, J. (1990). *Basics of qualitative research: Grounded theory procedures and techniques*. Newbury Park, CA: SAGE.

van den Akker, J., Gravemeijer, K., McKenny, S., & Nieveen, N. (Eds.). (2006). *Educational design research*. London, England and New York, NY: Routledge.

Vygotsky, L. S. (1978). *Mind in society: The development of higher psychological processes*. Cambridge, MA: Harvard University Press.

Vgotsky, L. S. (1986). Thought and language (A. Kozuin, Ed. & Trans.). Cambridge, MA: MIT Press.

Vygotsky, L. S. (1987). Thinking and speech. In R. Rieber & A. Caron, (Eds), N. Minich, (Trans.), *L. S. Vygotsky: Collected works* (Vol.1, pp. 39–285). New York, NY: Plenum.

Yankelovich, D. (1972). *Corporate priorities: A continuing study of the new demands on business*. Stamford, CT: Daniel Yankelovich, Inc.

CHAPTER 6

FIDELITY OF PRACTICE

The Challenge of Transformative Change in Teacher Professional Development

Mary Hutchinson and Xenia Hadjioannou

INTRODUCTION AND THEORETICAL CONTEXT

Constructing robust bridges between teachers' pedagogical praxis and the theoretical frameworks and instructional recommendations of professional development is a fundamental challenge for teacher educators. Indeed, research on teacher professional development finds that such programs are often unsuccessful in substantively changing teachers' beliefs and attitudes and that, ultimately, course acquired knowledge does not necessarily make its way into instructional practice (Cohen & Hill, 2000; Dusenbury, Brannigan, Falco, & Hansen, 2003; and Fullan, 1982). In this chapter we investigate the notion of *fidelity of practice*—the reflective and productive implementation of development-recommended instructional practices— through a longitudinal mixed-methods case study examining the impact of training designed to prepare mainstream classroom teachers to work with English Learners (ELs).[1]

Transformative Pedagogies for Teacher Education:
Critical Action, Agency, and Dialogue in Teaching and Learning Contexts, pp. 87–102
Copyright © 2019 by Information Age Publishing
All rights of reproduction in any form reserved.

The spotlight on the preparation of mainstream classroom teachers to work with culturally and linguistically diverse learners has increased as more and more schools experience an upsurge in EL numbers. In response, a great deal of research has examined the kinds of professional development teachers need in order to support ELs in their mainstream classrooms (Casteel & Ballantyne, 2010; Lucas, 2015; Santos, Darling-Hammond, & Cheuk, 2012; Samson & Collins, 2012; Working Group on ELL Policy, 2009). The importance of this preparation cannot be understated, as ELs persistently suffer from low levels of academic achievement, high dropout rates and low rates of secondary enrollment (Abbate-Vaughn, 2008; Ballantyne, Sanderman, & Levy, 2008; DePaoli et al., 2015; Marin, 2015; Mitchell, 2016). Given this state of affairs, it is imperative to have mainstream classroom teachers who are well prepared to work with culturally and linguistically diverse students. And, although research to support the kinds of professional development needed to meet this demand exists, what is less known is the long-term effectiveness of this development, particularly the degree to which pedagogical approaches promoted through professional development become substantively and productively integrated into educators' teaching praxis in the long run. In other words, further investigation is needed into *fidelity of practice*— "how and at what point teachers appropriate new understandings with regards to the education of [ELs]" (Teague, 2010, p. 6). Ultimately, insight into this issue can facilitate the process of "bridging research and practice," which "is a persistent problem in education and a perennial impediment to the implementation of education reforms" (Stein et al., 2008, p. 368).

THE IMPERATIVE TO EXAMINE FIDELITY OF PRACTICE

When educational reform and curricular interventions are put in place, their aspirational claim is that their faithful implementation will lead to improvements in the outcomes of the educational process. Indeed, to make an authoritative claim about the effectiveness of any approach or program, it first needs to be ascertained that it was actually implemented and that pedagogical praxis was transformed in ways compatible to the intentions of the innovation. Consequently, there is widespread agreement that educational researchers must study the fidelity with which curricular interventions are implemented, especially for programs that receive federal and state funding and/or are executed with the belief that they will bring about significant change. In reality, over a billion dollars in federal government funds alone is sent annually to school districts, yet according to Pamela Grossman, a leading researcher in the field, "we know less than we should about professional development, particularly given the money that is invested in it" (Fertig & Garland, 2012). A report by the U.S. Department of Education (2011) underscored this concern: "Despite the presumed importance of high-quality implementation, reviews of the research literature indicate that implementation fidelity is often lacking" (p. 7). Indeed, "research on the factors associated with high-quality implementation is even rarer than that on the levels of implementation fidelity achieved" (p. 7).

Efforts to determine the degree of faithfulness to educational reform and adopted programs have often been pursued through the notion of Fidelity of Implementation (FOI), which is defined as "adherence to both the proper execution of the specific practices and the effective coordination of all the practices as they are intended to be combined" (Perlman & Redding, 2011, p. 81). However, O'Donnell (2008) reports that FOI research is often encumbered by inconsistent definitions, whereas others find the term problematic because it is persistently delimited to wholesale implementation of programmatic interventions that require "strict adherence" to programmatic scripts (Achinstein & Ogawa, 2006, p. 32) in ways that often "deskill" teachers who are forced to apply these programs into their classrooms (Achinstein & Ogawa, 2006; Shelton, 2010).

However, *fidelity* can and should also be understood in light of current effective professional development practices, which focus more on the teachers as learners in their own classrooms and less on "a repertoire of activities and methods for learning [which] follows more or less directly from the frequency with which professional development programs use these specific activities" (Opfer & Pedder, 2011, p. 377). Aware of the importance of examining the transformative effects of professional development in teaching praxis and mindful of the deprofessionalizing connotations of *fidelity of implementation,* here we propose the idea of *fidelity of practice* (FOP), a more open-ended process involving teachers identifying how to effectively implement best practices recommended through professional development into their particular contexts. Through this perspective, teachers are not mere implementers, but are viewed as "users and creators of legitimate forms of knowledge who make decisions about how best to teach ... within complex socially, culturally, and historically situated contexts" (Johnson, 2006, p. 239). This approach relies on teachers having strong theoretical understandings of how to support the academic growth of ELs and a variety of evidence-based practices to implement as necessary depending on the learning context. FOP accounts for the various opportunities that teachers have to not only construct their understanding about working with ELs, but also shape a vision and philosophy that informs their practice about how to effectively serve their needs.

THE STUDY

Professional development on teaching English as a second or additional language typically seeks to bring about transformative changes to teachers' instructional praxis in ways that support ELs. The aspiration of such programs is for participants to become knowledgeable about the processes of second language acquisition, to add Teaching English as a Second Language (TESL) practices to their methodological repertoires, and, ultimately, to effectively and appropriately deploy these practices and knowledge when they are planning and enacting instruction. This study examines the effect of a Professional Development Program (PDP)[2] on teachers' thinking and their instructional practice and investigates (a) program participants' perceptions regarding the transformative (or not) influence of the PDP on their knowledge and ability to respond to ELs' needs; and (b) the degree to which PDP knowledge became present in participants' teaching (fidelity of practice).

The goals of the PDP were (1) to provide a solid foundation in understanding second language acquisition, cultural awareness and its impact on language learning; (2) to share effective teaching strategies aligned with State standards and assessment, and (3) to provide support through school-based learning communities organized to design, implement, and evaluate classroom practices and teacher-research inquiry projects. Participants enrolled in a two-course, six credit series over two semesters. The courses, each divided into a three module sequence, combined web-based and face-to-face interactions that built knowledge and application skills. In Module 1, teachers read, discussed and analyzed conceptual frameworks for second language acquisition/assessment through interactive online discussions and activities incorporating readings, podcast lectures, teacher interviews, and analysis of online resources. In Module 2, participants, led by grade-level/content area specialists interacted in small, online communities grouped by level/subject and conducted extensive literature reviews about ESL teaching issues, created and implemented lesson plans/units, and participated in self- and peer-assessment activities. In Module 3, participants, grouped by schools, worked with PDP instructors and met regularly to design action research projects based on individual classroom needs.

This mixed-methods case study involved survey and classroom observation data from 26 members of a program cohort and follow up observations and interviews from three of those teachers: Mr. Smith,[3] a middle school science teacher in a rural district (12% ELs); Ms. Robinson, a fourth grade teacher in an urban district (4% ELs), and Ms. Jackson, a bilingual kindergarten teacher in a dual language charter school.

Data sources for this case study included:

1. Pre-/Post-Knowledge Assessment Surveys (KAS): Before and after the program, participants completed a survey of 23 Likert-scale items closely reflecting the state certification standards and representing four conceptual categories:

    a. Language and literacy: knowledge of language acquisition and the process of literacy development; ability to apply this knowledge to facilitate English language development and promote English literacy
    b. Planning and managing instruction: knowledge of effective practices and strategies for planning, implementing, adapting, modifying and evaluating curriculum and instruction for ELs; ability to collaborate with ESL support professionals and services
    c. Assessment: knowledge about issues, principles, methods, and culturally-appropriate tools of assessment of ELs, use of a variety of instruments and tools to inform instruction and monitor EL progress
    d. Classroom practice: application of principles of second language instructional techniques to lessons and activities; ability to analyze the learning environment and instructional practices that impact ELs' academic achievement

The content and construct validity of KAS is supported by its close association with widely used standards both in terms of conceptual categories and specific items. Validity and reliability were further corroborated in a previous study where the KAS results were found to be closely aligned with the findings of a thematic content analysis of program participants' reflective writings (Hutchinson & Hadjioannou, 2011).

2. Observations of Teaching Practice: Participants' were observed once at the beginning and once at the end of the program with a focus on the presence of PDP-recommended practices in their teaching (fidelity of practice). Observations were guided by a 23-item rubric mirroring the KAS items, and sought to capture the degree to which knowledge of second language acquisition and research-supported TESL practices were utilized by participants. Items were rated on a three-point scale. The focal participants' teaching was also observed two years after program completion.
3. Follow-Up Interviews: The focal participants were interviewed two years after program completion and were asked open-ended

questions seeking to explore the focal participants' perceptions and impact of the program on their thinking and instructional practice.

This multipronged approach created a detailed and nuanced understanding of how program processes impacted participants' TESL knowledge base and their teaching praxis.

SELF-REPORTED TRANSFORMATION

The intention of this study was to examine how, if at all, participation in a TESL PDP had a transformative effect on our program participants. Participants' self-reports in reflective writings and course discussions suggested that participation in the PDP was a highly transformative experience for many of them: they reported that their eyes were opened to significant new knowledge about the processes of second language acquisition; that they now understood ELs' behaviors, language patterns and challenges in more informed ways; and that they were excited to be learning and experimenting with new instructional strategies. Even less effusive participants reported that program knowledge offered newfound insight, and that they were interested in trying out new techniques. As presented in what follows, these informal reports were corroborated by the post-program KAS: as a group, participants reported feeling categorically more confident in their TESL knowledge and in their ability to teach ELs. However, when the impact on instructional praxis was considered, a more complex and less uniform picture emerged.

Self-Perceptions of Program Impact. Upon their entry in the PDP, participants completed the KAS, through which respondents were asked to self-evaluate their knowledge of second language acquisition and their abilities regarding various aspects of working with ELs. The survey was also administered to participants at the end of the program. A comparative analysis of the per-item averages between the pre- and post-PDP surveys strongly suggests that participants felt more confident in all examined aspects of their knowledge and their ability to effectively work with ELs by the end of the program. The highest average differences between the two survey administrations involved knowledge of strategies to assist ELs in the different stages of language acquisition and knowledge of how to develop, implement, and evaluate a variety of curricular and instructional activities for ELs. Additionally, an analysis of the per-participant average difference between the pre- and post-program KAS administration showed that all participants reported statistically significant higher levels of confidence at the end of the program. The three focal participants' responses to the pre- and post-program administrations of the KAS show them to be following the group trend. In their interviews, two years after program completion, they all seemed to echo the confidence and optimism of their post-program KAS responses in regards to the program's impact on their professional knowledge and beliefs.

Language and literacy. All three focal participants described professional growth that affected their classroom practice in the area of language and literacy. Ms. Jackson reported that she increasingly incorporates a lot of picture cues, chunks new information in smaller quantities, and initiates verbal comprehension checks with her students on a very frequent basis. Similarly, Mr. Smith reported thinking more deeply about the levels of language proficiency represented by his ELs and how these different levels require different adaptations of his lesson content. He claimed to differentiate instruction by giving students choice and providing modified versions of assignments and tests for his ELs, and credited these positive changes to the learning accomplished in the PDP.

Planning and managing instruction. All focal participants reported increased conscious effort to meet the needs of all learners in their classrooms. When discussing their lesson planning, all participants spoke of the need to make adaptations and offered examples such as providing sentence starters, vocabulary and rate of speech modification, repetition of instructions/key points with added visual support, and varying the medium through which the lesson and assignments are delivered and required (auditory, visual, written, etc.). Additionally, Mr. Smith and Ms. Jackson spoke directly of an increased understanding of grouping students in strategic ways to support language development and content learning.

Assessment. All three focal participants highlighted the significance of appropriate adaptations. Ms. Jackson explained how important it has become to her, since participating in the PDP, to be knowledgeable of her students' levels of language proficiency in order to informally assess daily progress and growth. Mr. Smith and Ms. Robinson echoed these sentiments of the importance of understanding the individual student and the value of classroom-based assessment.

Classroom practice. All three participants acknowledged the presence of support in their particular school buildings. However, all agreed that these resources were not being used to the fullest potential. Specifically, all three participants noted that they, as classroom teachers, would like to see the ESL specialists in their buildings "push in" to their classrooms more often in order to support ELs in the content areas, as opposed to pulling the EL students out of their content classrooms for instruction. In all, a call for more collaborative practice was clearly echoed throughout all three interviews.

When asked what they saw as their biggest, continuing challenge in working with ELs in their content area classrooms, all three focal participants pointed to the task of remaining acutely conscious of each student's particular needs in order to meet them. Ms. Jackson framed this challenge in terms of the need she sees to deliberately and consistently provide not only verbal repetition of instructions, directions, and key content material, but also to provide visual and concrete cues as frequently as possible. Ms. Jackson also spoke to her need for diligence in checking for understanding in multiple ways to ensure ELs understand the content.

In general, the data (KAS and focal participant interviews) presented in this section paint a very promising picture in regards to fidelity of practice (FOP): (a) there was a clear, positive shift in the KAS responses between the pre- and post- administration, and (b) the focal participants provided very positive and confident interview responses regarding the implementation of tenets learned through participation in the PDP. The remaining question was whether this very positive outlook gleaned through study participants' self-reports aligned with the realities of classroom practice.

MEASURING TRANSFORMATION THROUGH OBSERVATIONS OF CLASSROOM PRACTICE

All study participants were visited in their classrooms or other educational settings and were observed while teaching both at the beginning of their participation in the PDP and then again at the end. The observations revealed a general positive trend, though a handful of areas showed negative or no change. The areas that showed positive change ran the spectrum across all four categories (language and literacy acquisition, planning and managing instruction, assessment, and classroom practice). Participants used knowledge of second language acquisition to support English language and literacy development, they were more knowledgeable of school-based support services for ELs, they implemented a variety of supportive learning environments, they applied several resources to promote English literacy, and they applied a variety of classroom-based assessment tools. The only negative average difference that was statistically significant referred to the use of a variety of language proficiency instruments and assessment methods for various purposes. Though disappointing, this seeming failure is rather deceptive given the time of the year pre- and post-observations were performed: teachers are much more likely to utilize formal language proficiency instruments to determine eligibility for and placement in support programs in the beginning of the academic year versus the end. Nevertheless, the use of both formative and summative alternative assessment strategies should still be apparent.

In general, the comparison between the pre- and post-program observations can be characterized as positive but rather underwhelming. Though not in direct contrast with the self-assessments discussed in the previous section, this lukewarm trend in the classroom observation data suggests an incongruence between the program participants' self-perceptions and their actual teaching practice. This incongruence is further explored and substantiated in the discussion of the focal participant data that follows.

FOCAL PARTICIPANTS: INCONGRUENCE IS A PROBLEM OF FIDELITY OF PRACTICE

As mentioned in the section on "Self-Perceptions of Program Impact," the focal participants shared the rest of the group's confidence and affirmative outlook on a perceived positive impact of the PDP on their knowledge and their ability to effectively address the needs of the ELs in their classrooms. A comparison of the pre- and post-observations for the focal participants showed them also following the rather tepid but positive trend of the group in terms of successfully incorporating effective TESL practices in their classrooms. Two years after program completion, the three focal participants were again observed. When compared to each focal participant's past observation rubrics, this follow-up observation was mixed, showing some stable areas, some areas of improvement, and some areas of decline.

Language and literacy. Most focal participants demonstrated a decline in competency in language and literacy support, when compared to their post-program observation nearly two years previously. While Mr. Smith self-reported to be more cognizant of students' levels of language proficiency and corresponding instructional implications, he failed to provide significant instructional modifications or appropriate scaffolds to an all-verbal instructional session. In addition, the modified assignments and assessments he provided for the ELs were not further differentiated by individual students' proficiency levels. During this instructional session there was a marked absence of student engagement, which may be related to the lack of adequate support.

Similarly, Ms. Robinson clearly articulated her understanding of the importance of specific differentiation based upon individual student need:

> ...(I) often pull students aside and do one-on-one.... So whenever someone is struggling in here, one of us (she or her co-teacher) always just goes to one-on-one.

However, during observation, there was no evidence of significant use of any need-based modifications. Instead, Ms. Robinson focused only on providing undifferentiated scaffolds for the whole group of students. Two years prior, during the same participant's post-program observation, the researcher had noticed a more heightened level of attention paid to such language and literacy-related scaffolds for individual students.

In contrast, with Ms. Jackson, the observer noticed a decidedly positive increase in practices aimed at supporting ELs' language and literacy development during the follow-up observation, as the participant paid very deliberate attention to scaffolding elements in the classroom. For instance, while introducing a new project, Ms. Jackson used both words and picture cues to make visible the steps in a process that students needed to follow.

Planning and managing instruction. In observation of concepts related to planning and managing instruction, there was no common trend among the three focal participants when compared with observation data two years prior.

Mr. Smith demonstrated modest growth in understanding effective planning practices for ELs and in ways to appropriately modify his teaching to support the ELs in his classroom. For example, in preparation for a quiz, Mr. Smith organized an interactive review activity in which students had the opportunity to collaboratively review their notes and ask questions of their peers and of the teacher. Though this activity has several desirable qualities when considering the needs of ELs, the prudence of its timing is somewhat doubtful, as Mr. Smith chose to enact it right before the actual quiz was administered.

Ms. Jackson also demonstrated some level of growth in terms of providing modification to classroom activities and planning a variety of appropriate classroom activities. The participant was very intentional in providing native language support, when possible, to help aid the comprehension of her students during a science project. Additionally, the participant also provided visual and concrete cues, as well as songs and chants, in order to demonstrate and expand verbal meaning. As she explained, "My inquiry project in the (PDP) program was how songs and chants and patterns help students learn vocabulary and words and that's what I try to do every day."

Conversely, Ms. Robinson did not demonstrate the same level of competence in the modification and variety of instructional activities as she had done two years prior. Rather, all students in the class were given the same task to complete, without significant differentiation based upon ELs' proficiency levels.

Assessment. In terms of assessment, only one participant showed growth in the level of scaffolding and number of accommodations provided for students on content area assessments. Mr. Smith provided a modified EL test version during the observation, and although actual test versions were not further differentiated for individual ELs' linguistic needs, the researcher did notice that the teacher provided varying levels of additional scaffolds during the assessment period, including text, note-based, and verbal support, based upon student need. Additionally, in the interview,

Mr. Smith recounted an experience he had in trying to grade an EL student's writing on a test. When he saw that the student was having difficulty responding to an essay question, he asked her about it:

> *I knew that she had verbalized it correctly ... [and] I can ... take that into consideration if she wrote something that didn't make sense grammatically.*

The other two focal participants demonstrated a decline in competencies regarding principles of assessment as they relate to ELs, as well as in employing a variety of classroom-based assessment tools to inform instruction and monitor progress. During the follow-up observations, the observer did not witness any deliberate actions taken to address the specific assessment-based needs of ELs in either classroom, despite the presence of circumstances where such actions were warranted.

Classroom practice. Finally, the observer looked for clear evidence of the overall application of second language instructional techniques and of a cognizant and deliberate monitoring of the mainstream classroom environment in terms of its appropriateness for ELs. Compared to the observation data collected two years prior, all three of the participants remained static in their growth related to the application of second language instructional techniques and lesson development. Two of the three remained static in the monitoring of the mainstream classroom environment, while Mr. Smith did demonstrate growth, exemplified by his very conscious effort to monitor the comprehension level of the ELs throughout the class period. Additionally, during a class read-aloud, Mr. Smith spent time clarifying the meaning of the word "detain" in terms of a word most school students, including those in his class, know: "detention." The class discussion that ensued was enlightening, as the students were able to draw on the meaning of the word they already knew ("detention") to derive the meaning of the newer word ("detain").

In conclusion, observation data two years after completion of the PDP showed inconsistencies in the application of the concepts learned during program participation. Each of the three focal participants demonstrated both growth and decline across the observation elements evaluated. Overall, the observer noted that while some growth may have been exemplified through practice, there were still essential elements of practice that were missing in the midst of that growth.

INFERENCES FOR PRAXIS

There is little doubt that the need to prepare mainstream classroom teachers to work with culturally and linguistically diverse learners is critical. It is imperative that all educators have a firm foundation in understanding the challenges faced by ELs and a secure grasp in applying classroom strategies that support their academic success, literacy, and English proficiency. Indeed, the professional development under study sought to develop these understandings and to support fidelity of practice by nurturing participants' theoretical knowledge and facilitating the construction of solid pathways between that knowledge and their teaching praxis. There is evidence that participants in this study grew in their capacity to understand and support ELs as a result of their involvement in the PDP. The pre- and post-program KAS revealed positive changes in the participants' confidence and perceived ability in fostering the kinds of learning environments that have the capacity to significantly impact ELs' personal and academic development. Though decidedly more muted than the confidence reflected in the KAS, the comparison between pre- and post-program observations of instruction suggested promising improvement in the participants' instructional practices. However, the classroom observation data collected from three focal participants two years after program completion exposed a widening incongruence between the self-reports and the actual implementation of desired practices. This confirms findings from other research studies that identified a dissonance between what participants believed they had changed in their practice and what researchers actually observed (Ebert-May, Derting, Hodder, Momsen, Long, & Jardeleza, 2011; Emshoff, Blakely, Gottschalk, Mayer, Davidson, & Erickson, 1987). Woodbury and Gess-Newsome (2002) refer to this phenomenon as "the paradox of change without difference" (p. 768). This appeared to indeed be the case for the participants in this study. Despite the participants' perceptions that their instructional practice in regards to ELs had been and remained positively transformed through the incorporation of PDP-acquired knowledge, observations of their teaching praxis were not supportive that such a transformation had persisted long-term. Though some changes were present, we cannot claim that *fidelity of practice* had been achieved.

Some possible explanations for the regression of application two years after program participation could be due to a number of factors, including new student populations, shifting educational policies, or perhaps to the lack of collaborative support as described by the focal participants—variables identified by other researchers as impacting teacher learning and change (Foster, 2011; Gess-Newsome, Southerland, Johnston, & Woodbury, 2003; Woodbury & Gess-Newsome, 2002). One such powerful factor appeared to be at play in this study, as the follow up observations occurred during the first year of implementation of the Common Core Standards in the state. As has been the case across the United States, this implementation brought about a significant wave of curricular changes, new instructional programs, new evaluation systems for students and teachers, and a grueling load of required trainings and workshops. Combined, these factors may have detracted from a focused effort to adapt instruction for ELs.

In addition, the call from the focal participants for more collaborative practice indicates the need to provide more sustained support for teachers through collaborative communities, mentoring and coaching, as such practices can create structures for embedded and sustained feedback and support. Our participants had received this in-depth support through Professional Learning Communities incorporated in the PDP. Throughout the year, participants had the opportunity to engage in online discussion forums about teaching practice, to work directly with faculty and teacher consultants (who were in-service teachers themselves), to develop their classroom-based inquiry projects, and to collaborate with other teachers at the same grade level who might be experiencing similar concerns. The research on Professional Learning Communities indicates that this aspect of professional development is highly effective (Archibald, Coggshall, Croft, & Goe, 2011; Hill, Stumbo, Palioka, Hansen, & McWalters, 2010), which may point to the reason why the focal participants in this study had shown some improvement in instructional practice by the end of the program. Unfortunately, the focal participants did not have access to this kind of high-quality professional learning network post program. Indeed, one of the participants spoke candidly about the lack of collaboration even between mainstream classroom teachers and ESL-support teachers, which he felt was due to the seclusion of the ESL classrooms in outdoor trailers in an adjoining parking lot. The two other participants lamented the lack of having the ESL support teacher in the mainstream classroom with them, helping to not only support their ELs, but also providing guidance and direction for their own practice. This lack of connectedness and teamwork may also have contributed to the lack of fidelity of practice.

Finally, the contrast between the self-reported assessment in the interviews and the actual observation of practice in this study is particularly worrisome because the focal participants seemed to be unaware of the attrition of effective TESL practices from their instructional praxis. What is known from the research about teacher development and change is that it is a gradual and organic process—"a way of knowing, of seeing, and of being" (Cohen & Ball, 1990, p. 335). Without teachers invested in the process of change, change will not occur. However, given our findings, the question that must be raised is "What if teachers believe that they have changed but in reality they have not?" We fear that this could lead to a false sense of expertise to appropriately respond to the needs of ELs, and may in effect serve as a limiting factor in the academic achievement and progress of the English learners in their classrooms. Teachers cannot move toward transformative praxis they erroneously believe they are already implementing. Therefore, in order to employ and sustain crucial professional development initiatives on a protracted basis, the focus must be on "teachers' thinking—their understandings, conceptions, implicit theories, preferences, and so forth—about traditional patterns of pedagogy and the necessity for change" (Woodbury & Gess-Newsome, 2002, p. 776) that can only be sustained through the kinds of questioning and seeking that occur in concert with other teachers in communities of professional learning. Only with this continuous critical reflection of ideology and practice will *fidelity of practice* of high-quality professional development be obtainable.

NOTES

1. The term English Learners (also designated as English Language Learners, Emergent Bilinguals, Limited English Proficient, or English as a Second Language in the literature) will be used throughout the chapter to denote students whose native language is not English and who are benefitting from various types of language support programs in schools.
2. Special thanks are due to Dr. Marisa Hockman, Project Manager of the PDP, for her help in participant recruitment and data collection.
3. All participants' names are pseudonyms to protect their anonymity.

REFERENCES

Abbate-Vaughn, J. (2008). Highly qualified teachers for our schools: Developing knowledge, skills, and dispositions to teach culturally and linguistically diverse students. In M. E. Brisk (Ed.), *Language, culture, and community in teacher education* (pp. 175–202). New York, NY: Erlbaum.

Achinstein, B., & Ogawa, R. T. (2006). (In)fidelity: What the resistance of new teachers reveals about professional principles and prescriptive educational policies. *Harvard Educational Review, 76,* 30–63.

Archibald, S., Coggshall, J. G., Croft, A., & Goe, L. (2011). High-quality professional development for all teachers: Effectively allocating resources. Washington, DC: National Comprehensive Center for Teacher Quality. Retrieved from HighQualityProfessionalDevelopment.pdf

Ballantyne, K. G., Sanderman, A. R., & Levy, J. (2008). Educating English language learners: Building teacher capacity. *National Clearinghouse for English Language Acquisition.* Retrieved from http://www.eric.ed.gov/ERICWebPortal/search/detailmini.jsp?_nfpb=true&_&ERICExtSearch_SearchValue_0=ED521360&ERICExtSearch_SearchType_0=no&accno=ED521360

Casteel, C.J. & Ballantyne, K.G. (Eds.). (2010). *Professional development in action: Improving teaching for English learners.* Washington, DC: National Clearinghouse for English Language Acquisition. Retrieved from http://www.ncela.gwu.edu/files/uploads/3/PD_in_Action.pdf

Cohen, D. K., & Ball, D.L. (1990). Relations between policy and practice: A commentary. *Educational Evaluation and Policy Analysis, 12*(3), 331–338.

Cohen, D., & Hill, H. (2000) Instructional policy and classroom performance: The mathematics reform in California. *Teachers College Record, 102*(2), 294–343.

DePaoli, J. L., Fox, J. H., Ingram, E. S., Maushard, M., Bridgeland, J.M., & Balfanz, R. (2015). Building a grad nation: Progress and challenge in ending the high school dropout epidemic. Retrieved from http://gradnation.org/report/2015-building-grad-nation-report

Dusenbury, L., Brannigan, R., Falco, M., & Hansen, W. (2003). A review of the fidelity of implementation: Implications for drug abuse prevention in school settings. *Health Education Research: Theory and Practice, 18*(2), 237–256.

Ebert-May, D., Derting, T. L., Hodder, J., Momsen, J. L., Long, T. M., & Jardeleza, S. E. (2011). What we say in not what we do: Effective evaluation of faculty professional development. *Bioscience, 61*(7), 550–558

Emshoff, J. G., Blakely, C., Gottschalk, R., Mayer, J., Davidson, W. S., & Erickson, S. (1987). Innovation in education and criminal justice: Measuring fidelity of implementation and program effectiveness. *Educational Evaluation and Policy Analysis, 9*(4), 300–311.

Fertig, B. & Garland, S. (2012). Millions spent on improving teachers, but little is done to make sure it's working. *The Heckinger Report*. Retrieved from http://hechingerreport.org/content/millions-spent-on-improving-teachers-but-little-done-to-make-sure-its-working_8696/

Foster, L. H. (2011). Fidelity: Snapshots of implementation of a curricular intervention (Unpublished doctoral dissertation). University of Virginia, Charlottesville, VA.

Fullan, M. (1982). *The meaning of educational change*. Toronto, ON: OISE.

Gess-Newsome, J., Southerland, S. A., Johnston, A., & Woodbury, S. (2003). Educational reform, personal practical theories, and dissatisfaction: The anatomy of change in college science teaching. *American Educational Research Journal, 40*(3), 731–767.

Hill, D., Stumbo, C., Paliokas, K., Hansen, D., & McWalters, P. (2010). *State policy implications of the Model Core Teaching Standards (InTASC draft discussion document)*. Washington, DC: Council of Chief State School Officers. Retrieved from http://www.ccsso.org/Documents/2010/State_Policy_Implications_Model_Core_Teaching_DRAFT_DISCUSSION_DOCUMENT_2010.pdf

Hutchinson, M., & Hadjioannou, X. (2011). Better serving the needs of Limited English Proficient (LEP) students in the mainstream classroom: Examining the impact of an inquiry-based hybrid professional development program. *Teachers and Teaching: Theory and Practice, 11*(1), 91-113.

Johnson, K. E. (2006). The sociocultural turn and its challenges for second language teacher education. *TESOL Quarterly, 40*(1), 235–257.

Lucas, T. (2015). Building a knowledge base for preparing teachers of English language learners. In L. C. de Oliveira & M. Yough (Eds.), *Preparing teachers to work with English language learners in mainstream classrooms* (pp. vii–xi). Charlotte, NC: Information Age Publishing.

Marin, A. M. (2015). *Determining the academic achievement of English Language Learners (ELLs) by using additional measures of growth* (Unpublished doctoral dissertation). University of Southern Mississippi, Hattiesburg, Mississippi. Retrieved from http://aquila.usm.edu/cgi/viewcontent.cgi?article=1130&context=dissertations

Mitchell, C. (2016). English-Language-Learner graduation rates are all over the map. Retrieved from http://blogs.edweek.org/edweek/learning-the-language/2016/01/english-language_learner_gradu.html

O'Donnell, C. L. (2008). Defining, conceptualizing, and measuring fidelity of implementation and its relationship to outcomes in K–12 curriculum intervention research. *Review of Educational Research, 78*(1), 33–84.

Opfer, V. D., & Pedder, D. (2011). Conceptualizing teacher professional development. *Review of Educational Research, 81*(3), 376–407.

Perlman, C. L., & Redding, S. (Eds.). (2011). *Handbook on effective implementation of school improvement grants*. Lincoln, IL: Center on Innovation & Improvement. Retrieved from http://www.centerii.org/handbook/Resources/Handbook_on_Effective_Implementation_of_School_Improvement_Grants.pdf

Samson, J. F., & Collins, B. A. (2012). *Preparing all teachers to meet the needs of English language learners: Applying research to policy and practice for teacher effectiveness*. Washington, DC: Center for American Progress. Retrieved from https://www.americanprogress.org/issues/education/report/2012/04/30/11372/preparing-all-teachers-to-meet-the-needs-of-english-language-learners/

Santos, M., Darling-Hammond, L., & Cheuk, T. (2012). *Teacher development to support English language learners in the context of Common Core State Standards*. Paper presented at the Understanding Language Conference, Standord, CA. Retrieved from http://ell.stanford.edu/sites/default/files/pdf/academic-papers/10-Santos%20LDH%20Teacher%20Development%20FINAL.pdf

Shelton, N. R. (2010). Program fidelity in two reading mastery classrooms: A view from the inside. *Literacy Research and Instruction, 49*(4), 315–333.

Stein, M. L., Berends, M., Fuchs, D., McMaster, K., Sáenz, L., Yen, L., Fuchs, L. S., & Compton, D. L. (2008). Scaling up an early reading program: Relationships among teacher support, fidelity of implementation and student performance across different sites and years. *Educational Evaluation and Policy Analysis, 30*(4), 368–388.

Teague, B.L. (2010). *Preparing effective teachers of English language learners: The impact of a cross-cultural field experience* (Unpublished doctoral dissertation). Vanderbilt University, Nashville, Tennessee.

U.S. Department of Education, Office of Planning, Evaluation and Policy Development, Policy and Program Studies Service. (2011). Prevalence and Implementation Fidelity of Research-Based Prevention Program in Public Schools: Final Report. Washington, DC: Author. Retrieved from http://www2.ed.gov/rschstat/eval/other/research-based-prevention.pdf

Working Group on ELL Policy. (2009). The American Recovery and Reinvestment Act: Recommendations for addressing the needs of English language learners. Retrieved from http://www.stanford.edu/~hakuta/ARRA/

Woodbury, S., & Gess-Newsome, J. (2002). Overcoming the paradox of change without difference. A model of change in the arena of fundamental school reform. *Educational Policy, 16*(5), 763–782.

CHAPTER 7

EXPERIENCE OF TRANSFORMATION

Educator Perspectives

Amanda Jo Cordova, Encarnación Garza, Jr., and Juan Manuel Niño

EXPERIENCE OF TRANSFORMATION: EDUCATOR PERSPECTIVES

> "Students are part of our lives and we are part of theirs' long after they are gone."
>
> —Carmelita

This chapter is conceptualized to illuminate an alternative way of thinking about education, as a transformative pedagogy where engaging in self-critical inquiry is the conduit to authentic, reciprocal learning relationships necessary for knowledge acquisition. As educators, the concept of transformation, is shaped within the sociohistorical context of the public school system where it is negotiated much like "the concept of justice is a negotiated concept that depends on the representative viewpoints"

(Willie & Willie, 2005, p. 475). For example, historically, education in the United States transformed dramatically over the last 100 years from a sporadic, mobile array of schoolhouses, established within small communities (Drennon, 2006), to mandatory school attendance for all children established through compulsory attendance laws (Katz, 1976). However, since this historic transformation to legally require inclusive educational opportunity, an exclusive societal negotiation of educational purpose, accessibility, equity, oversight, socialization, and intellectual development, has brought about new waves of school transformation. Thus, for educators, the concept of transformation must first be deconstructed in the reality, of the influence of its sociohistorical context before it can be understood as a pedagogy informed by theory.

To center the concept of transformation at the individual educator level, relevant literature is discussed to detect when the notion of public school transformation emerges, the shape it takes as defined by the corresponding sociohistorical landscape, and the conduit by which it appears at the individual educator level. In doing so individual transformation is realistically framed within a broader sociohistorical context of school transformation. This comprehensive perspective is necessary to affirm the totality of an educator's lived experience and to differentiate their individual transformation from the transformation of schools. With this perspective in mind, this chapter is divided into two main sections. First, the varying configuration of transformation, or waves of transformation, beginning with the nation-wide initiation of public schools to the present time, is presented in its sociohistorical context. This provides a broad description of what transformation looks like in public schools thus far. Second, a qualitative case study exploring transformation from the perspective of 21 educators examines a more in-depth, personal account of their experience, followed by a discussion of the findings.

WAVES OF TRANSFORMATION

Public schools are complex organizations designed as institutions of the state and as such can be understood as developing in sociohistorical contexts, with varying degrees of oversight at the federal level. Examining the configuration of transformation in public education over time, within a historical context, provides a broad portrait of the spaces in and direction toward which it operates. This broad portrait is necessary to situate transformation at the individual educator level as centered within the larger organization of the public school system, that is also is molded by waves of transformation. The literature reveals four distinct efforts toward public school transformation connected to: the Post-Civil War Era, school accountability, theories of educational leadership and theories of social justice. Within each wave of intended transformation it becomes evident the transformation of schools without transformation of our intra/interpersonal relationships is like expecting a seed to blossom without proper nutrients of water and sunshine.

Post-Civil War Era

Key events such as the ratification of the 13th Amendment of 1865 to abolish slavery (Finkleman, 2010), the passage of the 14th Amendment of 1866 for the protection of equal rights, and compulsory school attendance laws passed by 1918 (Katz, 1976) contributed to the conceptualization of a nation-wide public school system for all children. Since then, two major court cases heard by the U.S. Supreme Court reflect a progression of conflicts centered on challenging the interpretation of the protection of equal rights in public institutions, including schools. The divergent, Supreme Court rulings of these cases greatly influenced a long-term struggle for the transformation of schools to embody equal opportunity for all students. First, in the 1896 ruling of *Plessy v. Ferguson*, the court upheld "states and their agencies were free to use racial categorization to segregate public places" (Hoffer, 2012, p. 1) affirming constitutional protection of separate but equal. Second, in *Brown v. Board of Education*, the Supreme Court ruled segregation unconstitutional, signaling the transformation of schools into racially integrated institutions and an opposing interpretation of the 14th Amendment, when compared to the ruling in *Plessy v. Ferguson* (Lopez & Burciaga, 2014). Unfortunately, even with a constitutional mandate for educational equality, in following decades the cases of *Milken v. Bradley* of 1974 and *D. Missouri v. Jenkins* of 1995 made it virtually impossible for any legal impetus at the local and state level to dismantle de jure segregation (laws allowing segregation to flourish) (Bryant, 2008).

School Accountability. A new era of school transformation was advanced with the passage of The Elementary And Secondary Education Act of 1965 (ESEA), stipulating "federal policy could affect school financing, curriculum, classification of students and teachers, and placement of students and teachers" (Radin & Hawley, 2013, p. 13). Specifically, ESEA legislation declared "it to be the policy of the United States to provide financial assistance ... to local educational agencies serving areas with concentrations of children from low-income families" (Viteritti, 2012, p. 2). Criticism of the ESEA from research conducted on behalf of the NAACP demonstrated that "Title I monies were misused by school districts" who did not spend funds on "low-income children" (Viteritti, 2012, p. 3). By 1984, ESEA longitudinal studies indicated educational gains "were not sustained over time and the Nation At Risk Report (NAR) "documented high rates of adult illiteracy, declining scores on college entrance examinations, and a rise in remedial programs in colleges, corporations, and the military" (Viteritti, 2012, p. 3).

The reauthorization of the ESEA through the No Child Left Behind legislation of 2002 emphasized recommendations of the NAR related to more rigorous performance standards and assessment (Viteritti, 2012). However, "it relies not on the small federal bureaucracy but on state education agencies to play the crucial role in implementing the federal mandates" (Sunderman & Orfield, 2006, p. 526). Cost analysis conducted by several states argue that Title I funds diverted to meet NCLB requirements exceed these funds stating "implementation of the administrative and learning opportunities aspects of the law would require a new sum of $144.5 billion or an increase of 29% in educational spending" (Mathis, 2005, p. 91).

School reform legislation re-envisioned academic accountability as the mechanism to transform schools toward equitable outcomes. The focus shifts away from racial integration and equality of opportunity toward meeting acceptable academic outcomes with the teaching of standardized curriculum and implementation of standardized assessments. The implications of school transformation through accountability removes the burden of the local and state actors to dismantle institutional racism. Instead, this new concept of school transformation rests in the hands of individual school leaders and teachers to equalize educational outcomes without equitable funding. This compounds the complexity of the configuration of transformation for the individual educator as they bear the full weight of school transformation, as dictated by federal and state accountability legislation, without the autonomy to assess and procure resources deemed as necessary. Students, teachers, and schools are categorized as meeting or not meeting standards and school transformation is reduced to assessment results steering teachers even further away from their own transformation.

Educational Leadership

The concept of transformational leadership can be traced to research of leadership theory during the 1970s and 1980s, initially studied in the realm of politics and business (Berkovich, 2016), and evolving as an alternate framework to transactional leadership. James Burns's (2012) examination of political leaders frames transformational leadership as "the process of leadership [that] must be seen as part of the dynamics of conflict and of power; that leadership is nothing if not tied to collective purpose" (p. 25), with the intent of satisfying human needs and expectations. He differentiates transformational leadership from transactional leadership, emphasizing transformation as cultivated in "a relationship of mutual stimulation and elevation that converts followers into leaders" (p. 26), in which all feel a moral responsibility to consciously choose a desired reality as the driver of change. Bass and Avolio (1993) elaborate on transformational leadership as facilitating change by first seeking to understand the culture of an organization, collectively shaping a vision, and then altering assumptions, values, and norms to match this shared vision.

Leithwood (1992) argued transformational leadership ought to "subsume instructional leadership as the dominant image of school administration, at least during the 90's" (p. 17), while Hallinger's (2003) review of leadership development discovered "refocusing ofattention on the improvement of learning and teaching has once again brought instructional leadership to the fore" (p. 342). Although both models are focused on initiating change toward improved school achievement, they differ in their locus of control for change. In instructional leadership the locus of control rests with the principal and measures for change are carried through from top to bottom (Hallinger, 2003). In transformational leadership the target for change is prompted from a shared vision and leading change within the school is implemented as a shared responsibility (Hallinger, 2003). Additionally, hierarchal power is viewed as less effective and "promoting change by operating on the emotions, motivations, and identity of followers" as more relevant to the current era of school reform (Berkovich, 2016, p. 617).

The research of educational leadership theory is significant to the individual educator in their struggle to decipher the effectiveness of leadership models in advancing school transformation. However, the lack of consensus in research findings suggest any one leadership model may not address the goals of school transformation. Thus, individual educational leaders are responsible for transforming leadership pedagogy to meet accountability, with full awareness leadership models are like unconnected puzzle pieces in the bigger picture of school transformation. With these models, transformational leadership pedagogy is central and relational between principal and teacher, viewed as the leaders of a school, but only as tied to accountability. The transformation does not permeate the relationships between teachers and/or students and once again steers the teacher away from their individual transformation.

Social Justice Theory

Theories of social justice in education conceptualize transformation of schools at the individual and institutional level with emphasis on community driven transformation. Where educational reformers focus their attention on an achievement gap, social justice leaders point to an opportunity gap

(Carter, Welner, & Ladson-Billing, 2013) stemming from interconnected cumulative effects (Rothstein, 2014) of institutional racism, also referred to as educational debt (Ladson-Billings, 2006). Framing educational outcomes through opportunity gaps "shifts our attention from outcomes to inputs—to the deficiencies in the foundational components of societies, schools, and communities that produce significant differences in educational—and ultimately socioeconomic—outcomes" (Carter, Welner, & Ladson-Billings, 2013, p. 3).

In Freire's (2000) book, *The Pedagogy of the Oppressed*, he methodically explains why the transformation of education is enabled by a praxis of emancipation of the oppressed by the oppressed. Freire stated "people must first critically recognize" the causes of oppression, "so that through transforming action they can create a new situation" (p. 47), defining people, as the individuals who are closest to the struggle. This means educators and the communities they serve must engage in the process of transformation together, in which they simultaneously unravel the insidious nature of perpetuating the roles of oppressor and oppressed. This process enables the strength of their collective consciousness to transform the totality of social inequity. In this manner transformation is placed in the hands of the community and those closest to the community (educators and students), through "the action and reflection of men and women upon their world" (p. 79), to awaken their power to discover a new reality of education; thereby transforming it.

These transformed relationships collectively engage in critical inquiry into the structures and norms that result in inequitable schooling for many students, and together refashion educational policies resulting in more socially just schools. (Cambron-McCabe & McCarthy, 1995; Marshall, 2004). Collective transformation in an urban context means:

> Urban educators and community workers must also cultivate their students' transformational resistance strategies to challenge anti- affirmative-action, anti-bilingual-education, anti-immigrant, and heterosexist legislation and policies. Indeed, this is crucial to counteracting the results of ineffective, inappropriate, and often racist and sexist educational practices and policies that continue to fail many Students of Color in an urban context. (Solorzano & Bernal, 2001, p. 336)

Transformation as envisioned by social justice theory reverses previous waves of school transformation to place the starting point of change at the individual and on a personal level, to critique their everyday thinking and actions contributing to social injustice. Transformation then manifests in relationships as individual changes, whereby classrooms become claimed spaces of reciprocal learning (Friere, 2000; Pane & Rocco, 2014). It centers the negotiation of the problematic social constructs of schools in a socially driven transformation of its individuals. The measure of transformation then becomes the ability of educators to value all ways of knowing, to facilitate authentic teaching and learning resulting in outputs of unrestricted, non-standardized student development and creativity. Where school transformation measured by standardized outcomes, from its definition constrains intellect; transforming individuals measured by their transforming relationships liberates intellect. In sum, individual transformation directed toward social justice, gives rise to a collective movement of transformation embracing knowledge as the creativity of its people, instead of their conformity to hegemonic standards.

TRANSFORMATION AS EXPERIENCED BY 21 EDUCATORS

The first part of this chapter describes the educator as situated within the tension of school transformation aimed at educational equality, that has yet to overcome the status quo of segregation, discrimination, and inequity as it pertains to public education. While school transformation initiated in a top-down fashion works toward standardized educational outcomes as a measure of equality, educator transformation is more focused on the changes of individual thinking and actions that contribute to equitable spaces of learning. This means researching the transformation of educators, emphasizes "tracing one's past" as "a key way to understand what you believe and how those beliefs were formed" (Warren, 2011, p. 140), making us conscious of why we educate the way we do and what we count as knowledge. Warren asserts "rigorous research centered in our own pedagogical histories" (p. 141) is necessary to engage in rigorous education because it elevates our understanding of how students are shaped by the praxis of individual educators. Thus, at the heart of exploring individual educator transformation, is the examination of how they change, why they change, their perceptions of the benefits of this change, and the sustainability of transformation. This research is unique in that it centers individual educators' experience of transformation and their perceptions of its influence, they express in auto-ethnographic writings, video, and interviews. We ask, what does the theoretical concept of transformation, driven by social justice, look like in the real lives of urban educators?

Positionality

This study was conceptualized within reflections of the authors they shared with one another from personal and professional reflections the authors' shared with one another as their relationships deepened over the last four years. Dr. Garza and Dr. Niño are professors and co-coordinators of the cohort graduate program discussed in this study known as the Urban School Leadership Collaborative (USLC) at the University of Texas in San Antonio. Dr. Garza has devoted his career to developing a teaching pedagogy in his professional experiences within secondary and higher education that models education as a liberating process he coined the *Pedagogy of Collective Critical Consciousness* (Garza, 2015). In the classroom this pedagogy is modeled through authentic care while simultaneously engaging in reciprocal learning alongside students. Together, learners (students and professors) engage in individual and collective reflection about connections between coursework focused on social justice in education, lived experiences, and the many forms of oppression. Dr. Niño began working as a professor at the University of Texas at San Antonio (UTSA) in 2013 and accepted the opportunity to co-teach with Dr. Garza. As co-directors of the USLC, Dr. Garza and Dr. Niño facilitate the *Pedagogy of Collective Critical Consciousness* in both graduate and doctoral educator programs, working closely with UTSA colleagues, urban school districts, and rural regions, to provide graduate coursework in these underserved areas. Amanda worked as an urban school teacher, graduated as a student of the USLC, and works as a doctoral fellow for both professors. All of us experienced transformation as members of USLC and listened to other members reflect about their own transformation. It is within these reflections we began to think about the importance of sharing how transformation is experienced by urban educators beyond these conversations, and in the spaces of research, as a way to center the the ways in which graduate students of the USLC program experienced transformation.

Theoretical Framework

This study is grounded in transformational learning theory as developed by Jack Mezirow, who initially researched the engagement of community discourse as a means to resolve social conflicts, and enhance the ability of Pakistani local communities to prioritize as well as plan community action, in the mid-1950s (Mezirow & Santopolo, 1960). Meizrow's theory of transformational learning further developed in the following decades, maintained its emphasis on an individual's ability to transform their own thinking and actions as a consequence of discourse, inclusive to members of the community. He later defines this as participation in the "critical reflection on assimilated epistemic assumptions and critical dialectical judgment" (Mezirow, 2004, pp. 69–70), as the mechanisms employed to validate new assumptions that then, guide new actions to bring about transformation (Mezirow, 2003). The underpinnings of transformation from this theory require the educator to critically reflect upon "taken for granted frames of reference" (Mezirow, 2003, p. 59) across the entirety of their lived experiences as the first step in making their praxis "more inclusive, discriminating, open, reflective, and emotionally able to change" (Mezirow, 2003, p. 58). Mezirow asserts critical reflection, unlike reflection alone, results in "significant personal and social transformations" (Mezirow, 1998, p. 186) giving credence to the idea that schools are social institutions, and any transformation for the benefit of all students, must precisely address the maintenance of epistemologies of privilege and power.

Thus, educator transformation is observable through participation in critical reflection, a willingness to discard old, fixated ways of being that do not make sense in within a transforming perspective of education. Adult learners are believed to be "empathetic and open to other perspectives; are willing to listen and to search for common ground or a synthesis of different points of view; and can make a tentative best judgment to guide actions" (Mezirow, 1997, p. 10). In addition, transformation guided by Meizrow's theory, affirms it is an ongoing process defined by our ability to continually evolve as educational traditions change (Meizrow, 1998). In sum, transformational learning theory recognizes transformation as beginning on an individual level, in which critical reflection with others, allow us to discover the origin of assumptions facilitating thinking and actions working against change and/or improvement. For educators, unraveling our own thinking and behaviors that do not align with an equitable education, is the basis of critical reflection informing individual transformation, leading to actions capable of fashioning inclusive, social transformations of educational systems.

Purpose

The purpose of this study is to explore the experience of transformation, among educators, who are also students of a uniquely designed graduate, cohort program. The uniqueness of this program is that it is informed by the *Pedagogy of Collective Critical Consciousness* (Garza, 2015) as the foundation of individual transformation, deemed necessary to develop authentic, educational leaders of social justice.

Research Questions

The purpose of this inquiry is to explore the experience of transformation, how it may inform practice, and perceptions of its sustainability. Research questions include:

1. How do educators' experience transformation?
2. In what ways do educators' perceive their transformation to influence practice?
3. What are the perceptions of educators related to the sustainability of transformation in educational settings?

Methodology

Study design. A qualitative, case study design anchors this examination of the experience of transformation by educators. The study sample was purposefully selected for participants' ability to provide rich, thick, textual data about their experience of transformation documented throughout their two year graduate cohort program coursework. Data collected includes 21 individually written auto-ethnographies, 1 student led and produced video incorporating all participants, and 4 randomly selected, follow-up interviews, (conducted 1½ years post-graduation). Data was secured on a password protected computer and downloaded to Dedoose, a password protected qualitative analysis software program.

Participants. Participants include 21 graduate students from a south Texas university who completed an Educational Leadership and Policy Study program in December of 2014 while working full-time in an urban school setting whose population is predominantly Latina/o. The participants' early educational experiences and undergraduate college level experiences were based on traditional direct teaching pedagogies. In contrast, the participants' graduate program was specifically designed for aspiring, urban educational leaders and founded upon principles of social justice, purposefully embedded throughout the sequence of coursework. A true cohort model, in which students take all classes together and graduate together was followed, along with a co-teaching methodology. Graduate students engaged in weekly reflection practices among their peers to promote collective critical consciousness (Garza, 2015) as a means of thinking about, challenging, and confronting personal and professional barriers to centering practices of equity. All graduate students worked full-time in the same school district with a predominantly Hispanic student population, of low socioeconomic status, with a large population of English language learners, whose particular schools struggled with overall academic achievement.

The participants range in age from 23 to 43, with 7 males and 14 females. Five males are of Hispanic descent and two are White. Eleven females are of Hispanic descent, two are African American, and one is White. Three males worked as curriculum instruction specialists, one as a special education coordinator, and three as teachers in elementary, alternative, and high school settings. One female worked as a preschool director, two as curriculum instruction specialists, and 11 as teachers (four elementary school teachers, two middle school teachers, one alternative school teacher, and 4 high school teachers).

Data analysis procedures. Triangulation of data, and rich, thick description are trustworthiness measures of the study. The primary researcher is bracketed within the study as a complete participant. Internal validity is optimized by the use of multiple coding cycles, independent coding, and inter-coder agreement, among two researchers. In addition, to ensure the primary researcher did not code her own data, a third researcher participated in the first coding cycle to specifically code data from the primary researcher, and the second researcher completed the second cycle. Two cycles of coding (Saldana, 2008) were conducted, with the first cycle as emic coding including inductive, descriptive methods. This type of coding was chosen to focus on how each participant described their experience of transformation and to minimize the bias of the researchers' personal experiences of transformation. Coding descriptions were added with the initial analysis of each auto-ethnography, with no coding descriptions decided upon in advance. During the second cycle of coding, researchers worked independently meeting four times to confer and reach inter-coder agreement. As descriptive codes were added with each auto-ethnography, the second round of coding served to apply newer codes to the analysis of auto-ethnographies completed prior to the discovery of these codes, whenever appropriate. Researchers then worked together to collapse descriptive codes into conceptual categories of the transformative experience. These categories were used as a priori codes for the analysis of student produced video documentation of their overall graduate cohort experience and four randomly selected follow-up interviews to complete the triangulation of data.

ANALYSIS

Data analysis of graduate student auto-ethnographies reveals a shared emphasis on five primary elements of transformation, common to their transformational experience. These common elements among all 21 participants, emerge as the primary themes including: (1) Distinct differences between traditional and transformational learning environments (2) Transformation is integrated across personal and professional spheres, (3) Specific readings influence the direction of transformation, (4) Transformation is an ongoing and collective process sustained in relationships, and (5) Dispositions of social justice in leadership and the collective critical consciousness of social justice ground transformation. Analysis of video and four randomly selected follow-up interviews served to triangulate data.

Theme 1: Differences of Traditional and Transformational Learning Environments

All participants described distinct differences between traditional learning environments and the transformational learning environment of their graduate cohort experience. Participant writings illuminate the tensions of teaching in a traditional educational system, they perceive as minimizing the importance of teaching relationships. Traditional learning environments were described as based on hierarchy, focused on teaching to the test, and engrossed in labeling students where teaching becomes disconnected from student-teacher relationships. Julia, a reading intervention teacher, describes teaching as more directed by expectations in a top-down hierarchy:

> I was forced to acknowledge that the stress of a broken educational system and the demands of complying with administrative tasks left me little energy or time to devote to building authentic professional or student relationships. Teaching seemed more like a being a surgeon without proper instruments, the classroom more like a factory than a learning environment, and the student more like a standardized test result than a child discovering their potential.

In contrast, the transformational learning environment of the participants' graduate cohort program was described as grounded in reciprocal learning, whereby learning is culturally constructed. Karen emphasizes the role of dialogue in the reciprocity of transformational learning relationships, "The dialogue of the classes permeated my thoughts between class sessions and became my reference for teaching and living. In effect our professors taught us to deviate from a banking concept (Freire, 2000) of learning in which the teacher deposits knowledge." James, speaks to the tendency of traditional classrooms to discourage the cultural constructs of knowledge when he explains:

> Traditional classrooms do not see color, nor the cultures of people of color. Their histories, cultures, and languages are omitted, or even discouraged in the classroom. This omission produces negative energy in which the students of color come not to value their own unique wealth of knowledge, and understanding of the world.

Opposing this tendency Juan relates the importance of how the transformational learning environment of the cohort program felt safe and allowed him to grapple with his lived experiences as an educator:

> Finally, this program has provided an environment in which I have felt safe to be—safe to learn, safe to ask questions, safe to express concerns and problems and opinions, safe to struggle with the challenges we face as educators. The manner in which the program has been set up—from beginning to end—has been thoughtful and reflective.

In sum, Doris, relates the nature of oppressive, hegemonic nature of teaching relationships in a traditional classroom when she states, "I was distinctly aware that the message about the importance of education often translated for students into one of the importance of assimilation and acculturation to white, middle-class culture." Finally, Juanita further explains the difference of the transformational environment when she taps into how the consistent collective discourse of the cohort program led her to critically evaluate herself personally and professionally as a unique individual:

> Instead, I think, the experience [cohort] has permeated my being in such a way that all facets of my life have been dramatically altered. The process has forced me to constantly reflect upon myself as a professional, colleague, friend, and mother. Whereas other programs are purely academic in nature, our cohort was challenged to unravel the true motivations of what made us choose to work toward becoming an educational leader and how that leadership is carried out in the academic world.

Transformational classrooms. Whereas the learning of traditional classrooms focuses on mastery of standardized content; transformational classrooms emphasize the development of the individual with deep respect for the students' own funds of knowledge and experiences as relevant to their education. Their experience of this pedagogy in the graduate cohort program redefined how they attended to this concept of transformational learning in the classrooms of their workplace signaling a change in praxis. Becky models her cohort experience in the classroom of her workplace:

> It requires the educator to cultivate a safe, nurturing environment in which the student is encouraged to share their lived experiences without judgment or fear to relate and engage in the process of learning. The sharing of their experiences must come first, it must be honored and valued, so that students are encouraged and free to relate their learning. The emphasis upon the relationship of learning is paramount with continuous dialogue as the catalyst, and cannot flourish in a hierarchical, banking system learning stance.

Monique agrees her classroom began to mirror the openness and dialogue of her cohort experience she also connects to what she will focus on as an administrator, "This is more how my classroom is now. I really listen to my students. We have open dialogue and their ideas are shared and valued. This will definitely be something that I will stress when I become an administrator." Participants also begin to focus on learning as connected to the development of the individual. Jose makes this connection as a way of educating more holistically, "Educating the whole student, beyond academics, means attending to a student's affective and cultural needs. It is a sense of caring that goes beyond the grade book to the purpose and the motivation of learning, and self-identity of being human." Brianna delves into the importance of reflecting about lived experiences with her students to engage them in a collective process of working toward educational goals in their overall development:

> We discuss identity and race and culture in my classroom as well as the negatives—discrimination, bias, injustice. My students express their thoughts, feelings, and perspectives about their experiences—and they have had so many experiences for their young age. We reflect on our past experiences, and we write about how we have changed and what has changed us, about what our goals are for the future and the path we are going to take to reach them. We need to be strategic about getting to know our students and students knowing us.

Transformational leadership. In addition, transformational learning environments, are spaces shaped by the diversity of students and the surrounding community. Participants agree inclusive leadership is crucial. Jake articulates he believes socially just schools must be open to diversity:

> As a school leader in the future, and even now as a teacher leader, my mission is to create a school in which the intersections of race, ethnicity, culture, and education are discussed and addressed with students and teachers in such a way as to create a socially just school.

Carmelita specifies the importance of the school community in being more inclusive of the surrounding neighborhood:

> It is my responsibility as a school leader to find those ways to help all families become part of the school community. Meeting parents in their homes opens true dialogue. Especially when they are in charge of their own agenda. How powerful this would be if all principals did this?

Mikayla prefaces inclusivity must envision a shared leadership with the entire community:

With having my experiences with my current principal and being part of the [cohort] program, I have learned to truly value working collaboratively as a team on campus. When decisions are shared amongst each other we as a team are more apt to carry out our tasks and follow through on our assignments. Not only does the voice of the staff matter and should be heard, but so should the voices of the students, parents and community. I now see how their voices matter.

Theme 2: Reflection on Specific Readings Influence the Direction of Transformation

Participants identified specific course readings, assigned in their graduate cohort program, as influential in the direction of their transformation. In particular, course reflections about Paulo Freire's (2000), *Pedagogy of The Oppressed* and *Subtractive Schooling: U.S.-Mexican Youth and the Politics of Caring* by Angela Valenzuela (1999), challenged participants to think differently about themselves, students, and educational systems. Carlos explains,

> Other readings stood out in terms of prompting change within me, but none as significantly as the first two. All my course work there after was framed within those two readings. Does this action take away from my students' identity of self? Does this action build upon the culturally relevant curriculum I am trying to implement? These two questions framed the rest of my work.

Reflections on readings of Paulo Friere. Participants grappled with reflecting about the role of the oppressor as discussed by Freire (2000). Karina relates how she gained insight into her perpetuation of the oppressor,

> Two years ago, I was the woman who stayed silent when I heard teachers talking negatively to students or indirectly speaking ill of students before colleagues. I was the woman who had many questions about why things were done the way they were at school, yet never asked those questions. I was a woman who had subconsciously chosen the side of the oppressor by not speaking up.

Guadalupe interprets intellectual oppression from Friere's (2000) work, in which the knowledge of students and their communities are often unrecognized, "This revisits the premise of social capital that we as humans and conductors of knowledge each contain. To ignore the knowledge of an individual is oppression in and of itself." Lastly, Juan explains his critical reflection of oppression altered his practice, "Freire's theory of oppression in education altered how I thought about both my practice as a social justice educator and my actions as a person in an unjust society."

Reflections on readings of Angela Valenzuela. Valenzuela (1999), specifically her articulation of subtractive schooling prompted participants' to critique and transform their relationships with students. Karen discusses the consequences of student learning when they are not valued for their diversity:

> In Valenzuela's (1999) book, *Subtractive Schooling*, I learned how a dominant group can deplete other groups of its culture, language, and beliefs in order to invest in mainstream American culture and beliefs into these groups. Through this course, I developed an awareness of subtractive assimilation and its effect on students by depleting them of their identity, giving feelings of isolation, and promoting hostile resentment and most importantly lack of achievement.

Julia gains insight into her contribution to methods of subtractive schooling in her relations with other Latinos:

> However, after learning about various ways that U.S.-born youth were stripped of their cultural identities, I began to understand how subtractive schooling had driven a division and misunderstanding among various types of Latino groups, including a division among myself and my school's community.

James agrees, he was able to more readily see his own ignorance, helping him to take action to move away from participation in subtractive schooling:

> Subtractive Schooling acted like coarse sand-paper, stripping the pretense and the layers of ignorance away. Reading this, the definitive case study, showcasing the effects of decades of ignorance; anger and incredulity boiled inside of me, I found myself compelled to act. Without reading the abhorrent accounts chronicled by Valenzuela, I might not have seen the price of ignorance.

Doris, also explains how reading Valenzuela's (1999) work inspired introspection ultimately influencing her praxis:

> My thoughts and reflections turned inward and I began to look at where in my own praxis, I was being subtractive. While I can say much of my teaching was inclusive, it was not conscientious of inclusion and therein the subtractive nature of schooling emerged. Valenzuela (1999) made me conscious of the positive impacts a student's culture brings to their education and made me ask myself how I showed my students I valued their culture. Since that text I have found myself including that cultural aspect of education to a greater extent and have been rewarded with a greater depth of understanding from my students.

Theme 3: Transformation Is Personally and Professionally Integrated

Participants' experience of transformation within the cohort program is integrated across their personal and professional lives where relationships take center stage. Who one is as an individual, becomes who they are as educators. Enrique notes, "The past two years [in the cohort], I have noticed a transformation taking place not only in my professional life but personal one as well." Selena concurs, "it all makes sense now through such readings, experiences, and projects that have enabled me to transform not only as an educator, but also as an individual." Critical reflection about personal and professional relationships guide their experience of transformation as Vanessa describes:

> Transforming through the cohort was of course about academia, but it was more about transforming as a person who could embody the importance of relationships in all aspects of an educational system. It requires constant, sometimes, brutal reflection on how these relationships are or are not being nurtured and how to improve listening and collaborative skills.

Participants continually reflect upon how personal and professional relationships influence one another, and without critique can falter in their ability to value each individual. Delia makes this connection as a parent and teacher:

> I consider how my personal life affects the decisions I make and the relationships I build. Through my own reflections, I am reassuring myself that I am making quality decisions, and that I am doing what is best as a parent and a teacher.

Ramona expresses the cohort program's emphasis on self-development helped her strengthen relationships in and out of the classroom:

> This program was more than academics; it was fundamental in helping me establish who I am as a person both professionally and personally. I have unraveled my selfish ways as a human being and I have truly redefined myself into someone who truly cares about people. It has helped me establish strong relationships with my students, friends, and family.

Alejandra's transformation within her relationships is affirmed by herself and others solidifies it is not a compartmentalized experience:

> Since I started this [cohort] program, I see a drastic change within me that my family, friends, students, and colleagues have noticed. A change that aims towards building meaningful authentic relationships that focuses on valuing people's identities, perceptions, and experiences.

Theme 4: Transformation Is Ongoing and Sustained in Relationships

Participants experience transformation as an ongoing, unfinished process. Ramona stresses the continuous nature of transformation when she states, "I view and define transformation as a process in which we continuously are changing ourselves through our experience in life." Alejandra also notes transformation is ongoing when she says, "I am still being transformed and I believe that I will continue to do so even after I graduate from the program." In addition, Carlos relates "Transformation as a journey and struggle to know myself best describes my experience to this point." Their insights convey transformation as consistently excavating deeper understanding of the self in which Karina conveys "I still see remnants of my former self, however I am content with the idea that I am still transforming into the person that I will become." In developing this deeper understanding of ourselves, Jose informs us transformation is also ongoing interpersonally when he declares, "I will continue to transform and see what I can do to become the best husband, father, brother, teacher, student, and social justice leader in my life." The expression of the participants discern transformation as an ongoing process both intra and interpersonally.

Theme 5: Social Justice Grounds Transformation

Participants specify they experience transformation as they become more connected to the social justice during their two year participation in the cohort, graduate program. Karen explains, "I really was transformed during this time of my life not just because of what I read in books or heard my professors say, but because the professors practiced [social justice] what they were teaching." Julia also relates the cohort as instrumental in grounding her transformation as visible in the alignment of socially just thoughts and acts:

> As a result, being a member of this cohort initiated a deeper process of evaluating my interaction with the world from a social justice perspective and prompted me to question if my thoughts and actions are or are not representative of this ideal.

Karen delineates how the program's pedagogy is linked to social justice:

> When I reflect back on what I have learned in this cohort program about social justice and how this program has helped me to transform, I ask myself, "how can I be that change agent?" I believe the first thing I must do is to

understand that there is injustice in our world. We have two sets of groups – privileged and disadvantaged. We must understand how privilege operates and how disadvantage occurs. I must also recognize that oppression comes in multiple forms, and I must take action to interrupt the cycle of this oppression.

As the participants' continue in their graduate program, they begin to link specific dispositions of social justice leadership to their transformation, including consistently engaging in critical, individual and collective reflection, treating others with authentic care, and becoming part of a collective critical consciousness for social justice as praxis.

Individual and collective critical reflection. James explores how he connects critical collective reflection to his relationships with students:

> As I continued in the cohort and we used a reflective process to allow ourselves the time and freedom to speak openly about our real experience in the school system as well as opposing professional perspectives, I became keenly aware of how much time I spent feeling frustrated, overwhelmed, and stressed with forces out of my control that ultimately impacted the time and effort I put into developing stronger relationships with my students. Was it possible that I didn't have as much faith in relationships as the foundation of learning as I thought? Was I truly forging relationships with students in which they felt nurtured as a person developing and maturing academically and personally?

Juan notes how collective reflection pushed him to critique his thinking:

> This reflection was particularly helpful because we were required to actively listen to other people's thoughts. While I may not have expressed myself eloquently during my reflection, the thinking that occurred before sharing was, for me, the most enriching part of the exercise. My thoughts were pushed and challenged by what I heard others say. In addition, actively listening to classmates helped me find shared experiences that brought us closer together.

Doris summarizes improved discourse as an outcome of collective reflection:

> After two years of engaging in reflection with the twenty cohort members in the program, I now feel equipped to invite others to share in the process of developing patience, enhancing their skill of reflection, and practicing listening to others so that we all may understand one another's perspective and respect different opinions.

Participants learn from the modeling of this collective reflection to initiate individual reflection as described by Juanita, "My greatest area of transformation is the use of personal reflection. I am continuously trying to make meaning of my experiences." Becky affirms individual reflection is occurring daily:

> I reflect almost daily on events that occurred in class, considering whether or not I have oppressed my students, evaluating what my actions and my words express to them about values and privileges and power. I reflect on the balance that must be struck between teaching students to fit into middle-class culture and encouraging them to value the culture in which they were raised. Moreover, I reflect on what the actions and the systems of the school express to my students and their families. Do we value them? Do we value their perspective? Have we created a space in which students and families feel safe to express themselves?

Monique explains transformation stems from critical reflection, "Transformation comes from one's self-experiences, but one needs to understand and be able to reflect on those experiences in order to change. Transformation only happens with honest self-reflection through valuing yourself and others."

Authentic caring. Participants connect authentic care as a disposition of social justice leadership central to their experience of transformation. Juanita explains how authentic caring becomes the central focus of her transformation:

> All in all, my transformation during this cohort can be summed up through authentic caring. I believe that if we build relationships with students, parents, teachers, staff, administrators, and the community and have authentic caring everything should take care of itself—with hard work of course.

Becky explains her experience of authentic caring transformed her practices and relationships as a classroom teacher:

> How has authentic caring transformed me? For one thing, I listen more. I used to think the old school banking system was a great system. I told my students what I wanted them to know and they were supposed to write it down and memorize it. I did not think that my students had anything of value to contribute their education. I always thought, "If it was good enough for me, it should be good enough for them." However, I quickly learned in this cohort that I was not taught to think. I was only good at regurgitating information.

Monique concurs the authentic care of student relationships promotes deeper understanding, "When I started the cohort, I learned that authentic caring was a more than being good to others. It meant that working with students, such as ours, required a connection with them on a much deeper level." Lastly, Jose, connects the tenet of authentic caring in social justice leadership within multiple school relationships:

> As a future social justice leader I plan on establishing the same relationships with my students, parents, and staff. I feel enthusiastic about what I have learned through this program in regards to social justice and establishing relationships through authentic caring.

Collective critical consciousness. Individual and collective critical reflection are perceived as dispositions of social justice leaders, however, critical collective critical consciousness is specifically focused on our collective ability to see ourselves as connected to the reality of oppression. Participants begin to experience this connection to their transformation as a "we" experience specifically focused on social justice. It calls for a collective critical consciousness of social justice that engages in a collective transformation of the social constructs that maintain injustice. Brianna explains how this applies to educators:

> We all must examine our attitudes, perceptions, and beliefs as educators. How does our pedagogy affect our students? Do the challenges that hold our students back also diminish the way we see them too? Does the lack of literacy and math skills encourage our perception of deficit thinking in our students? In addition to addressing the organizational relations that create oppression, we must also address the thinking behind our behavior and pedagogy, in order, to change ourselves from within as leaders for justice.

Carmelita concurs collective critical conscious is about recognizing thinking and behaviors misaligned with social justice to fashion transformation in a new pedagogical direction "In addition to addressing the organizational relations that create oppression, we must also address the thinking behind our behavior and pedagogy, in order, to change ourselves from within as leaders for justice." Jake speaks to joining in the struggle for liberation, at the heart of collective critical consciousness for social justice:

> Certainly, in many ways, I fit into the category of both the oppressor and the oppressed. In knowing this, it is I who must continue to change, to constantly renew my own involvement in the struggle for liberation. As teachers, we often engage in dialogue about quality learning in the absence of students without first recognizing that we too are students.

Collective critical consciousness in praxis. Specific visible actions of social justice within relationships are perceived as integral to participant's transformation. Without action, their transformation remains constrained in thoughts and words. Vanessa depicts these daily actions of social justice:

> Social justice is a way of life and a mindful measure of implementation. In the beginning, social justice seemed like a disingenuous motto that anyone who wanted to create the impression of integrity would use. It seemed like the popular jargon of the moment. Now I know that social justice is a creed that I bear wherever I go and is present within everything that I do. It is my moral compass that I regard when I am uncertain or weary.

Mikayla further describes these actions as connected to stirring the critical consciousness of others, "Today, I speak. I question. I challenge. I share my knowledge with others to raise awareness for the development of critical consciousness. I am far from perfect, but I today, I choose to take action." Delia's transformation connects authentic caring as an action of social justice that occurs for the duration of one's career, "My transformation occurs in sustaining that method of relationship [authentic caring] throughout my career." Brianna concludes the practice of reflection leads her to enact social justice to center equitable relationships, as a leader of change, and to address systematic injustice of school systems collectively:

> With this constant reflection I am better able to place relationships with students and colleagues at the forefront, more effectively seek leadership opportunities to collaborate in a social justice change process; and confront a faulty, inequitable, hierarchical, and often racist educational system.

FINDINGS

Transformation for these participants, is nestled within the tension of teaching in a traditional educational system that contrasts with their experience as students in a non-traditional graduate program. Transformation is perceived as an ongoing, sustainable, individual and collective process in which their praxis becomes more aligned with a collective critical consciousness of social justice. This finding affirms transformation as put forth by Mezirow (2003, 2004) and Freire (2000) in which transformation is a social construct that is not internalized without action. Furthermore, transformation is perceived to be sustained by the reproduction of the transformative process within personal and professional relationships. The transformational process can begin at any point, but is connected by each element as depicted in Figure 7.1.

The transformative pedagogy of their graduate cohort program is grounded in the dispositions of social justice leadership and the collective critical consciousness of social justice. This pedagogy is aligned with Freire's *Pedagogy of the Oppressed* (2000), Valenzuela's conceptualization of authentic care (1999), and Garza's (2015) *Pedagogy of Collective Critical Con-*

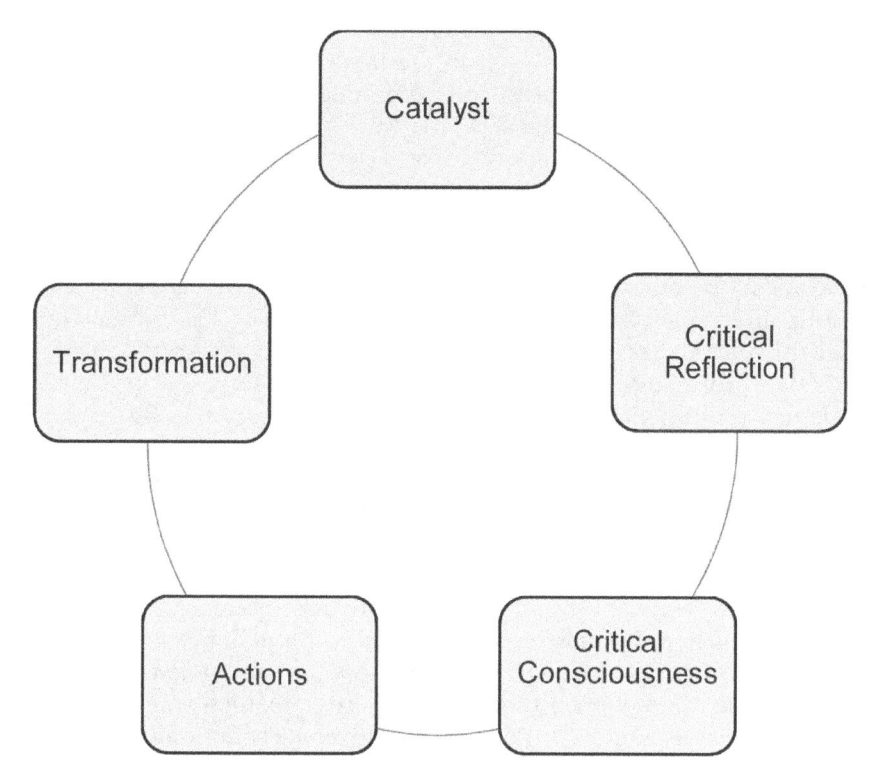

Figure 7.1. Experience of transformation as a process.

sciousness. This pedagogy served as the catalyst for participants participate in the process of transformation as depicted above. Their transformation begins when they engage as students in a new way, in which professors' model learning relationships established in reciprocity and the value of student's lived experiences. In this learning environment, the hierarchy of teacher and student, was replaced with a learner-learner stance facilitated with discourse about their personal and professional lives, as well as their assigned coursework. Their interpretation of coursework is integrated within their personal and professional lives. Students freely choose how and to what extent this integration occurs.

Transformation is not perceived as compartmentalized, or conceptualized through direct teaching methods. Instead, week by week, participants unravel their personal and professional beliefs, through individual and collective critical reflection. They come to know each other through these reflections enabling trusting, authentic relationships to develop. How they know themselves individually, is shared collectively, where they feel safe to question themselves and their peers in the critique of their praxis both, personally and professionally. From the first semester, the participants practice critical individual and collective reflection that engages them in a profound critique of who they are, what counts as knowledge, their understanding of educational systems and coursework, their pedagogy as educators, and their ability to form authentic relationships.

As they engage in this transformative learning process, they become critically conscious of the tension between their personal and professional beliefs. They become conscious of how these tensions in thought and action derails their vision of equitable educational systems. The participants engage in the process of transformation to continually work toward aligning their newly formed collective critical consciousness of social justice across both their professional and personal lives in their daily praxis. Participants also specifically identify collective critical consciousness as necessary for all educators to become aware of the dynamics of oppression, perpetuated by individuals and systems. Their transformational experience is cemented with visible actions of social justice.

Interpersonal relationships are critical to sustaining their ongoing transformation because the process of transformation becomes re-produced, within personal and professional relationships throughout their lifetime. Thus, at the same time many participants move into traditional leadership roles with the completion of their graduate program, their transformative pedagogy, has the potential to be carried out in broader educational settings.

DISCUSSION

We assert the transformational experience is a process of discovering who we are as individuals to integrate our personal and professional lives, through actions that align to a collective critical consciousness of social justice that continually informs praxis. This suggests, in the realm of education, the critical consciousness of social justice is capable of deconstructing social constructs maintaining educational inequity. It is evident from the findings of this study, that participants experienced a significant transformation they articulate as a distinct process, realized as a consequence of their participation in their cohort graduate program. However, both co-coordinators of the program emphasize that "transforming" students is not a deliberate goal of the program. They stress that the program is designed to engage students in a process where students "transform" themselves. In discussion with Dr. Garza and Dr. Niño they insist their goal is to "facilitate a process to help students see themselves in the students they serve." It is a process that encourages students to claim the space that has always belonged to them. "As professors, we do not create the space because the space belongs to all of us" (Garza, E., personal communication, June, 8, 2016).

In order to facilitate a process in which individuals define what transformation means to them and how they experience it, in an educational setting, professors of USLC demonstrate their own unique ongoing, transformation as it progresses in real time, in both their personal and professional lives. It is not a class titled, "The Process of Transformation," instead it is the sharing of their daily lived experience of their own ongoing transformation seen in how they design the program, their struggles, their teaching pedagogy, and their relationships that serve to facilitate transformation without defining the experience for others.

The facilitation of this process begins the moment student becomes interested in the USLC program. Students have shared that they felt something immediately "different" in the way they were recruited, selected, and admitted into the program. Students are recruited by past members of the USLC because they believe they have the dispositions that make them good candidates for the program. In most cases, they are asked permission to be nominated and usually have several candid discussions with their nominator about the program before applications are completed. Many times the students nominated are not the same educators' principals might choose, and nominators take time to express the specific qualities they see in their peer that would make them a good candidate. Once they are nominated, the program coordinators are in constant contact with potential students to answer questions and help them through the application process. The coordinators are also in constant contact with the department staff, to make sure the application process is working smoothly. They also continue to speak to their nominator to process practical concerns such as anxiety about comprehending advanced readings and writing formal papers, and financial burdens, as well as balancing family and work as graduate students. From the beginning, through personal interaction with the coordinators, students have expressed that they feel invited and important, that their personal lives matter, and that they have potential to earn a graduate degree.

Their potential is not reliant upon academic prowess, accolades, high grade point averages, professional accolades, perceived expertise, or traditionally highly regarded recommendations. In fact, program coordinators have consistently found ways to admit students often rejected by universities. A student's potential is instead seen through their "*ganas*," a Spanish word meaning, desire, that is taken from the Spanish verb *ganar*, meaning to win or gain. Dr. Garza has often said, "I don't care about anything else. If you have the ganas, you will get in." He does not save this discussion for after candidates are accepted; he tells them this at every orientation. What he suggests is, only we have the power to determine the expansiveness of our intellect, and the strength of our desire to claim who we are in the halls of education and beyond. Potential candidate's interest in the program, and their experience in applying connect to initiate the catalyst of their transformation, they continue long after they graduate. This recruitment, application, and selection experience models the process of transformation that turns the hierarchical, traditional college screening process on its head.

The program design of the USLC also facilitates a transformational experience for students. Once again, it starts with a deep interest in the personal development of the individual. In this case these individuals are educators serving in diverse, ambiguous, and challenging contexts who are struggling to move forward in the social constructs of unjust, inequitable educational systems. To affirm their personal lived experiences, the USLC program centers social justice to prepare educators as social justice leaders, and not as educational managers. The program, at its core, expresses this deep interest with its innovative design. First, the program is driven by a philosophy of social justice advocacy, focused initially on the development of asset-based attitudes and mindsets, and then on the cultivation of collaboration, analytical and leadership skills. Second, as an authentically collaborative partnership, both the school district and university are actively involved in the selection, planning, teaching, and evaluation of the program. This is essential to the department's capacity building and results in a praxis-oriented curriculum that benefits the student and faculty. Third, the USLC is a closed cohort model that serves the employees of the partnering school district. Leadership preparation is customized to meet the needs of the children of SAISD while promoting buy-in and a level of ownership from central administration. Fourth, because all classes are taught by department faculty on campuses throughout the school district, university faculty engage with issues and problems in the field, across the district and at multiple levels of the district organization. And finally, student support continues via a mentoring component in which faculty continue to mentor graduates as they assume leadership positions. As one graduate noted, "We may graduate, but we never finish." With this innovation, transformation is modeled as a collective reality within the community.

Once students begin the program, professors also use a pedagogy that is aligned with social justice in which students witness professors grappling with their ongoing transformation as educators. Teaching and learning in this program are driven by a constructivist theoretical approach. In a constructivist classroom, students, together and collectively, engage in critical reflection. Coupled with constructivist learning theory, the *Pedagogy of Collective Critical Consciousness* (Garza, 2015) engages students intensely in collective learning activities, including shared critical reflection, the writing of auto-ethnographies, and ultimately, the implementation of praxis (Freire, 1993). Students learn together and from each other. As co-constructors of knowledge, they are both teachers and learners. The central premise of the *Pedagogy of Collective Critical Consciousness* framework is to engage students in a continuous cycle of collective learning experiences. The intensive critical reflection and auto-ethnography are extremely demanding and require students to develop a deep understanding of who they are, personally and professionally. It is critical that these activities be carried out in a context of trust and respect, which deepens over the course of the program. Professors become students as well, engaging alongside them in critical reflective practices, sharing personal auto-ethnographies, working on research projects together, and making new meaning of past and present lived experiences—including coursework. Incorporating instructors from both the district and university who have particular understandings of the experiences of participants in the USLC has been critical to the success of these activities to continue this pedagogy in each class. This intense collective dynamic as learners, informs their collective critical consciousness enacted daily within personal and professional settings.

When the authors of this chapter reflect on the findings, it is clear that while the experience of transformation is facilitated by professors of the program before and during the student's graduate experience, it can only be understood through the collective expression of those telling their stories. In their own words they have defined what transformation is like for them, how it has been shaped, and how it informs their practice. Educators of this program have left an indelible print to sustain the experience of transformation by helping to grow this program. Their nominations and mentoring of potential applicants has helped to triple enrollment for 2017. In addition, several are halfway-through completing an educational doctoral program with several more applying that will build the capacity of professors needed to support this program modeling the *Pedagogy of Collective Critical Consciousness*. With these actions, they are collectively transforming educator preparation as we know it, to support the readiness of college professors to grow programs such as these that facilitate a transformative process, grounded in the ideals of social justice. Their experience began with their individual transformation, shared collectively, and carried out in critically conscious, socially just actions. Their transformation process extends beyond themselves, beyond their schools, beyond their personal lives—it never ends as others join the ongoing process.

REFERENCES

Bass, B. & Avolio, B. (1993). Transformational leadership and organizational culture. *Public Administration Quarterly. 17*(1), 112–112.

Berkovich, I. (2016). School leaders and transformational leadership theory: Time to part ways? *Journal of Educational Administration, 54*(5), 609–622.

Burns, J. M. (2012). *Leadership*. New York, NY: Open Road Media.

Bryant, D., III, & J. D. (2008). "A failure to act" from *Brown v. Board of Education* to *Sheff v. O'neill*: The American educational system will remain segregated. *Thomas M. Cooley Law Review, 25*, 1–555.

Cambron-McCabe, N., & McCarthy, M. M. (2005). Educating school leaders for social justice. *Educational Policy, 19*(1), 201–222.

Drennon, C. M. (2006). Social relations spatially fixed: Construction and maintenance of school districts in San Antonio, Texas. *Geographical Review, 96*(4), 567–593.

Finkelman, P. (2010). Lincoln and emancipation: Constitutional theory, practical politics, and the basic practice of law. *Journal of Supreme Court History, 35*(3), 243–266.

Freire, P. (2000). *Pedagogy of the oppressed* (30th anniversary ed.). New York, NY: Continuum.

Gándara, P., & Contreras, F. (2009). *The Latino education crisis: The consequences of failed social policies*. Cambridge, MA: Harvard University Press.

Garza, E. (2015, November). *The pedagogy of collective critical consciousness: The praxis of preparing leaders for social justice*. Paper presented at UCEA Conference, Denver, CO.

Hallinger, P. (2003). Leading educational change: Reflections on the practice of instructional and transformational leadership. *Cambridge Journal of Education, 33*(3), 329–352.

Hillstrom, L. C. (2013). *Plessy V. Ferguson*. Omnigraphics.

Hoffer, W. (2012). *Plessy v. Ferguson: Race and inequality in Jim Crow America*. Lawrence, KS: University Press of Kansas.

Katz, M. S. (1976). *A history of compulsory education laws*. Bloomington, ID: Phi Delta Kappa Educational Foundation.

Ladson-Billings, G. (2006). From the achievement gap to education debt: Understanding achievement in U.S. schools. *Educational Researcher, 35*(7), 3–12.

Leithwood, K. A. (1992). Transformational leadership: Where does it stand? *Education Digest, 58*(3), 17–20.

Lopez, G., & Burciaga, R. (2014). The troublesome legacy of *Brown v. Board of Education*. *Educational Administration Quarterly, 50*(5), 796–811.

Marshall, C. (2004). Social justice challenges to educational administration: Introduction to a special issue. *Educational Administration Quarterly, 40*(1), 3–13.

Mathis, W. (2005). The cost of implementing the federal No Child Left Behind Act: Different assumptions, different Answers. *Peabody Journal of Education, 80*(2), 90–119.

Mezirow, J. D., & Santopolo, F. A. (1960). Community—development in Pakistan—the 1st 5 years. *International Social Science Journal, 12*(3), 433–439.

Mezirow, J. (1997). Transformative learning: Theory to practice. *New Directions for Adult and Continuing Education, 1997*(74), 5–12.

Mezirow, J. (2003). Transformative learning as discourse. *Journal of Transformative Education, 1*(1), 58–63.

Mezirow, J. (2004). Forum comment on Sharan Merriam's "the role of cognitive development in Mezirow's transformational learning theory." *Adult Education Quarterly, 55*(1), 69–70.

Mezirow, J. (1998). On critical reflection. *Adult Education Quarterly, 48*(3), 185–198.

Pane, D. M., & Rocco, T. S. (2014). *Transforming the school-to-prison pipeline: Lessons from the classroom* (1st ed). Rotterdam, the Netherlands: Sense.

Radin, B. A., & Hawley, W. D. (2013). *The politics of federal reorganization: Creating the U.S. department of education.* New York, NY: Pergamon Press.

Rothstein, R. (2015). The racial achievement gap, segregated schools, and segregated neighborhoods: A constitutional insult. *Race and Social Problems, 7*(1), 21–30.

Saldana, J. (2008). *Coding manual for qualitative researchers.* Los Angeles, CA: SAGE.

Solorzano, D., & Bernal, D. (2001). Examining transformational resistance through a Critical Race and Latcrit Theory Framework: Chicana and Chicano students in an urban context. *Urban Education, 36*(3), 308–342.

Sunderman, G., & Orfield, G. (2006). Domesticating a revolution: No Child Left Behind reforms and state administrative response. *Harvard Educational Review, 76*(4), 526–556.

Valenzuela, A. (1999). *Subtractive schooling: U.S.-Mexican youth and the politics of caring.* Albany, NY: State University of New York Press.

Viteritti, J. (2012). *Choosing equality: School choice, the constitution, and civil society.* Washington, DC: Brookings Institution Press.

Walsh, C. (2007). Erasing race, dismissing class: San Antonio Independent School District v. Rodriguez. *LaRaza Law Journal, 21,* 133–177.

Warren, J. T. (2011). Reflexive teaching: Toward critical autoethnographic practices of/in/on pedagogy. *Cultural Studies ↔ Critical Methodologies, 11*(2), 139–144.

Willie, C. V., & Willie, S. S. (2005). Black, White, and Brown: The transformation of public education in America. *Teachers College Record, 107*(3), 475–495.

CHAPTER 8

STUDENT RESPONSES TO CRITICALLY COMPASSIONATE INTELLECTUALISM IN TEACHER EDUCATION FOR SOCIAL JUSTICE

Amy Rector-Aranda

INTRODUCTION

Enacting socially just practices in both the education of our future teachers and in how we study our work within teacher education should be a logical aim of any movement for social justice in education as a whole. Aligning my means with these ends has been an imperative underlying my work, as with many other scholars (Carter Andrews, Bartell, & Richmond, 2016; Conklin, 2008; Kincheloe & Steinberg, 1998; Picower, 2012). In this spirit, over the course of two years, I conducted critical qualitative practitioner and participatory action research on my use of *critically compassionate intellectualism* (CCI) (Cammarota & Romero, 2006) in the educational foundations course I taught at an urban Midwestern research university. Work with Latinx youth in the original CCI projects showed that its combination of critical pedagogy, authentic caring, and a social justice purpose fostered

Transformative Pedagogies for Teacher Education:
Critical Action, Agency, and Dialogue in Teaching and Learning Contexts, pp. 133–151
Copyright © 2019 by Information Age Publishing
All rights of reproduction in any form reserved.

these students' critical consciousness and deeper academic and life competencies, so it holds promising implications as a transformative pedagogy in the education of future teachers.

Remembering to honor the roots of CCI as a social justice project for ethnic minority high school students, I have expanded on the project in order to study how CCI can enrich the learning experiences of future educators, especially those from minoritized backgrounds and those who will end up teaching diverse students and/or in high-poverty communities. This is particularly significant for many teacher education programs where students largely come from more demographically homogenous locales and have had minimal exposure to individuals who are racially, culturally, socioeconomically, linguistically, ably, academically, and otherwise different from themselves. Literature shows that these students often resist or resent our efforts to enlighten them to the perspectives and experiences of marginalized pre-K–12 students with whom they cannot personally relate (Conklin, 2008; King, 1991; Matias, 2015). Simultaneously, catering our efforts to this majority further neglects minoritized teacher education students' ways of being and knowing. Instead, CCI foregrounds these students' needs and lived experiences.

While it is important to remember that many forces beyond teachers' control contribute to the educational disparities experienced by students with socioeconomic, racial, and otherwise disempowered identities (Cochran-Smith & Villegas, 2016), in a context where these students remain underserved, we must do our best to prepare teachers who are fully aware of these forces and ready to confront this reality. Specifically, in order for them to successfully teach and advocate for their future students, teacher education programs must nurture all preservice teachers' sense of their own and others' humanity and inherent worth, co-empower them to understand both the material and existential purposes of education, and facilitate their learning about the relational, social, political, historical, economic, and other structural contexts that influence the varied learning experiences of students in all settings. Examining the nature of teaching and learning as enacted through CCI illuminates some ways teacher educators—and by extension, our students—might become better conductors of as well as activists for socially just educational practices.

Because action research of this nature is context-specific, it is not meant to be generalizable, but can potentially be transferable to other teacher education contexts. The main purpose of this chapter is to make visible the kinds of behaviors and dispositions that resulted in my students' being receptive to social justice messages and ideals, and to show how CCI principles facilitated this in my classroom. While the ways in which I enacted CCI are particular to my own character and positionality, to the groups of students and the program in which I taught, as well as influenced by countless other contextual factors, teacher educators reading this chapter will hopefully be able to envision similar ways they might put CCI into practice in contextually and personally meaningful ways.

As part of a larger project that also examined CCI's influence on other aspects of my research and practice, here I focus on answering: *How did students respond to my CCI policies, practices, and pedagogy, and how did this shape their engagement with concepts of social justice education?* Findings show that students consistently did not resist efforts to help them examine their assumptions and acknowledge various social and educational advantages, but instead valued the respect and care they experienced through this pedagogical framework and were able to envision affording their own students the same dignity and support. They felt empowered to take charge of their own learning and goals, to become critically reflective practitioners, and to act as advocates and change agents for their future students. Regarding social justice ideals, they emerged much more aware of the complicated role that teachers play within society and in the individual lives of students. Simultaneously, I was able to enact my own moral vision of socially just teacher preparation, where my unconventional, reflexive, and compassionate pedagogy became assets to both my students' learning and my own continuing growth as a teacher educator.

CRITICAL CONSCIOUSNESS, CARE, AND JUSTICE

The theoretical framework for this study is built into CCI, consisting of critical pedagogy (Freire, 1970/1993), authentic caring (Valenzuela, 1999), and a social justice curriculum and purpose (Ginwright & Cammarota, 2002). The original CCI framework resulted from several projects Cammarota and Romero enacted with Latinx youth in Arizona high schools to counter the injustices ethnic and racial minorities face in our education system. Findings from these projects confirmed the importance of CCI's conceptual trifecta when working toward educational justice with marginalized youth (Cammarota & Romero, 2006).

Critical pedagogy draws attention to the ways power is enacted in education, asserting that traditional hierarchies of power, privilege, and knowledge production perpetuate relationships of dominance and oppression in society at large (Freire, 1970/1993; Giroux, 2001; McLaren, 2003). Instead, in critical pedagogy, students and teachers democratically negotiate knowledge creation and re-creation around issues relevant to students' lived experiences, investigating the contextual and ideological forces that either maintain or disrupt the status quo (McLaren, 2003). Even when used with students who do not personally experience educational struggles, critical pedagogy still "poses a variety of important counterlogics to the positivistic, ahistorical, and depoliticized" (McLaren, 2003, p. 185) predominant forms of schooling, opening a space for all students to more deeply question, comprehend, and reflect upon existential injustices.

Valenzuela's (1999) notion of "authentic care" is based on her work with Latinx youth who perceived their experiences of schooling as uncaring and "subtractive," denying them any connection with their cultural and community identities and ways of knowing. She found teachers who uncritically maintained the colonizing effects of the dominant culture through curriculum, policy, and practice were not authentically caring, but merely aesthetically caring, claiming to care for students but limiting this care to ensuring student achievement while neglecting essential aspects of students' humanity. Authentic caring instead means creating more meaningful, personal relationships with students, embracing and affirming their identities, and generally establishing a loving and genuine interest in students' overall well-being.

Adding to Valenzuela's framework in order to extend considerations of care and compassion beyond the original context of educating Latinx youth into this new context of teacher education, I have incorporated relational-cultural theory (RCT) and care ethics into my interpretation of CCI. RCT is a feminist theory of psychosocial development that draws attention to the impacts of culture on relationships, proposing that successful relational connections that lead to healing and growth are achieved through aspects of trust, mutual empathy, authenticity, shared power, and growth-in-connection (Miller & Stiver, 1997; Rector-Aranda, 2018; Rodgers & Raider-Roth, 2006; Spencer, 2000). An ethic of care was first articulated by Gilligan (1982) and Noddings (1984), who proposed that moral choices should be motivated by emotion, empathy, and a concern for the cared-for (Noddings, 2012). Like authentic caring, which shifts our view of the traditional teacher–student affiliation, care ethics shift our view of moral responsibility from rule-oriented to relationship-oriented.

Finally, while "social justice" has come to mean many things to many people (North, 2006), in this framework, it very specifically entails conceptualizing the lives of marginalized students "within the terrain of the changing political, economic, and social landscape" (Ginwright & Cammarota, 2002, p. 83), through the study of difficult and important issues from multiple perspectives, and particularly aligning content, pedagogy, and purpose with students' histories and lived experiences. A social justice purpose in CCI means aiming to effect changes in the larger structures that underserve these youth, and paying close attention to how schooling is implicated in perpetuating or interrupting enduring disparities.

COLORING MY PRACTICE

Whenever I discuss my use of CCI in teacher preparation, I feel it is crucial that I also remain conscious of and am able to justify using a framework first created on behalf of marginalized students of color with the students in teacher education classrooms who have generally been advantaged by their race, class, ability, and other privileged statuses in our culture. Because many current educational trends around multiculturalism and diversity have tended to "filter out the most radical parts" of theories that were first conceptualized by scholars of color (Matias, 2015, p. 8), I want to affirm that my use of CCI has been wholly unfiltered, and indeed, the most radical parts of the framework are what I have tried most to exemplify for my students. I believe my adoption of CCI has been further justified because it supports that small percentage of my students who do not affiliate with the mainstream, while offering all students an unambiguous model from which to draw ideas about how they might enact their own more humanizing pedagogies. My students are mainly college freshmen, with little beyond their traditional pre-K–12 experiences from which to fashion their ideas about what education should be. Most of the topics we explore and what I do are so very unfamiliar compared to the types of knowledge and pedagogy to which they have grown accustomed, fundamentally challenging their ideas about what "education" means, and what defines "good" students and "effective" educators.

Because CCI is an anti-oppressive pedagogy meant to alleviate racial/ethnic inequities, in my classes we also pay specific attention to the role of race in the U.S. institution of education through an overall curriculum and pedagogy meant to sensitize my students to the historical and modern injustices disproportionately borne by students of color. Like others, I believe this content and purpose should be included across teacher education curricula rather than isolated to a single "multicultural education" course (Matias, 2015). I have therefore incorporated it alongside the other foundations curriculum in this course, which is additionally aimed at raising students' awareness of educational injustices based in ability, gender, SES, sexuality, religion, and so forth.

MODES OF INQUIRY

Four semesters of this research represented four action research cycles of action and reflection if viewed broadly, and many microcycles throughout each semester as I navigated students' implicit and explicit responses and made constant adjustments in all the myriad choices I had to make as an instructor (Hill, 2015; Kemmis, McTaggart, & Nixon, 2014). Throughout, CCI and my action research stance dictated that the research remain intuitive and organic. It was also imperative that the research not alter or interrupt students' regular course experience since the primary purpose of examining these concepts was for students to benefit from improvements to my pedagogy and curriculum. To triangulate and get the most detailed impression of students' needs and reactions, I used several qualitative data forms, of which the following were analyzed here: anonymous early-term feedback via open-ended prompts; semi-structured interviews and individual meetings at the end of the course; open-ended end-of-course reflection questionnaires; and the anonymous written response sections of formal course evaluations. For example, end-of-course reflection questionnaires asked:

1. How did the relationship with your **peers** help or hinder your learning in this class?
2. How did the relationship with your **instructor** help or hinder your learning in this class?
3. How was your experience in this course different or similar to **other courses**?
4. What **ONE THING** about this course do you wish all courses had?
5. Did you feel comfortable **communicating** with your instructor for this course? Please explain.
6. What **ideas** have been most important to you and your learning this semester?
7. What aspects of the course have been most **supportive** of your learning?
8. What aspects of the course have interrupted or **hindered** your learning?

My personal data included planning and observation notes, syllabi and other curricular artifacts, and critical reflective journaling using Napan's (2011) *Questions for Co-Creative Inquiry*. For the participatory action research component, students in two classes did a Photovoice project near the end of the semester, a method in which participants are no longer the subjects but the creators of inquiry through their own photography and a group analysis process (Janesick, 2014) (see Figure 8.1 depicting collaborative analysis and discussion of themes from the Photovoice during class).

Another participatory method we used was Group-Level Understanding (Raider-Roth et al., 2019; Vaughn & Lohmueller, 2014), an anonymous, student-driven approach for them to make meaning of their evolving learning and to assess course content and practices.

While the majority response reflected an overall positive student experience of CCI, there were, of course, that handful of students for whom

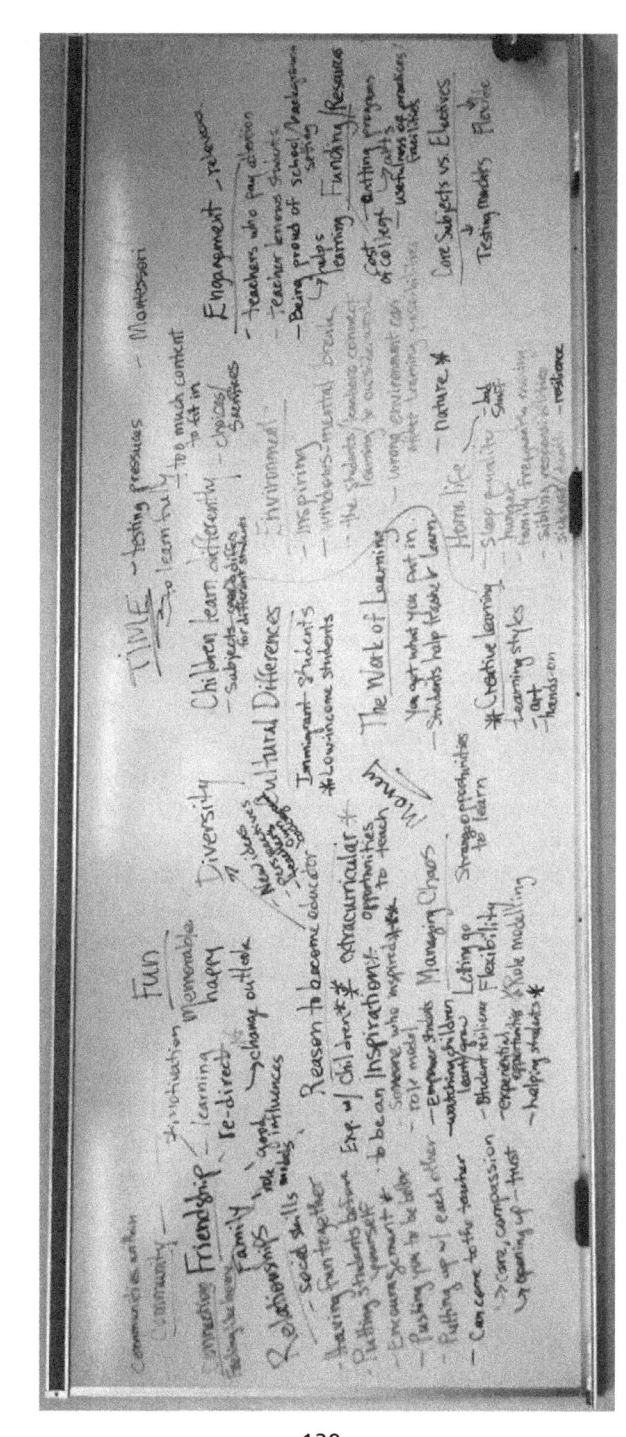

Figure 8.1. Collaborative analysis and discussion of themes from the Photovoice during class.

the course did not appear to have much impact on their thinking or ways of seeing things, who failed to successfully complete the course despite my very deliberate academic and relational supports, who maintained resistance to ideals of socially just education, and so forth. Some of their own perspectives on this are difficult to account for with specific evidence because not all gave formal consent for me to use their artifacts in my study, so this is a limitation to the examples I am permitted to disseminate. However, as a practitioner, I was still able to reflect on the types of barriers these students encountered and continually try to address these discrepancies in new iterations of my practice.

THE STUDENT RESPONSE

As mentioned in the introduction, the main goal of this chapter is to illuminate how the theoretical tenets of CCI influenced my personal practice, and how this helped my students move from having minimal consciousness of social justice concepts at the beginning of the course, to a place of deeper awareness and having gained the dispositions to act on these ideals by the end of the course. While my specific procedures are not presumed to be directly applicable in either my students' future practice nor the reader's, I share them in order to show examples of how I implemented CCI, and in what ways my students consequently changed their perspectives and mindsets and are now primed to imagine more just practices in their future work.

So much more emerged from the data than can be described in this space, therefore, a purposeful selection of themes and examples of students' responses are presented here. These findings fall into somewhat of an arc that is built on relationships, flows through the students' course experiences, and ends up in their important learning. Recognize that within and between each topic there is a lot of overlap among the concepts and students' responses, suggesting that rich educational experiences cannot be easily reduced to discrete particulars, and that multiple factors interact in this kind of teaching and learning—which also reinforces the need for frameworks like CCI that provide a holistic approach.

Relationships

Overall, students valued and felt that many relational aspects of the course were uncommon, such as the amount of freedom and time to work with and learn from peers, the fact that I sat with and talked to them like equals, or the ability to approach me about anything and trust that I would value their ideas or be compassionate to their needs. Findings around authenticity and vulnerability, confidence and safety, trust and respect, and care and engagement follow.

Authenticity and vulnerability. From day one, I go against norms that assume teachers and students should maintain strict personal boundaries, instead attempting to help students feel at ease by sharing a lot about myself, especially my vulnerabilities, and asking to learn more about their lives and experiences beyond school. I believe this transparency and "being real" are the kinds of actions transformative pedagogues must take to show our students the value in authentically engaging with their future students, which is especially important when they are teaching students who may face challenges many of us cannot even imagine enduring. I proceed similarly throughout the semester to model the sharing of personal experiences, ideas, and opinions, and invite them to do the same—importantly, without judgment or correction from me, only further question-posing when appropriate—pointing out how instructors do, indeed, have human lives and minds of their own.

> *Having such a level relationship without fear of always being told I was wrong really helped me be more honest with myself which helped me figure out more about who I want to be as a teacher one day.*

Educators of already vulnerable students' whose identities have been marginalized by mainstream norms must realize how mutual empathy through the disclosure of vulnerability can actually lead to stronger levels of respect between students and their instructors.

> *I wish I could have a honest and personal relationship with all my professors because sometimes people are just having a rough day and need a break. Some professors don't even know your name they just know you by a clicker number or a ID number. I think that the personal relationship shared made me more willing to connect with the teacher and the class.*

The assumption that teachers cannot love or share their lives with students is based on a culture of separation in which we are taught to be competitive and self-protect, rather than to collaborate, connect, and share our real feelings or the most authentic parts of ourselves (Jordan, 1995; Miller & Stiver, 1997).

Confidence and safety. Students attributed their feeling self-confident in the space of our classroom to the relationships they were able to build, both with their peers and with me.

> *I felt comfortable to speak my mind and be engaged in discussions with my peers which was crucial for my learning in this class. I never felt intimidated to share my opinions around my peers.*

Some described this as feeling "safe" or similar terminology. I do not necessarily connect these statements with formal notions of "safe space," in which guidelines for dialogue across difference are devised that can actually inhibit a lot of the "unsafe" talk necessary to truly get at topics of injustice, and which have a tendency to privilege the dominant groups' ways of feeling safe. Instead, I follow Sensoy and DiAngelo's (2014) "less-orthodox adaptations" (p. 8) of the typical safe space guidelines, which I think contribute to the feelings students describe while retaining a focus on finding comfort with our discomfort.

Trust and respect. In our class, trust between students and myself, students and their peers, and students' trust in their own funds of knowledge (Rodgers & Raider-Roth, 2006) creates a context of shared power and respect in which students felt confident enough to explore intimidating topics, attempt creative modes of conveying their learning, and otherwise test unfamiliar waters. Students found the trust and respect they received "refreshing."

> *I usually never have professors who care what I think or believe in. This instructor was different. She showed me how she really respects me, and this made me respect her and what she teaches in class.*

I believe it is this trust and respect that made it possible for students to explore their own privileges, assumptions, and other positionalities without getting defensive, as so much of the literature says our mostly White, middle-class preservice teachers tend to do.

I also make it clear to students that I believe they are capable of thinking deeply, acting for themselves, and learning in their own ways. All policies, assignments, and other requirements for which I am able to offer options are negotiable (within the constraints of our program requirements). This means anything from encouraging students to propose variations on how they complete a project, to letting them be responsible for their own attendance. This also translates into mostly flexible due dates, individual and collaborative projects in place of tests and quizzes, and extensive qualitative feedback instead of quantitative evaluation of their work (Kohn, 2012). I believe these policies also helped mediate the potential that students would "tell me what I want to hear" for the sake of their grade.

> *I actually spent more time trying to make it as good as possible before turning it in and really upped the quality of my work.*

While some might wonder about the objectivity of such a system for ensuring a "level" playing field, especially in light of the standardized forms of assessment so dominant in education today, students actually expressed that they thought this individualized approach was more *fair* and *effective*, allowing their achievement to be based on their own growth rather than on comparison or competition with classmates. I also provide a lot of structure for those students who want it, and students always have the option to receive traditional instructions and grades for everything they do, an option that even the most self-proclaimed extrinsically motivated students never exercised and without which, they seemed delighted to discover, they did as good or better work.

Not only do these policies alleviate an immense amount of stress for students—which may be one of the most repeated appreciations in their feedback—I am also able to trust in my own understandings of education, prioritizing my compassion for students as human beings and their authentic expressions of learning and engagement.

> *Overall, my relationship with my instructor I think was built on mutual trust that we would both complete our work and put effort into learning together, and I think this really helped my learning throughout the course.*

Overly regulative practices and policies that prevent students from questioning, challenging, exploring, and experimenting are, from the perspective of critical pedagogy, the epitome of oppressive education—a means of privileging the kinds of docility and conforming that maintain the status quo. Rather, because I uphold my values by trusting students to make the most of their learning, they live up to that trust, and also learn to trust in themselves.

> *While we still had responsibilities and work to do, this course felt a lot more self-lead in that I could get out of it whatever I put in, and it is my responsibility to learn rather than the professor forcing the information upon the students.*

In place of banking methods, this trust entails another kind of vulnerability from instructors—acknowledging the possibility that what we think is the most important idea or the best way to do something is not always necessarily so. Because of the trusting and respectful relationships we had built, students were able to trust in their own abilities to create knowledge and wanted to extend their existing thinking in new directions and do their best work.

Care and engagement. Care in this class was perceived as my compassion and concern for the overall wellbeing of my students, care for their genuine learning that went beyond their achievement, and care for the subject matter that made students want to care as well.

> *I truly believe I tried my hardest in this class because I knew the instructor cared about my learning which made me care about my growth as a learner.*

Returning to the earlier topic of authenticity, students could tell that my care for them and their learning was a priority and was genuine.

> *Most of my other courses are very strict and have little to no compassion. This instructor showed so much love and care for her students inside and outside of the classroom and I do not receive that from a majority of college professors. I felt very comfortable sharing my opinion in class which is very difficult for me to do in other courses.*

My approachability also facilitated students' greater engagement with learning.

> *I never felt weird asking her questions, often times instructors or professors are really intimidating and it scares you away from asking questions which is stupid because the professors and instructors are there to help you learn and if you don't feel comfortable talking to them that stinks because that affects your learning.*

I had apprehensions that my sensitivity or relaxed policies might inhibit students' levels of commitment and engagement, which I always candidly discussed with them early on. Overwhelmingly, students showed the opposite response, stating that is was precisely these policies that made them want to turn in assignments in a timely fashion, come to class, do their best work, fully participate, and so on.

> *I was never bored, stressed, or frustrated during class and I think that is a big part of why I never procrastinated with assignments and always came to class because it was actually enjoyable.*

My solicitation for feedback in all data forms included space for students to tell me what interrupted or hindered their learning. The interesting thing about their responses to these questions was that students typically took responsibility for these hindrances, such as for procrastination, or attributed such interruption to other students, such as others' lack of preparation or contribution. They admitted that while certain assets of the course could also be drawbacks, they tended to conclude that this was "on them," and that the benefits far outweighed the negatives.

The Course Experience

Students expressed the most enthusiasm about having their voices heard, exploring alternative perspectives, and our student-centered policies, activities, and assignments. These prominent aspects of the course included a calm learning environment, emphasis on student voice, agency, and questioning, discussion and collaboration, field experiences in urban youth spaces, and reflection and reflexivity.

Calm learning environment. Students attributed feeling at ease, calm, less stressed, comfortable, engaged, motivated, interested, and so on to the overall student-centered feel of the classroom environment, the ease of relationships between students and with me, and the relaxed policies and ways of learning.

> *I think that this is the only class I have ever taken where I didn't feel a little nervous walking in the door each day. It had a very calm and relaxed feel to it and I really appreciated that. I feel like it really helped me learn the material because I wasn't constantly on the edge of my seat feeling like I was missing something or doing something wrong.*

Students were able to enjoy the environment of our classroom because they were not intimidated or constantly worried about repercussions for their actions. They felt like they mattered, their presence was vital to our classroom community, and what they had to say was important, which made them want to be there.

Voice, agency, and questioning. Students very consistently cited the ability to voice their ideas and opinions, to make their own choices about their learning, and to question previously taken-for-granted knowledge and ways of seeing education as essential to their ability to construct new knowledge in the course. Given the current era's emphasis on developing students' "critical thinking skills," it was interesting to hear that the critical aspects of the course were what students considered the most novel.

> *I liked being able to develop my own ideas and opinions for subjects rather than being told the instructors opinions of the story and being expected to agree with it. This has helped me to learn and dig deeper and find a greater meaning in my learning. I was able to discover things for my own, rather than just think about one persons ideas and not dig deeper to develop my own.*

Considering that social justice educators are often accused of indoctrinating their students to their own liberal or radical perspectives, this shows that when we simply present the evidence, foregrounding multiple perspectives and options for understanding a phenomenon, students are perfectly able to choose for themselves. This kind of problem-posing (Shor, 1992) particularly sets the stage for students to comprehend marginalized perspectives as part of their own process of discovery.

> *Most classes just view the facts to students, are asked to memorize it, and apply it on a test. But this class challenged our own thoughts, allowed us to think about overlooked minorities and how they feel about education, and for once we were allowed to question the education system.*

This form of criticality was different than mainstream views of critical thinking, which focus too much on the technical aspects of deconstructing passages of information, rather than questioning that information and its validity in the first place, comparing it with one's own experience of the world, and judging its contribution to a just society.

Discussion and collaboration. The types of questioning just described were facilitated by the course's use of discussion and collaboration in place of lectures and exams. Discussions and the ability to hear other people's ideas and perspectives were common responses when students were asked what was different or most important about this course.

> *Open ended discussion, because sometimes it's just the teachers ranting the entirety of the period and by the end everyone just has the same views as the prof. which doesn't make for the greatest thing.*

Students particularly liked that we discussed topics relevant to their personal experiences of education, as well as to the contexts they would themselves face as teachers.

> *We talked about real world situations and approached education at a realistic level, so it provided for an interesting class with controversial discussions and topics.*

Throughout the semester, each class included small or large group discussions, activities, and cooperative projects. Establishing caring relationships between us all made it easier in these activities for students to venture out and say things they would normally keep to themselves. I want to note, however, that I also never require students to speak in the way that some instructors do in order for students to receive participation credit, because there are many types of participation that need to be honored besides the privileged mode of speaking publicly.

Field experiences. Students in this course also engage in ten hours of service-learning field experience (Tinkler, hannah, Tinkler, & Miller, 2015) in local schools and other youth settings that serve racially, economically, and otherwise disadvantaged students in the urban neighborhoods surrounding the university. Here they are able to take the foundational topical and theoretical knowledge they have gained in the course and turn it into action with and on behalf of actual students. This connection of theory to practice is vital in order to avoid reinforcing preservice teachers' potential deficit mindsets about students in these settings (Gorski, 2016). The field experiences helped them develop personally meaningful views on teaching.

> *Students respond very well when they trust the person helping them. The students taught me patience, understanding, and perseverance, everything necessary, in my opinion, to be a good teacher.*

In a connected observation assignment, students critically examine their taken-for-granted assumptions about teaching and learning, using description vs. interpretation to explore alternative explanations for everyday student behaviors.

Reflection and reflexivity. Almost weekly reflective journal assignments are also central to students' overall learning, especially for those quieter students who explore more of their thoughts in this private space in which the students and I dialogue. For each journal, students are able to answer a prompt or choice of prompts, or to write an open-ended personal reflection on that week's topics. Prompts encourage them to explore their own varied positionalities of privilege and vulnerability, to connect topics to their personal experiences, and to think about how these positions and experiences have influenced their assumptions about teaching, learning, and learners.

> *This course taught us to not be self-centered and not take education for granted.*

In my responses, I pose questions for them to think further about the ideas they express and how they express them.

> *She not only affirmed what I was doing was correct but she also challenged my opinions and how I supported my opinions. It developed my debating skills as well as myself as a learner.*

Through these journals I was able to see, which students corroborated, that their thinking evolved and their consciousness of the complexities of education increased.

Important Learning

Because my main aim in this chapter is to illustrate some ways students arrived at important learning around topics of social justice in order to offer options others may be able to translate into their own transformative pedagogical strategies, here I only briefly inventory the learning products students considered most important from their time in this course. From my own vantage point, students showed an increasingly critical awareness, frequently discussing the importance of classroom relationships, supporting diverse perspectives, thinking outside the box, and otherwise pushing up against educational and societal norms. They clearly grew in both their ability to recognize relational connection/disconnection and educational justice/injustice, and to envision change through their own purposeful thinking and future action. Importantly, they made a lot of connections between these forms of consciousness and specific aspects of how I operated and what we learned or did within the course.

Students themselves said they were able to apply their learning to figuring out what kinds of teachers they want to be in their future classrooms. They now better understand the importance of forming close and caring relationships with and between students. They are able to recognize their own positionalities, assumptions, advantages, and vulnerabilities, and to better comprehend issues of equity that impact underprivileged students, schools, and communities, as well as how teachers and systems have the power to perpetuate or disrupt these inequities. In place of difference- and color-blindness, they now want to fully recognize and value the diversity of students' identities, backgrounds, abilities, knowledges, and lived experiences. They believe that students' self-expression, criticality, and engagement are as important as their measurable achievements, and teachers must create learning environments that are conducive to supporting the total wellbeing and growth of all types of learners. They acknowledge that there are a lot of challenges both students and teachers face, and that it is educators' responsibility to be proactive in confronting these challenges, rather than feign neutrality or complacently accept situations as given and unalterable.

CONCLUSION

I have had teachers that complain about the system and explain that they don't want to do it that way but they never change anything.

The student quote above both troubles me and reaffirms the importance of this work for educating future teachers. Our students, perhaps more than in any other field, need to see what they are learning put into action. An instructor who is clearly critical of the very things he or she is expected to do, yet fails to ever do anything to change the situation, is setting an example to students that teachers are basically powerless—powerless to truly question what we do and why we do it, and powerless to change things that do not work or do not align with our personal philosophies about what education should be. As teacher educators, we must hold ourselves to a higher standard. When we do feel powerless, we need to discuss this with students transparently. We need to give them the opportunity to help us figure out what does not work and to envision alternatives, and we need to actually implement those alternatives ourselves to the greatest extent possible. I recognize that not every change is possible, and not all problems even have solutions, at least not in some contexts, but we need to talk to our students about these complexities. If we complain but then do nothing, we are reinforcing a "that's just the way it's always been done" mentality, rather than showing future teachers that improvement and innovation are always possible.

I also recognize that the majority of education instructors are constantly assessing and re-creating their pedagogy and content, and thus, what I have endeavored to do in this project is not something revolutionary. Hopefully, the value of this work will be in its naming and making visible the kinds of things *social-justice minded* instructors *in particular* can do, and to show through concrete examples what actually worked to help me achieve the goals I have set for my teacher candidates. Specifically, I wanted to show some evidence that CCI could be a worthwhile pedagogical framework for use in teacher education so that readers may decide whether this is a transformative pedagogy they can see adapting to their own settings.

REFERENCES

Cammarota, J., & Romero, A. (2006). A critically compassionate intellectualism for Latina/o students: Raising voices above the silencing in our schools. *Multicultural Education, 14*(2), 16–23.

Carter Andrews, D. J., Bartell, T., & Richmond, G. (2016). Teaching in dehumanizing times: The professionalization imperative. *Journal of Teacher Education, 67*(3), 170–172.

Cochran-Smith, M., & Villegas, A. M. (2016). Preparing teachers for diversity and high-poverty schools: A research-based perspective. In J. Lampert & B. Burnett (Eds.), *Teacher education for high poverty schools* (pp. 10–31). New York, NY: Springer International.

Conklin, H. G. (2008). Modeling compassion in critical, justice-oriented teacher education. *Harvard Educational Review, 78*(4), 652–674.

Freire, P. (1970/1993). *Pedagogy of the oppressed*. New York, NY: Continuum.

Gilligan, C. (1982). *In a different voice*. Cambridge, MA: Harvard University Press.

Ginwright, S., & Cammarota, J. (2002). New terrain in youth development: The promise of a social justice approach. *Social Justice, 29*(4), 82–95.

Giroux, H. (2001). *Theory and resistance in education: Towards a pedagogy for the opposition*. Westport, CT: Bergin & Garvey.

Gorski, P. C. (2016). Poverty and the ideological imperative: A call to unhook from deficit and grit ideology and to strive for structural ideology in teacher education. *Journal of Education for Teaching, 42*(4), 378–386.

Hill, J. (2015). Cycles of action and reflection. In D. Coghlan, & M. Brydon-Miller (Eds.), *The SAGE encyclopedia of action research* (pp. 233–237). London, England: SAGE.

Janesick, V. J. (2014). No bystanders in authentic assessment: Critical pedagogies for youth empowerment. In A. Ibrahim & S. R. Steinberg (Eds.), *Critical youth studies reader* (pp. 452–460). New York: Peter Lang.

Jordan, J. (1995). *Relational awareness: Transforming disconnection*. Wellesley, MA: The Stone Center Working Paper Series.

Kemmis, S., McTaggart, R., & Nixon, R. (2014). *The action research planner: Doing critical participatory action research* (6th ed.). Singapore: Springer.

Kincheloe, J. L., & Steinberg, S. R. (Eds.) (1998). *Unauthorized methods: Strategies for critical teaching*. London, England: Routledge.

King, J. E. (1991). Dysconscious racism: Ideology, identity, and the miseducation of teachers. *Journal of Negro Education, 60*(2), 133–146.

Kohn, A. (2012). The case against grades. *The Education Digest, 77*(5), 8–16.

Matias, C. E. (2015). "Why do you make me hate myself?" Re-teaching whiteness, abuse, and love in urban teacher education. *Teaching Education*, 1–18.

McLaren, P. (2003). *Life in schools: An introduction to critical pedagogy in the foundations of education* (4th ed.). Boston, MA: Allyn and Bacon.

Miller, J. B., & Stiver, I. P. (1997). *The healing connection: How women form relationships in therapy and in life*. Boston: Beacon.

Napan, K. (2011). How do I teach? *Higher Education Research and Development Society of Australasia Inc., 32*(3), 17–18.

Noddings, N. (1984). *Caring: A feminine approach to ethics and moral education*. Berkeley and Los Angeles, CA: University of California Press.

Noddings, N. (2012). The language of care ethics. *Knowledge Quest, 40*(4), 52–56.

North, C. E. (2006). More than words? Delving into the substantive meaning(s) of "social justice" in education. *Review of Educational Research, 76*(4), 507–535.

Picower, B. (2012). *Practice what you teach: Social justice education in the classroom and the streets*. Florence, KY: Routledge.

Raider-Roth, M. B., Rector-Aranda, A., Kaiser, T., Lipinsky Saltarik, L., Weikel, A., Wolkenfeld, S., & Zaidenberg, L. (2019). Shared power, risk-taking, and innovation: Participatory action research in Jewish education. *Journal of Jewish Education, 85*(2).

Rector-Aranda, A. (2016). School norms and reforms, critical race theory, and the fairytale of equitable education. *Critical Questions in Education, 7*(1), 1–16.

Rector-Aranda, A. (2018). Critically compassionate intellectualism in teacher education: The contributions of relational-cultural theory. *Journal of Teacher Education* (online first).

Rodgers, C. R., & Raider-Roth, M. B. (2006). Presence in teaching. *Teachers and Teaching: Theory and Practice, 12*(3), 265–287.

Sensoy, Ö, & DiAngelo, R. (2014). Respect differences? Challenging the common guidelines in social justice education. *Democracy and Education, 22*(2), 1–10.

Shor, I. (1992). *Empowering education: Critical teaching for social change*. Chicago, IL: University of Chicago Press.

Spencer, R. (2000). *A comparison of relational psychologies*. Wellesley, MA: Wellesley College Stone Center.

Tinkler, B., hannah, c. l., Tinkler, A., & Miller, E. (2015). The impact of a social justice service-learning field experience in a social foundations course. *Critical Questions in Education, 6*(1), 16–29.

Valenzuela, A. (1999). *Subtractive schooling: U.S.-Mexican youth and the politics of caring*. Albany: State University of New York Press.

Vaughn, L., & Lohmueller, M. (2014). Calling all stakeholders: Group-level assessment (GLA)—A qualitative and participatory method for large groups. *Evaluation Review, 38*, 336–355.

CHAPTER 9

ENACTING SOCIAL JUSTICE COLLOQUIA AS A KEY COMPONENT OF A TRANSFORMATIVE TEACHER EDUCATION PROGRAM

Todd S. Hawley, Lisa A. Borgerding, and Kristine E. Pytash

INTRODUCTION

Writing about the social reconstructionist tradition of teacher education, Liston and Zeichner (1990) highlighted how, "teacher educators are supposed to enable prospective teachers to articulate defensible justifications for their educational actions, to take into account the larger institutional and larger social contexts of schooling, and to examine their own implicit social, cultural, and political beliefs" (p. 193). Additionally, they argue that teacher educators should explicitly work to position preservice teachers to be "aware of and develop capabilities to implement alternatives to practices they find questionable or objectionable" (p. 193). To be successful, Liston and Zeichner proposed that teacher educators, "maintain an integration of theory and practice by focusing attention on issues of equity and justice when they arise out of the students' experiences in schools"

(p. 193). Although written in the early 1990s, their thinking continues to speak to the influence the social reconstructionist tradition can have on the work of justice-oriented teacher educators today.

Currently teacher education programs framed on a social justice mission and vision are under attack (Sleeter, 2009; Westheimer & suurtamm, 2009). Writing about critiques of social justice teacher education, Cochran-Smith et al. (2009) summed up the common critique offered from both inside and outside of teacher education as, "teacher education for social justice centers on kids feeling good and teachers being politically correct, while nobody pays attention to learning" (p. 625). The common critiques they discuss are *"the ambiguity critique, the knowledge critique, the ideology critique,* and *the free speech critique"* (emphasis in original, p. 625). Cochran-Smith Barnatt, Lahann, Shakman, and Terrell (2009) argued that:

> the critiques of teacher education for social justice are part of a larger political ideology based on a narrow view of learning, an individualistic notion of freedom, and a market-based perspective on education that substitutes accountability for democracy. What most of the critics want is not a value-free teacher education, but one that matches their values, not an apolitical teacher education, but one with a more hegemonic and therefore invisible politics. (p. 625)

Cochran-Smith et al. end their exploration of the common critiques of social justice teacher education by calling on teacher educators to develop, "carefully worked-out theories of teacher education for social justice that take into account the social, historical, and philosophical moorings of the term and carefully apply them to the educational scene" (p. 638).

Within this contentious climate are also calls for teacher educators committed to social justice to be more explicit about their vision of social justice. In their critique of the often vague notions of what counts as social justice teacher education, McDonald and Zeichner (2009), argued that:

> if social justice is to be more than rhetoric and more than merely a celebration of diversity, we argue that it must strive to take a different path. On this path, teacher educators would be challenged to further conceptualize social justice teacher education, to negotiate difficult political differences both within and outside the teacher education community, and to develop and identify specific program practices that prepare teachers to teach from a social justice perspective. (pp. 595–596)

To make this happen, they suggest teacher educators "challenge themselves and the field to develop a range of conceptions and practices that would provide some guidance in terms of the vision of teaching and learning and the process of such reform effort" (p. 606). Their argument, similar to Cochran-Smith et al.'s (2009), challenged teacher educators developing teacher education programs for social justice to be open, honest, and explicit about their commitments, approaches, practices. Our chapter addresses this call head on by exploring how we, as a program faculty, negotiated differences, developed a vision of social justice teacher education and created opportunities to expand and transform our teacher candidates' thinking about social justice issues and education.

Amid calls for teacher education programs to be more specific about their social justice mission, structure and practices, teacher educators also navigate increasing calls to anchor their programs in practice (Ball & Forzani, 2009; Grossman, Hammerness, & Mcdonald, 2009; National Council for Accreditation in Teacher Education, 2010). Much like the ambiguous definitions of social justice teacher education, little has been said about exactly what practice-based, or clinically-based teacher education is or looks like. This may be in part because of scholars warning that too narrow of a focus solely on clinical practice runs the risk of "narrowing the role of teachers to that of technicians who are able to implement a particular set of teaching strategies, but who do not develop a broad professional vision" (Zeichner, 2012, p. 379). As teacher educators who embrace the potential of meaningful, early clinical field experiences to expand and deepen the learning opportunities of our preservice teachers, we have felt the pressure to have early field experiences as a way to recruit more students and convince their parents that their child will receive a quality education. Our experience tells us that parents and students are comfortable asking about early field experiences when comparing teacher education programs. These same parents, however, never ask about social justice and compare programs based on the opportunities their children will have to develop powerful social justice pedagogies while learning to teach. We agree with Westheimer and suurtamm's (2009) argument that, "teaching teachers how to be concerned for and advance social justice in their classrooms should not be a controversial commitment" (p. 591).

But what happens as these two approaches mix in teacher education programs—a push for more clinical practice and a desire to develop justice-oriented preservice teachers? McDonald (2008) took a programmatic view and focused on the pedagogy of assignments in social justice teacher education programs and examined assignments as implemented across a number of courses. McDonald (2008), highlighted how a key tension of creating coherent teacher education programs focused on social justice is, "Providing teachers solely with broad principles related to justice will leave them with high ideals but with few practices achieving those ideals" (p. 165). Her work called on teacher education researchers to, "clarify how teacher education programs develop coherence around a vision of teaching and learning and how different settings within the program interpret and enact that particular vision" (p. 165).

Our chapter honors Cochran-Smith et al.'s (2009) and McDonald and Zeichner's (2009) efforts to better define, defend and enact the work of social justice teacher education. At the same time, we recognize Zeichner's (2012) concerns regarding the limits of clinically-based teacher education. As teacher educators committed to developing a teacher education program framed on a vision of social justice, we discuss the development and enactment of our Social Justice Colloquia as a key component of our teacher education program. These social justice colloquia were designed to expand and transform teacher candidates' thinking about issues of power, equity, and access as a key component of their learning to be secondary teachers. We then discuss specific steps that we have taken to further embed social justice throughout our program.

DEVELOPING SOCIAL JUSTICE PEDAGOGIES FOR OUR PROGRAM

For the past five years, the teacher education faculty in both the Adolescent to Young Adult Education (ADED) and secondary Master-of-Arts in Teaching (MAT) programs at Kent State University have developed a series of four (and now eight) social justice colloquia focused on culturally relevant pedagogy, service learning, issues of gender and sexuality in education, and the persistent problem of labeling students as "problems." These colloquia were created to reflect the faculty's commitment to enacting a vision of social justice teacher education and designed to become an explicit part of the teacher education curriculum. Here we provide specific examples of how a teacher education program committed to social justice designed specific pedagogical experiences to expand and transform candidates' thinking about issues of power, equity and access in education. We also explore how teacher education reform, reflection, and action can enable teacher educators to improve their practice while honoring their own diversity.

The Social Justice Colloquia

The social justice colloquia, as key components of our teacher education program, are a result of ongoing program review and reflection. Our goal is to focus on our innovative practices designed to make thoughtful and explicit connections between our commitments to social justice teacher education and the experiences teacher candidates have in our program. Specifically, we address the following questions: (1) What are the successful hallmarks of your programs and practices? How might these be adopted by other programs?, and, (2) How have your programs and practices managed core convictions such as academic freedom in relation to curriculum, instruction, and assessment when working toward a cohesive curriculum and experiences in teacher education? We hope to open up conversations regarding how other programs might utilize social justice colloquia within their own programs as part of preparing their teacher candidates to teach for social justice.

As policy initiatives continue to push teacher education programs to be more clinically focused and clinically based (National Council for Accreditation of Teacher Education, 2010), attention must remain on how teacher candidates are positioned to be advocates for all students. How and in what ways are teacher candidates developing an understanding of how issues of power, equity and access influence the lives of students in public school classrooms? As a successful practice, our social justice colloquia serve as examples for other teacher education programs and policy makers. We believe that all new educational initiatives, like the current push to expand clinical experiences provide ample opportunity for teacher candidates to explore issues of social justice while learning to be engaging professional teachers. We hope to expand this discussion and to maintaining a focus on justice-oriented teacher education programs and practices.

THE EVOLUTION OF THE SOCIAL JUSTICE COLLOQUIA

The faculty ADED program work with preservice teachers in mathematics, language arts, science and social studies. Students in the ADED program receive licensure to teach their content in grades 7–12. As part of our faculty retreat in 2009, we started discussing how Social Justice emerged in our separate courses as a part of our larger discussion about issues of Diversity in teacher education. In the summer of 2010, the ADED faculty participated in a Diversity retreat facilitated specifically for our group by an outside facilitator. At this retreat and through subsequent meetings, we began having sometimes difficult conversations with each other about our commitments to social justice and how we were attempting to enact these commitments in our work. To formalize our discussions we decided to start with readings focusing on social justice oriented teacher education. Examples of our social justice readings include, Anna E. Richert, David M. Donahue, and Vicki K. LaBoskey's chapter, "Preparing White Teachers to Teach in a Racist Nation: What Do They Need to Know and Be Able to Do?" from the *Handbook for Social Justice in Education* as well as

Keiser's (2005) chapter, "Learners Not Widgets: Teacher Education for Social Justice During Transformative Times."

ADED faculty began discussing social justice articles at our regular monthly meetings. As we engaged with the readings and each other, were troubled by several specific topics and desires. These included: How were we defining social justice?, a desire to take ACTION, and a desire to share our Social Justice commitments more formally with our students. We then developed a subcommittee to imagine how social justice could be emphasized during the senior year. We developed the social justice colloquia in fall semester 2012. The social justice colloquia have been part of our program from 2012 to 2017 with revolving and evolving topics.

TOPICS AND STRUCTURE

When we first started the Social Justice Colloquia, our topics were: Teaching LGBTQ students, Culturally-Relevant Pedagogy, Students Considered "At Risk," and Service Learning. We have since expanded the Social Justice Colloquia so preservice teachers are engaged in these opportunities throughout the entire senior year; therefore, some of the topics have shifted so we can address preservice teachers' learning needs when we think the information is most critical to their development and awareness.

The Social Justice Colloquia take place on two Fridays during the Fall semester. Every fall the Social Justice Colloquia consist of four 1-hour sessions. Students participate in two consecutive sessions on each of the two Fridays. Over the two Fridays students participate in each of the four colloquia sessions. Students are placed into interdisciplinary groups (math, SS, science, and language arts) of about 25–30 students per group. They are in the same group of students for each of the four colloquia.

Each of the Social Justice Colloquia sessions are facilitated by an ADED faculty member or program-affiliated doctoral student. During the fall semester, all ADED students take a content-specific practicum course that supports their fall field experience. Practicum instructors provide follow-up discussions and require a reflection paper as part of making connections between the colloquia and the students' experiences in the field. During spring semester, when students are in their full-time student teaching experience, the four topics from the social justice colloquia are integrated into the Inquiry (Student Teaching) Seminar. Students are encouraged to incorporate their new knowledge and skills into their practice as student teachers.

OVERVIEW OF EACH COLLOQUIA

LGBTQ Issues in Schools

The colloquia on LGBTQ Issues in Schools is designed to give preservice teachers an overview on three topics: Identity, Safe Spaces, Inclusive Curricula. Guided by GLSEN's mission statement, "We want every student, in every school, to be valued and treated with respect, regardless of their sexual orientation, gender identity or gender expression. We believe that all students deserve a safe and affirming school environment where they can learn and grow" (www.glsen.org). This colloquia provides background on gender identity, gender expression, biological sex, and sexual orientation and also addresses how LGBTQ issues arise in classrooms, extracurriculars, and policies. Before the colloquia students watch three short videos focused on LGBTQ Awareness, Transgendered Tweens and Kiri Davis's (2007) film, *A Girl Like Me*.

During the colloquia on LGBTQ Issues in Education, students begin by focusing on Identity. Preservice teachers are presented information on the vocabulary and an overview of some of the many identities within the LGBTQ community. There is discussion on the difference between sexual orientation and gender identity. Preservice teachers then explore how to create and sustain safe spaces. Preservice teachers discuss the need for creating safe spaces in their classrooms and within the school at large. This is supported by data from the GLSEN School Climate Survey. The focus here it makes these spaces warm and welcoming for all students. Finally, preservice teachers discuss creating and teaching from an Inclusive Curricula. After gaining some understanding of different identities and how to create safe spaces, the colloquia focuses on the need for including LGBTQ events, issues, and people into the curriculum, so LGBTQ students and their families feel a part of the course of study. Throughout, preservice teachers have space to ask questions and to consider how they can become allies for students as they enter their field placements.

Culturally-Relevant Pedagogy

The colloquia on culturally-relevant pedagogy was designed to provide preservice teachers with a background on culturally-relevant pedagogy and culturally-responsive teaching and to prepare them to honor, engage and integrate their students' cultures into their teaching. The colloquia invites preservice teachers to generate examples of 10 different "realms of culture" and to consider how culture influenced their high school as way to identify different aspects of culture. Before this colloquia preservice teachers watch the *Teaching Tolerance* (2010) video, "An Introduction to Culturally Relevant Pedagogy." Preservice teachers can access the video at. Preservice teachers also read Gloria Ladson-Billings's (1995) article, "But That's Just Good Teaching! The Case for Culturally Relevant Pedagogy."

During the colloquia, preservice teachers describe the culture of their high school by reflecting on aspects of the culture of the students who attended their school. To push them to focus in on how culture mattered in their high school, preservice teachers generate a list of the advice they would give to a student teacher placed at their high school. After this initial activity, students discuss the assigned video and article in small groups. Preservice teachers then generate examples of the 10 different "realms of culture" they are experiencing in their field placements. Using dry erase boards, preservice teachers compile lists focusing on topics such as: sexuality, family and social groups/subcultures. Finally, preservice teachers discuss ways that their teaching can honor the cultures students bring with them to school and how they can begin to engage students by drawing on their cultural knowledge as part of teaching the content of their courses. The goal is for preservice teachers to leave with a deeper sense of how leveraging their students' cultures can help make their classrooms spaces where all students feel welcome, valued and both intellectually and culturally capable of success.

Students Considered "At Risk"

Too often students are assigned labels that discursively and physically position them within schools and communities. The purpose of this session was to specifically untangle the label of "at risk." In order to invite preservice teachers to consider how this label might influence a student's learning, preservice teachers read selections from Jay MacLeod's (2008) *Ain't No Making It*. This reading served as a way to frame the conversation about youth in schools.

Preservice teachers were invited to consider their own preconceptions about who is "at risk" by drawing or sketching a picture or image of "at-risk." Following, preservice teachers participated in a discussion about factors that might place a student "at-risk." Preservice teachers discussed how this term if often used broadly to describe a variety of students who have found themselves in a variety of situations in and out of school. For example, preservice teachers shared that this could used to label students who are at-risk of academic failure, students who might be experiencing difficult personal relationships with parents, students who might have experienced incarceration, or those students who have had some sort of traumatic experience. This conversation continued to explore how this term might overlook the nuanced needs that all students have in schools and in classrooms. In addition, faculty asked preservice teachers to consider how certain federal, state, and district-level educational policies might further place students "at-risk." Preservice teachers were also asked to consider how labels might actually harm and perpetuate failure

Service-Learning

The service learning session explored elements of service-learning as a means to promote authentic learning tasks and civic engagement. To prepare for the session, students were invited to read Jonathan F. Zaff and Richard M. Lerner's (2010) article, "Service Learning Promotes Positive Youth Development In High School" and watch several brief YouTube videos highlighting examples of teachers incorporating service learning across disciplines.

At the session itself, we invited students to first define "service learning" and to reflect on any previous experiences they had had with service learning in their own K–12 education. We then shared a video highlighting interviews with students, teachers, and administrators involved in service learning projects, and asked students to get into small multi-content area groups to generate a list of service learning projects that could be embedded in secondary classrooms. As a whole class, we mapped these ideas on the board, noting when and how particular service learning projects crossed curricular boundaries, represented authentic opportunities to engage with content, and served as opportunities for meaningful community engagement. Next, student groups were assigned award-winning service learning projects to explore and present. While the previous discussion highlighted several positive aspects of service learning, we also wanted to confront ethical issues associated with this pedagogy. For the rest of the session, we discussed access issues associated with in-school versus out-of-school projects, authenticity issues connected to mandatory participation, and power differences inherent to salvation views of "service." Students brainstormed ways to be aware of and challenge these issues as they concluded the session by imagining a small service learning project that they could possibly pursue during their student teaching internship.

EXPANDING THE COLLOQUIA TO BETTER ENACT OUR SOCIAL JUSTICE MISSION

At the end of every school year the ADED faculty hold a retreat where we discuss ways to improve our program. During the 2016 retreat, we discussed ways that we could begin to expand on the four social justice colloquia that we had been facilitating each fall for the past five years. This developed into a larger conversation about finding ways to better integrate the social justice colloquia into our students' coursework. We wanted to find ways to provide more information on social justice approaches to teaching and to give students more opportunities to explore these issues in their schools as part of their field experiences and student teaching.

Faculty decided that there was a need to expand the social justice colloquia from four to eight. We would continue the four fall colloquia and add in a second set of social justice colloquia during the first week of Spring semester, before the start of student teaching. We now focus on eight different social justice topics in the colloquia. The topics are: race, poverty, LGBTQ Issues in Schools, Culturally-Relevant Pedagogy, Differentiated Instruction and Special Education, Human-Trafficking, Working With Families. In addition to expanding the social justice colloquia the faculty in the ADED program have also developed a new course, Introduction to Social Justice in Education. Faculty have also infused new field experiences (detention center, ESL placements, magnet schools) into the junior-year methods courses. We have also included social justice elements in the spring portfolio exhibition. Faculty have begun collaborating to conduct research about ADED students' cultural diversity awareness.

At the faculty retreat we also discussed ways that we could begin to enable students to explore issues of social justice in their schools and communities. Because our students are in the same school and working with the same teacher for their entire senior year (both the fall field experience and spring student teaching), we have always had assignments designed to give students the opportunity to make connections between their school contexts and student learning opportunities. Our hope was to make this learning and connections to social justice more explicit.

To facilitate this learning we adapted an Equity Audit and School History assignment (see Appendix A) for students to complete during their fall field experience (Alsup & Miller, 2014). The purpose of the Equity Audit and School History assignment is to:

> explore the resources available to the students at your student teaching location. Within this equity audit, you will examine the following: 1. What opportunities do all students have to learn? 2. Do students and teachers have access to high quality resources to support teaching and learning? (ADED 42292 Field Work Practicum Syllabus)

Students are encouraged to begin working on the Equity Audit and School History assignment as soon as they start their fall field experience. To complete the Equity Audit and School History assignment, preservice teachers are required to find data to answer questions like, "number of students in your school, students suspended in the past year, number of special education referrals each year, females teaching science/math classes, does your school have any active policies that address sexual orientation/gender identity?" (ADED 42292 Field Work Practicum Syllabus).

After collecting data related to each of the questions, preservice teachers create either an infographic or multimedia presentation of the data to represent their data analysis. Preservice teachers then write up a six to eight page reflection paper that addresses questions like, "Are there any injustices that you identified that might affect the people who live in this community?" (ADED 42292 Field Work Practicum Syllabus). Finally, preservice teachers interview a teacher and a parent/guardian from their school. After the interview, students reflect on their interviews and add to their initial reflection papers by addressing the following questions, "What does this mean for you as you actively develop as a professional educator? What will this mean for you as you engage in communities of English, Social Studies, Science and/or Mathematics educators?" (ADED 42292 Field Work Practicum Syllabus).

IMPLICATIONS FOR FUTURE ACTION

As teacher educators committed to preparing preservice teachers to develop social justice commitments and to enact social justice pedagogies, we realize that our work is ongoing. To sustain ourselves and to improve our practice as teacher educators we have found ways to expand our social justice colloquia into the student teaching experience. Through the use of the Equity Audit and the addition of four additional colloquia we believe that our preservice teachers are better prepared to enact their new knowledge about social justice teaching as student teachers. We also believe that these commitments will carry over into their professional practices after they graduate. Along with implications for our own program, we believe that our work has implications for others interested in justice-oriented teacher education.

To make this a reality beyond our own program we must continue to serve as an active example of how teacher education programs, committed to social justice, can design pedagogical experiences to expand and transform teacher candidates' thinking about issues of power, equity and access in education. We must model teacher education reform, reflection and action. Despite a wide-range of commitments and concerns, our story is an example of how teacher educators can collaborate to improve their practice and honor their own diversity. This is true even within a climate of accountability and oversight. Finally, we hope to provide a forum for future collaborative work between teacher education programs committed to social justice teacher education. By developing a network of committed programs and teacher educators, our goal is to develop collaborative research projects exploring the influence of social justice colloquium on the commitments, purposes and practices of our preservice teachers as they begin their work as professional teachers. To make this a reality we have been presenting at national and state-level teacher education conferences. These presentations have focused on our work developing and enacting the social justice colloquia.

CONCLUSION

As part of our efforts to integrate our social justice commitments into the ADED Program at Kent State University, the faculty developed and enacted four social justice colloquia. These initial colloquia focused on LGBTQ Issues in Schools, Culturally Relevant Pedagogy, Students Considered "At Risk," and Service Learning. After teaching the colloquia for four years, the faculty decided to expand the colloquia from four to eight and to create new assignments to further enact social justice throughout the program. Our preservice teachers now complete an Equity Audit and School History assignment during their fall field experience. The Equity Audit and School History assignment is part of our effort to honor Liston and Zeicher's (1990) call for teacher educators to focus "attention on issues of equity and justice when they arise out of the students' experiences in schools" (p. 193). As our preservice teachers engage with their students, cooperating teachers and their school community, the Equity Audit and School History assignment positions them to make connections between their school experiences and issues of equity and justice. It is also designed to enable preservice teachers to make use of the knowledge and skills they have developed in the social justice colloquia. This work has a great deal to offer teacher educators and teacher education programs working to enact a social justice mission. Our hope is that the social justice colloquia can serve as an example of what is possible when teacher educators work together to embed a social justice mission into their courses and program. We look forward to learning from and with other teacher educators as we continue to grow our efforts to develop a social justice oriented teacher education program.

RESOURCES USED IN THE SOCIAL JUSTICE COLLOQUIA

Davis, K. (Director). (2007, May 4). *A girl like me* [Video file]. Retrieved from https://www.youtube.com/watch?v=YWyI77Yh1Gg

Keiser, D.L. (2005). Learners not widgets: Teacher education for social justice during transformational times. In N. M. Michelli & D. L. Keiser (Eds.),

Teacher education for democracy and social justice (pp. 31–55). New York, NY: Routledge.
Ladson-Billings, G. (1995). But that's just good teaching! The case for culturally relevant teaching. *Theory Into Practice, 34*, 159–164.
MacLeod, J. (2008). *Ain't no makin' it: Aspirations and attainment in a low-income neighborhood* (3rd ed.). Boulder, CO: Westview Press.
Teaching Tolerance (Producer). (2010, June 17). *An introduction to culturally relevant pedagogy* [Video file]. Retrieved from http://www.tolerance.org/blog/introduction-culturally-relevant-pedagogy
Zaff, J. F, & Lerner, R. M. (2010). Service learning promotes positive youth development in high school. *Phi Delta Kappan, 91*(5), 21–23.

REFERENCES

Alsup, J., & Miller, sj. (2014). Reclaiming English education: Rooting social justice in dispositions. *English Education, 46*(3), 195–215.
Ball, D. L., & Forzani, F. (2009). The work of teaching and the challenge for teacher education. *Journal of Teacher Education, 60*(5), 497–511.
Cochran-Smith, M., Barnatt, J., Lahann, R., Shakman, K., & Terrell, D. (2009). Teacher education for social justice. In W. Ayers, T. Quinn, & D. Stovall (Eds.), *Handbook of social justice in education* (pp. 625–639). New York, NY: Routledge.
Grossman, P., Hammerness, K., & McDonald, M. (2009). Redefining teaching, reimaging teacher education. *Teachers and teaching: Theory and Practice, 15*(2), 273–289.
Liston, D. P., & Zeichner, K. M. (1990). *Teacher education and the social conditions of schooling*. New York, NY: Routledge.
McDonald, M. (2008). The pedagogy of assignments in social justice teacher education. *Equity and Excellence in Education, 41*(2) 151–167.
McDonald, M., & Zeichner, K. (2009). Social justice teacher education. In W. Ayers, T. Quinn, & D. Stovall (Eds.), *Handbook of social justice in education* (pp. 595–610). New York, NY: Routledge.
National Council for Accreditation of Teacher Education. (2010). *Transforming teacher education through clinical practice: A national strategy to prepare effective teachers*. Report of blue ribbon panel on clinical preparation and partnerships for improved student learning. Washington, DC: NCATE.
Sleeter, C. E. (2009). Teacher education, neoliberalism, and social justice. In W. Ayers, T. Quinn, & D. Stovall (Eds.), *Handbook of social justice in education* (pp. 611–624). New York, NY: Routledge.
Westheimer, J., & suurtamm, k. e. (2009). The politics of social justice meets practice. In W. Ayers, T. Quinn & D. Stovall (Eds.), *Handbook of social justice in education* (pp. 589–593). New York, NY: Routledge.
Zeichner, K. (2012). The turn once again toward practice-based teacher education. *Journal of Teacher Education, 63*(5), 376–382.

APPENDIX A:
EQUITY AUDIT AND COMMUNITY HISTORY ASSIGNMENT

The purpose of this assignment is to explore the resources available to the students at your student teaching location. Within this equity audit, you will examine the following:

- What opportunities do all students have to learn?
- Do students and teachers have access to high quality resources to support teaching and learning?

Your equity audit should include the following information:

1. Numbers of students in your school
2. Labels used at your school
3. Students suspended in the past year
4. Graduation rate
5. Drop-out rate
6. Students receiving free/reduced-price lunches
7. Students identified as special education
8. Percent of students identified as spec. ed receive free/reduced price lunches
9. Academic achievement data
10. Number of students of color
11. Of number of students labeled for Special Ed., how many are students of color?
12. Total staff who are people of color in your school
13. Certified staff who are people of color in your school
14. Uncertified staff who are people of color in your school
15. Number of ELL students in your school—what languages?
16. What is ELL service delivery model in your school?
17. Number of bilingual staff in your school
18. Number of special education referrals each year
19. Females on teaching staff
20. Females teaching science/math classes
21. Females teaching English
22. Females teaching highest level of math/AP
23. Out-of-school expulsions by gender
24. Does your school have any active policies that address sexual orientation/gender identity?
25. Does your school have a Gay/Straight Alliance?
26. To what extent are students teased or called names b/c of their gender identity or sexual orientation at your school?

27. Does your school have a gender specific dress code?
28. Other data you want to share

Once you have collected this data, you have the option to create either of the following:

- Infographic: a visualization of data, to represent your equity audit. You will use an app to create your infographic. You may use one of the apps or digital tools references through this link to generate your infographic.
- Multimedia Presentation: a multimodal visualization of the data, to represent your equity audit. You will use an app to create your presentation. You may use an app or digital tool such as Haiku Deck or iMovie to create your multimedia presentation.

Based on your equity audit, you will explore in more detail the community in which you will be teaching.

- What do you notice about your equity audit?
- What did you learn about the particular strengths of your school?
- Are there any social injustices?

In order to reflect on how the community and the local history of the community influences your findings from the equity audit, you will write a 6–8 page double-spaced reflection based on the following:

- Describe the context of the school's location: In your description, provide a sense of the geographic location of the school. If you identified a potential injustice, consider the community's economic, historical, and political history.
- Describe the people in the community: By approximating percentages, describe the mix of ethnicities, social classes, religions, typical family make-up, immigrants, persons with disabilities, English as a first language speakers, and the gay/lesbian/bi/transgender population.
- Describe the schools: Think about all the schools in the community. For example, how many public versus private schools and universities are there? Be exact. Check the department of education website for this information, and then cite it.
- Are there any injustices that you identified that might affect the people who live in this community?

Once you have thoroughly reflected on not only your school, but also the community where your school is located, you will interview one teacher and one parent/guardian to gain a more detailed view of the school and community. You should meet with the teacher and parent/guardian at a time convenient to the teacher and parent/guardian. Prepare 5–6 questions in advance. You can ask him/her how the data from the equity audit affects the classroom? What are the strengths of the community? The responses you receive from the teacher and parent/guardian interviews should be woven in throughout your community history reflection. In addition, you should reflect on how this information will shape your decisions as an English, social studies, science, and/or mathematice educator. What does this mean for you as you actively develop as a professional educator? What will this mean for you as you engage in communities of English, social studies, science and/or mathematics educators?

CHAPTER 10

SELF-STUDY AS A TRANSFORMATIVE METHODOLOGY AND PEDAGOGICAL PRACTICE IN A WRITING WORKSHOP

Elsie Lindy Olan

Introduction

This chapter explores the lived experiences of teacher educators conducting a 10-day writing workshop in central Florida and how they implement self-study as a transformative methodology that fosters self-reflection and critical reflection for teacher candidates, in-service teachers and myself (as a teacher educator) while disrupting our own prior assumptions about writing, sharing, teaching and engaging in dialogic inquiry.

During this 10-day writing workshop, the 17 participants (10 teachers, 5 teacher candidates and 2 teacher educators), revisited their writing literacies, pedagogical practices and beliefs. Through a series of dialogic interactions, they recognized their classrooms as transformative environments. And as a teacher educator dealing with changing practices and times, I pondered about what would constitute transformed teachers, students and classrooms.

Transformative Pedagogies for Teacher Education:
Critical Action, Agency, and Dialogue in Teaching and Learning Contexts, pp. 169–182
Copyright © 2019 by Information Age Publishing
All rights of reproduction in any form reserved.

I used self-study research as a lens to examine my own teaching practices and understandings. Data collected in a focus group explored teacher candidates', teachers', and teacher educator researcher's perceptions of narratives, writings, and dialogic interactions that influence their pedagogical practices, writing experiences, writing instruction and beliefs.

Using a lens of constructivist theory of teacher education, I examined participants' experiential narratives. Rex and Juzwik (2011) maintain that a constructivist theory of teacher education posits that repeatedly engaging preservice teachers and teachers in dialogues evoked from tense moments positions them to build discursive tools and strategies for opening meaningful dialogues in their own classrooms.

Perspectives and Context

I believe narrative and writing pedagogy affords teacher candidates and teachers the opportunity to craft and share narratives, writings and dialogic interactions. I perceive these narratives and writings as open opportunities for dialogic encounters and collaborative interpretation between teacher educators and teachers participating in the Atlantic Center for the Arts Writing Workshop. Narratives and "life history approaches am widely used in the study of teachers' lives" (Beattie, 2003; Cortazzi, 1992; Goodson & Gill, 2011; Goodson & Walker, 1991; Hargreaves & Goodson, 1996) and in teachers' thinking and personal and professional development (Alexander, 2008; Clandinin & Connelly, 2000; Cole & Knowles, 2001; Connelly & Clandinin, 1990; Goodson, 2008; Noddings, 2001, 2005)

Throughout the sharing of narratives, writings and exchanges of perceptions, teacher candidates, teachers and teacher educators are expected to experience profound and powerful encounters. Goodson and Gill (2011) define narrative pedagogy as the "facilitation of an educative journey through which learning takes place in profound encounters, and by engaging in meaning-making and deep dialogue and exchange." During this 10-day writing workshop, teacher candidates, teachers, and I engaged in sharing my personal narratives and writings and establishing relationships characterized by respect, care and dialogic interactions (Brooks, 1985; Reznitskyaya, 2012).Dialogic learning is learning that occurs through conversation. As mentioned, the concept of dialogic learning has been linked to various research perspectives and disciplines, most notably, the theory of dialogic action (Freire, 1970), the notion of dialogic imagination (Bahktin, 1981, 1986), the theory of communication action (Habermas, 1981/1984), the dialogic inquiry approach (Wells, 1999), and the dialogical self (Soler, 2004). I should include in this discussion the concept transformational learning theory (Mezirow & Taylor, 2009), the notion of students as radical agents of change (Fielding, 2001), the advantages of adopting dialogicality as the basis of educational reinvention (Koschmann, 1999) and the importance of dialogic-learning conditions to make significant gains in learning, especially in increasing vocabulary use for young children (Hargrave & Sénéchal, 2000).

Research Design

This research reported here was conducted as a qualitative self-study using self-study (as mentioned above) as the methodological approach. The use of self-study methodology in teacher education research (LaBoskey, 2004; Lyons & LaBoskey, 2002; Mitchell, Weber, & O'Reilly- Scanlon, 2005; Pinnegar & Hamilton, 2009; Samaras, 2011) invites teacher educator-researchers to answer the questions of how and why I teach what I teach.

By incorporating self-study and focus groups, I revisited my own beliefs, pedagogical practices, narratives and writing practices and learning. It was an opportunity to explore elucidate my perceptions regarding writing instruction, pedagogy, and dialogic interactions, with a goal of improving my practices as a teacher educator. I wanted to be assertive in moving myself and my teacher candidates and teachers from reflective practices to critical reflection.

Data Sources and Data Analysis

The majority of the data collected during this qualitative self-study included one questionnaire, one interview, personal reflective journals, drawings, recordings and photos of teaching and classroom discussions, critical reflections of narrative and writing practices (e.g., literacy autobiography and teaching philosophy) and the syllabus of the writing workshop.

Data also included 10-day field notes at the Atlantic Center for the Arts (site). In addition to the interview, questionnaire, and field notes, I collected a wide range of documents for analysis including assignments teacher candidates and teachers assignments participants completed during the 10-day writing workshop. These documents were useful for establishing participants' perceptions of narratives, dialogic interactions, pedagogical and writing practices and beliefs while I (teacher educator) revisited my goals for conducting this workshop and my own pedagogical beliefs, practices and responsibilities.

I employed Seidman's (2005) "tell a story" questioning techniques to visit the participant's day-to day experiences and teacher narratives and writings. As I began my analysis, the interview questions were framed by the work of Seidman. I noticed that I was primarily collecting and analyzing participants' stories. Working simultaneously with data collection and the analysis of it, it became evident that teacher narratives and my own stories were crucial to understanding teachers' perceptions of narratives and writings, dialogic interaction, reflections and critical reflections.

Rex and Juzwik (2011) explain how emerging themes were largely determined by narrative discourse while identifying "narrative discourse analysis for teacher educators" (p. 38). Rex and Juzwik state how "these methods of narrative analysis can help educators learn about themselves and others and to act more effectively."

I triangulated the themes from this analysis with the other forms of data collected through documents and observation, and identified significant themes, determined inductively, using open coding techniques to interpret the data and to identify patterns (Strauss & Corbin, 1990).

Challenges of Incorporating Dialogic Inquiry and Self-Study in a Writing Workshop

Wells (1999) defines "dialogic inquiry" as not a research methodology, but a predisposition for questioning, trying to analyze events and conditions by collaborating with others with the objective of seeking answers to resulting questions. This educational approach acknowledges the "dialectic relationship" between the individual and society, for acquiring and considering information through communicative interactions. Collaborative action and interaction is required in learning communities where dialogic inquiry is to occur. Dialogic inquiry not only enhances and enriches individuals' knowledge, but also transforms and ensures the survival and transformation of every social moment (Adler, Rougle, Kaiser, & Caughlan, 2003).

Still, despite being recognized as having significant pedagogical potential, dialogic teaching is often rare, sporadic and difficult to achieve in today's schools. In most secondary classrooms, what passes for so-called discussion is really nothing more than "question-answer discussion" (Alexander, 2008; Nystrand, Wu, Gamoran, Zeiser, & Long, 2003; Smith, Hardman, Wall, & Mroz, 2004).

This educational reality, though, stands in distinct contrast to the discussion among most educational circles on student-centered teaching, primarily aimed at developing independent critical thinkers. Moreover, academic theory and research links dialogic pedagogy to student development of higher order thinking (Murphy, Soter, Wilkinson, Hennesey, & Alexander, 2009; Nystrand, Wu, Gamoran, Zeiser, & Long, 2003; Wegerif, Mercer, & Dawes, 1999).

Of the many reasons for the prevalence of teacher-directed instruction in today's secondary classrooms is that one, teachers tend to teach in a style that they were taught, and two, teachers rarely are questioned about their tendency to use only direct instruction. Often, it is only in graduate programs, that teachers deliberately study their own teaching practice (Adler, Rougle, Kaiser, & Caughlan, 2003; Smith, Hardman, Wall, & Mroz, 2004).

Moreover, in a comprehensive review of teacher professional development literature, Elmore (2002) argued that teachers do not willfully engage in classroom practices that they consider to be ineffective; instead, most educators believe that they are doing the best they can. Thus, in order to bring about significant changes in classroom practice, teachers must reexamine their own interactions to better understand what they are doing in their respective teaching (Garet, Porter, Desimone, Birman, & Yoon, 2001; Walsh, 2002).

I acknowledged, that despite classroom particulars, the importance of dialogic interactions present in narratives, writings and conversations is most significant to the well-being of both classroom instruction and teacher preparation. It is my hope that through these dialogues, teachers inform their pedagogical practices and beliefs and are informed of current issues and initiatives affecting their teaching. Mezirow (1990, 1991, 2000) defines transformative learning as "the expansion of consciousness through the transformation of basic worldview and specificcapacities of the self-transformative learning results from a disorienting dilemma ... resulted from an accumulation of transformations in meaning schemes over a period of time" (p. 335).

When teachers experience difficult, troublesome events or experience situations they cannot immediately resolve, teachers step back to question and analyze their experiences. Teachers are "reflective practitioners and professionals who am able to play very active roles in curriculum development and educational reform" (Dewey, 1910, 1934, 1938; Schön, 1983,1987). When teachers use reflection as a collaborative act with an emphasis on rethinking assumptions, it involves learning to make decisions about teaching and learning based upon moral and political implications and an awareness of alternatives (Zeichner & Liston, 1996). I argue that when teachers and teacher educators are afforded writing practices, and opportunities to share their narratives, they will revisit their assumptions and make decisions regarding their writing instructions, pedagogical practices, and beliefs.

Results

A self-study of teacher education practices is never complete. The journey towards self- discovery of one's understanding is always marked by inherent contradictions and predilections. My analysis identified themes that seem significant for understanding participants' and my own perception of narrative and writing pedagogy, dialogic interactions, pedagogical practices and beliefs and writing instruction.

I found myself asking what would happen if I helped bring a group of teachers together, not for a class, but for a writing workshop. I then conferred with my colleagues about encouraging these teachers to write their autobiographies in a collaborative setting. A constant topic of those early conversations was, of course, whether I was achieving my educational purposes in assigning autobiography, but this conversation nearly always ended up, instead, focusing on the problem of understanding student motivation and classroom pedagogy.

I wanted a setting where students would be free to write their autobiography without the immediate constraints of their daily teaching lives—without fear of student and/or administrative approval. Gradually, I set about organizing such a group, inviting teachers from a local K–12 schools to join us in an autobiography writing workshop project.

During this 10-day writing workshop, the 17 participants revisited their writing literacy and pedagogical practices and beliefs. Although there was a lack of diversity in terms of gender (only 2 male teachers were included among the 17 participants), there was diversity in terms of age, ethnicity, socioeconomic class, and teaching experience.

As the workshop progressed, a shared and collaborative relationship was nurtured among teacher educators, teachers and preservice teachers. The primary intention was to provide a setting, place, and time when educators could write personal narratives and come together to talk about their pieces.

During my workshop, I used autobiographical reflections as an important teaching technique to produce critical reflection about participants' own classroom teaching. Their autobiographies were a reflection of their interpretations of their teaching and their perceptions of their strengths and needs. Students actively underscored ways in which their autobiographies aligned in substance and attitude with their peers. They found commonalities in their teaching lives. As students said,

> By sharing my stories, I recognized that I had more in common than I knew. My teaching lives was bonded by a shared purpose of working with teens.

> From hearing others, I was able to see how my teaching was similar to theirs. They spoke of teaching moments that I could relate to without question.

> Reading aloud is never easy and reading aloud about my own teaching is particularly hard. My shared reading, though, made learning about myself easier.

I recognized—as I suspected—that in the immediate sense, I was developing a community of learners who was engaged in dialogic interactions that was at that moment, making a significant impact on their teaching lives. I also discussed—as teacher educators—that issues such as diversity and multicultural education were intimately connected to my own understandings of what it means to be both a teacher educator and a classroom teacher.

With assigned selected readings, my workshop participants began to reflect on their personal teaching experiences to produce a more reflective understanding of the complex social, cultural and personal issues affecting both themselves and their students. Moreover, as I and my teacher participants delved deeper into our understandings of our own teaching, I began to see the interconnectedness of our experiences—regardless of background, race, ethnicity, or grade level taught.

I discussed at length how autobiography can be both a useful and cautious teaching strategy to be utilized in a classroom setting—and how I must be wary of how I handle the writing of autobiography—especially an adolescent—in a classroom setting. I recognized the importance of personal narrative in serving a larger educational purpose and the sensitivity required when assigning autobiography to adolescent readers and writers. As my participants wrote,

> Knowing my students' ability to speak freely and openly—without regard for whom it might hurt or harm—I am always hesitant to use autobiography as a classroom teaching strategy. Still, I know how powerful personal narratives can be in teaching students to write.
>
> Personal writing is always a sticky issue. How much do you allow students to write? How much do you allow them to say? Especially, aloud? And what is my responsibility as a teacher if I learn too much?
>
> I like personal writing—I especially think that it is important for students—but, I also know, that personal writing is not one of my standards—and thus, I hardly have room to use it in class."

Quickly, the nature of using autobiography as meaningful and relevant teaching strategy– particularly with emerging adolescents, —became the subject of my workshop discussion. I inquired whether I considered personal narrative instruction as an appropriate means by which to secure my educational aims. I discussed (1) if autobiography was appropriate in a classroomsetting (given the sensitive nature of writing about personal topics); (2) if autobiography was a legitimate teaching technique to improve students' writing (as the vast amount of writing in educational settings is academic); and (3) if autobiographical writing opened teachers to revealing certain aspects of self—especially among adolescents—that would leave them vulnerable and self-serving. As workshop members said,

> Writing about self—sounds romantic and legitimate—but as a teacher, I wonder if I am asking for more trouble than its worth…?

> Whenever I have used personal writing, I always have students who write about stuff that leaves me numb—do I report this stuff? Or, am they just saying these things because they can…?

I recognized—in my working with teachers during this ten-day workshop,—that I was attracted by the promise of autobiography,—the writing of personal narratives and the connections made—but slowly, I began to wonder whether this was the appropriate technique to achieve my educational objectives and goals. I seemed to be combining classroom pedagogy and group therapy.

Nevertheless, I recognized that personal narrative is the heart and mind of educational instruction. All writing, I acknowledged, was personal—no matter the genre or subject—and that as an educator, I had a responsibility to help my students not only learn to write, but to appreciate the role of "self" in developing and curating a "voice" of their own. After all, what else should my roles as teacher educators, as writing workshop leaders, as facilitators of communication be—if not the moderators of teachers who are developing a sense of community and commonality.

The power of autobiographical writing as a reflective tool—a technique to help teachers manage their own perceptions of their teaching and to sham in their understandings with others—was just too potent a strategy to dismiss as simply too dangerous to explore. True, autobiographical construction has its inherent problems and concerns—but, with judicial and reflective practice, teachers can use personal writing in their teaching and in their classrooms to underscore their own perceptions of their perceived strengths and improvements.

I explored the promise of autobiography as a reflective tool—while remaining cautious of the problems associated with using personal narratives in classroom instruction. As such, I found myself preparing to share my own autobiographies for the first time—and feeling the "jitters" and "churning,"—associated with revealing myself with my newly formed community of writing workshop participants. Throughout my initial meetings, I concentrated on establishing among my workshop members the ground rules for establishing an open, inviting, and cooperative group dynamic. I wanted to be a facilitator of a group that shared in the decision-making process as well as the group discussions.

I doubled-down on my efforts to ensure that my workshop participants would feel welcomed and engaged. I did not impose on them any rules of autobiography besides acknowledging that their writing—and their forms of expression (drawings, photos, videos, drama presentations)—would be most welcomed.

Moreover, I began my teaching by sharing my own teaching stories—which led in turn to other personal recollections about how their teaching experiences were similar to mine. Gradually, I put into words—myself as a teacher educator included—my own life, giving texture and feeling to what I previously had only said aloud.

As I said in my own writing, "I began to realize the impact of my teaching when I shared my thoughts About my teaching with my workshop participants."

Moving from the position of teacher educator, with overall responsibility, to equal participant in a democratic group shifted my perspective on audience. I began to understand how the role of teacher as participant—instead as teacher as teacher and/or facilitator—would change my understanding of what it meant to be a truly embedded and engaged writer—a member of a learning community—and the value of autobiography in education.

Looking back at my first meeting of my workshop participants, I was taken aback at how deeply personal my teaching would and could be. While initially unaware of myself in my teaching experience, I became increasingly aware of my presence—and the sharing of my life both aloud and on paper—would reveal and change the dynamic of my teaching life.

After two weeks, I found my concerns—the apprehension that I would change my workshop dynamics by imposing myself in my instruction—to be lessened and to be more fully aware of how sharing my unvarnished and unpolished pieces about current issues and concerns would increase my understanding of not only my students, but myself as well.

As my students recognized,

> Having my teachers share their stories made a difference. They are no longer watching us—but sharing with us. This was real and good and honest.

> Listening to them tell about their own lives helped me share my life. I realized that my life was similar to theirs—and that their teaching was full of the same mistakes that I knew…

By sharing my life—my personal and teaching life—with my workshop participants, I revealed who I was both intentionally and unintentionally.

Through writing autobiography within a community, I learned to recognize positive aspects of audience as a result, I developed reflective lenses to better perceive, define, and underline my teaching beliefs and practices. The value of my writing workshop learning community was based on a true democratic process where all members took on the various roles of writers, readers, and researchers, all reflecting on their own autobiographies to underscore and interconnect the experience we were sharing together.

Member checking—having workshop participants review and validate their colleagues' personal narratives—enhanced the democratic framework of this writing workshop. In fact, the workshop became more focused on sharing communal stories than searching for tacit approval from the workshop instructors.

As I shared my autobiographies, I recognized new and often, unresolved tensions; thus, We became cautious as a group, and not just workshop leaders, of the necessity to make build a safe, non-threatening space for my autobiographical writing community. As my participants wrote,

> I learned to listen without commenting—and if I did, I learned to accept before criticizing … so that my colleagues heard my caring before all else.

> Learning to listen is always tough—especially, when listening must come before judging—always hard, always difficult, always real…

My personal narratives led to a realization of my shared vulnerability. My insecurity served as the most important teaching tool in establishing a caring, congruent, and complementary community of learners. The recognition of my common humanity—my dedication to conducting research on myself, on my presenting who I was, and sharing with a larger world became first and foremost prevalent to my workshop participants.

The equal sharing of responsibilities such as writing, reading, leading discussions, conducting research on myself, presenting, and writing for publication led to a shared ownership of the writing community and its goals. My community could not have developed without the unique procedures established by its members. Again, the format for my meetings was not preplanned; rather, the improvised rituals of my meetings developed through our discussions and interactions.

Scientifically and Scholarly Significance of the Study

As a self-study researcher, I identified four themes that revealed the depth and breadth of my self-study and underscore the following four implications for further educational research. This chapter has relevance for contributing to scholarship in at least four areas of inquiry:

- ***Implication for Teacher Education:*** Research related to teacher education and preparation that considers approaches to foster the maintenance of critical reflection and narrative and writing pedagogy for beginning and novice teachers.

- ***Implication for Teachers:*** Research related to narratives and dialogic interactions indicate how narrative and writing pedagogy and dialogic interactions afford teachers with narrative crafting, revisiting and sharing beliefs and inequities regarding educational settings.
- ***Implication for School Contexts:*** Research related to how curricula can be designed to foster opportunities for students to improve writing via narratives and dialogue.
- ***Implication for Self-Study Research:*** Research related to narrative and writing pedagogy, dialogic interactions and Self-Study afford teacher educators a shift from intuitive, emotional and systematic thinking to rationale thinking based on inquiry-driven activities.

Attention in recent decades has turned to the significant and vital role that conversation plays in mediating student learning and understanding. Talk—real, realistic, and meaningful conversation among and between individuals in a classroom setting—can stimulate and extend students' learning and understanding. Engaging students in reciprocal and reiterative dialogues helps individuals explore issues, engage in ideas in a cooperative and collaborative arena that is supportive and engaging of these often, difficult, but necessary conversations.

I began my self-study from the viewpoint of a teacher educator, actively searching for ways to incorporate the writing of autobiographies as a means of critical reflection into the coursework of my writing workshop students. My journey led us to work in and write within an autobiographical group composed of preservice teachers, teachers, and teacher educators in a setting where all members write, discuss, and analyze pieces.

My self-study demonstrated the importance of writing, sharing, and conversing within a democratic community to facilitate the critical dialogue of my narratives. I believe a democratic, non-hierarchical autobiographical community where students open the space for reflection is integral not only to developing strong and vital workshops for teaching writing, but essential, to all my teacher education instruction. And as I learned, dialogical communities can only emerge and develop over time—as teachers and students learn to express their values and beliefs in a safe, non-threatening environment.

REFERENCES

Adler, M., Rougle, E., Kaiser, E., & Caughlan, S. (2003). Closing the gap between concept and practice: Toward more dialogic discussion in the language arts classroom. *Journal of Adolescent & Adult Literacy, 47*(4), 312–322.

Alexander, R. (2008). *Essays on pedagogy*. New York, NY: Routledge.
Bahktin, M. M. (1981). *The dialogic imagination* (C. Emerson & M. Helquist, Trans.). Austin, TX: University of Texas Press.
Bakhtin, M. M. (1986). *Speech genres and other late essays*. Caryl Emerson & Michael Holquist (Eds.), (Vern W. McGee, Trans). Austin, TX: University of Texas Press.
Beattie, G. (2003). *Visible thought: The new psychology of body language*. London, England: Routledge
Brooks, P. (1985). *Reading for the plot: Design and intention in narrative*. New York, NY: Vintage Books.
Clandinin, D. J., & Connelly, F. M. (2000). *Narrative inquiry: Experience and story in qualitative research*. San Francisco, CA: Jossey-Bass.
Cole, A. L., & Knowles, J. G. (2001). *Lives in context: The art of life history research*. Walnut Creek, CA: AltaMira Press.
Connelly, F. M., & Clandinin, D. J. (1990). Stories of experience and narrative inquiry. *Educational Researcher*, *19*(5), 2–14.
Cortazzi, M. (1992). *Narrative analysis*. London, England: Falmer.
Dewey, J. (1910). *How I think*. Boston, MA: D. C. Health,
Dewey, J. (1934). *Art as experience*. New York, NY: Capricorn Books.
Dewey, J. (1938). *Experience and education*. New York, NY: Macmillan.
Elmore, R. F. (2002). *Bridging the gap between standards and achievement: The imperative for professional development in education*. Washington, DC: Albert Shanker Institute.
Fielding, M. (2001). Students as Radical Agents of Change. *Journal of Educational Change*, *2*(2), 123–141.
Freire, P. (1970) *Pedagogy of the oppressed*. New York, NY: Continuum Books.
Garet, M. S., Porter, A. C., Desimone, L., Birman, B. F., & Yoon, K. S. (2001). What makes professional development effective? Results from a national sample of teachers. *American Educational Research Journal*, *38*(4), 915–945.
Goodson, I. F. (2008). *Investigating the teacher's life and work*. Rotterdam, the Netherlands: Sense.
Goodson, I., & Gill, S. (2011). *Narrative pedagogy: Life history and learning*. New York, NY: Peter Lang.
Goodson, I. F., & Walker, R. (1991). *Biography, identity and schooling*. London, England: Falmer.
Habermas, J. (1984). *The theory of communicative action. Volume I: Reason and the rationalization of society and Volume II: Lifeworld and system: A critique of functionalist reason*. Boston, MA: Beacon Press. (Original work published 1981)
Hargrave, A., & Sénéchal, M. (2000). A book reading intervention with preschool children who have limited vocabularies: the benefits of regular reading and dialogic reading. *Elsevier Science Journal*, *15*(1), 75–90.
Hargreaves, A., & Goodson, I. (1996). Teacher professional lives: Aspirations and actualities. In I. Goodson & A. Hargreaves (Eds.), *Teachers' professional lives*. London, England: Falmer.
Koschmann, T. (1999). Toward a dialogic theory of learning: Bakhtin's contribution to understanding learning in settings of collaboration. *International Society of the Learning Sciences*, *38*.

Krueger, R. A. (1988). *Focus groups: a practical guide for applied research*. London, England: SAGE.

LaBoskey, V. K. (2004). The methodology of self-study and its theoretical underpinnings. In J. J. Loughran, M. L. Hamilton, V. K. LaBoskey, & T. Russell (Eds.), *International handbook of self-study of teacher education practices* (pp. 817–869), Dordrecht, the Netherlands: Kluwer.

Lyons, N., & LaBoskey, V. (Eds.). (2002). *Narrative inquiry in practice: Advancing the knowledge of teaching*. Retrieved from linkinghub.elsevier.com/retrieve/pii/S0742051X06000278

Mezirow, J. (1990). *Fostering critical reflection in adulthood*. San Francisco, CA: Jossey-Bass.

Mezirow, J. (1991). *Transformative dimensions of adult learning*. San Francisco, CA: Jossey-Bass.

Mezirow, J. (2000). *Learning as transformation: Critical perspectives on a theory in progress*. San Francisco, CA: Jossey-Bass.

Mezirow, J., & Taylor, E. W. (2009). *Transformative learning in practice: Insights from community, workplace, and higher education*. San Francisco, CA: Jossey-Bass.

Mitchell, C., Weber, S., & O'Reilly-Scanlon, K. (Eds.) (2005). *Just who do I think I am? Methodologies for autobiography and self-study in teaching*. London, England: Routledge-Falmer.

Murphy, P. K., Soter, A. O., Wilkinson, I. A., Hennessey, M. N., & Alexander, J. F. (2009). Examining the effects of classroom discussion on students' comprehension of text: A meta-analysis. *Journal of Educational Psychology, 101*(3), 740–764. doi:10.1037/a001557

Noddings, N. (2001). The caring teacher. In V. Richardson (Ed.), *Handbook of research on teaching* (4th ed., pp. 90–99). Washington, DC: American Educational Research Association.

Noddings, N. (2005). *The challenge to cam in schools* (2nd ed.). New York, NY: Teachers College Press.

Nystrand, M., Wu, L., Gamoran, A., Zeiser, S., & Long, D. A. (2003). Questions in time: Investigating the structure and dynamics of unfolding classroom discourse. *Discourse Processes, 35*(2), 135–198.

Pinnegar, S., & Hamilton, M. L. (2009). *Self-study of practice as a genre of qualitative research. Theory, methodology and practice*. Dordrecht, the Netherlands: Springer.

Rex, L. A., & Juzwick, M. (Eds.). (2011). *Narrative discourse for teacher educators: Managing cultural differences in classrooms*. Cresskill, NJ: Hampton, Press.

Reznitskyaya, A. (2012). Dialogic teaching: Rethinking language use during literature discussions. *The Reading Teacher, 65*(7), 446–456.

Samaras, A. P. (2011). *Self-study teacher research: Improving your practice through collaborative inquiry*. Los Angeles, CA: SAGE.

Schön, D. (1983). *The reflective practitioner*. New York, NY: Basic Books.

Schön, D. (1987). *Educating the reflective practitioner*. San Francisco, CA: Jossey-Bass:

Seidman, I. (2005). *Interviewing as qualitative research: A guide for researchers in education and the social sciences*. New York, NY: Teachers College Press.

Smith, F., Hardman, F., Wall, K., & Mroz, M. (2004). Interactive whole class teaching in the National Literacy and Numeracy Strategies. *British Educational Research Journal, 30*(3), 395–411.

Soler, M. (2004). *Reading to sham: Accounting for others in dialogic literary gatherings: Aspects of the dialogic self.* Berlín, Germany: Lehmans.

Strauss, A., & Corbin, J. M. (1998). *Basics of qualitative research: Techniques and procedures for developing a grounded theory.* Los Angeles, CA: SAGE.

Wegerif, R., Mercer, N., & Dawes, L. (1999). From social interaction to individual reasoning: An empirical investigation of a possible sociocultural model of cognitive development. *Learning and Instruction, 9*(6), 493–516.

Walsh, S. (2002). Construction or obstruction: Teacher talk and learner involvement in the EFL classroom. *Language Teaching Research, 6*(1), 3–23.

Wells, G. (1999). *Dialogic inquiry: Towards a sociocultural practice and theory of education.* Cambridge, England: Cambridge University Press.

Zeichner, K. M., & Liston, D. P. (1996). *Reflective teaching: An introduction.* Mahwah, NJ: Erlbaum Associates.

CHAPTER 11

VULNERABILITY STARTS WITH MYSELF

Bilingual Teacher Educator Identity as Pedagogy

Blanca Caldas Chumbes

INTRODUCTION

Bilingual education is a politicized field. The history of bilingual education—especially for Mexican American/Latinx populations—is intertwined with issues of immigration, racism, linguicism and discrimination (Menchaca, 2011; Valenzuela, 1999). Bilingual teacher preparation programs play a vital role in the professional development of future teachers. It is a site where both ideology (lived experiences, views of bilingualism, training, etc.) and language practices are decisive in that they shape practices and ideologies of future teachers. Since teacher preparation programs determine "how [future teachers] are trained, how they view themselves and what is envisioned for them" (Varghese, 2004), one can argue that professional development and the environment where this growth happens are connected with the emergence of professional identity (Korthagen, 2004).

The bilingual teacher preparation classroom becomes a space for the evolution of personal and professional identities while interacting and sharing understandings with other participants (Lave & Wenger, 1991). This learning environment is more than a place where cognitive processes take place; it is also a space for developing emergent identities, for becoming. Lave and Wenger (1991) propose situated learning to understand the process of identification, in which mentors—or in this case, teacher educators—influence future teachers' actions and speech as a marker of belonging (Kirshner & Whitson, 1997). This identification within a community of practice becomes clear through collective engagement and negotiation through a shared repertoire (Wenger, 1998). In a nutshell, identity is the created product due to social interaction and culture in a given context (Bucholtz & Hall, 2005).

As a bilingual teacher educator, I am a direct participant in the culture within the bilingual teacher preparation program, involved in collective engagement and sharing a similar linguistic and cultural repertoire. Therefore, my own identity becomes a pedagogy (Morgan, 2004) as I become a text through the performance of the facets of my identities (mestiza/bilingual/transnational) to either conform or resist normalized discourses that inform what teaching and teacher educators should or should not be (Marsh, 2003; Sleeter, 2008) or sound like. Though Ladson-Billings (1995) argues that teacher educators can do very little to influence future teachers' ideologies, as an educator and researcher, my quest to obtain a more politically clear educational philosophy (Bartolome, 1994) encourages me to look for ways to teach "against the grain" (Cochran-Smith, 2009). I take King's (1991) challenge to make myself vulnerable by showing the contradictions of my own practice, and the discrepancies between my intentions and my actual practice (Cochran-Smith & Lytle, 1993) to create a democratic space where future teachers can be safe to feel uncomfortable (Kumashiro, 2000). This chapter provides a window into a preservice bilingual teacher education classroom in the Southwest, teaching foundation classes in Spanish to Mexican American/Latinx future teachers.

METHODOLOGY

Drawing from data collected from a larger study, this study utilized a teacher/action research approach (Cochran-Smith & Lytle, 1993; Souto-Manning, 2009) from a critical perspective as I use my own experience as teacher educator/researcher as the focal point to problematize my "practice situations" (Feldman, 2002). Teacher research inquiry confronts the teacher/researcher by opening up their classroom for self-observation and scrutiny, documenting the intentions, outcomes, and contradictions of their teaching practice in the name of teacher learning and scholarship. I used the data I collected for a larger study on the development of "languages" (professional language and Spanish language proficiency) within a cohort of 21 future bilingual teachers in a teacher preparation program in the Southwest. I specifically focused on the data collected during a session during the first semester of this cohort's professional development coursework. I utilized an excerpt of my own teaching philosophy as a springboard into two different activities: developing metalinguistic skills and discussing power differentials at schools. The data was collected through videos showing classroom interactions and play during the drama-based activities, fieldnotes, self-reflection, and research assistant's observations. The two activities chosen for analysis correspond to two of my most vulnerable moments during this study: showing personal teaching reflections for the participants' analysis, and the release of control during the drama-based activity, in which the participants held the power to recreate injustice and oppression to then collectively imagining ways to rewrite the prescribed script in contrast with reality.

This chapter concentrates on an analysis of classroom instruction through translanguaging practices (Garcia, 2009) and pedagogies (Palmer, Martinez, Mateus, & Henderson, 2014) and drama-based pedagogy (Boal, 2000) in response to feelings of linguistic inadequacy among future bilingual teachers, need for Spanish language development support, and the examination of power differentials at schools. My analysis responds to two main research questions: in which ways can teacher educators help future bilingual teachers develop confidence in their Spanish proficiency while using all their language practices during their teacher preparation? How can teacher educators provide a space in which future bilingual teachers examine issues in bilingual education in engaging and non-threatening ways? The inclusion of *Theater of the Oppressed* (Boal, 2000) techniques helped participants warm up and build on one another's ideas to share their insights interactively in a safe space.

Theater of the Oppressed opens the possibility of the democratization of the stage where figured worlds (Holland, Lachicotte, Skinner, & Cain, 2003) can be imagined and rehearsed. Schaedler (2010) describes *Forum Theater*—one of the branches of *Theater of the Oppressed*—as a problem posed by the *spect-actors*. The word *spect-actors* is a play on words that gives the spectator a more active role in the improvisation. The *spect-actors*, are both the ones who do the performance and, at the same time, the ones who are not on the stage but have the power to interrupt the play, replace the oppressed character and offer a solution. *Forum Theater* is a way to connect *spect-actors* ideas and apply them to a real life situation, realizing the need for abandoning rhetorical solutions due to their impracticality in real life, and the ineffectiveness of individual action for permanent change

(Brown & Gillespie, 1999). In many ways, this contextualized problem-posing approach is critical and meaningful for future bilingual teachers since it provides them with a glimpse of the challenges they will invariably face and a chance to question their own ideologies and reflect on their own practices (Nieto, 1999).

POSITIONALITY

My positionality is a complex one; it is important to acknowledge the juggling of different roles by the researcher: teacher educator, researcher, *Theater of the Oppressed* facilitator, both an insider due to my professional preparation as a teacher, and an outsider, due to my role as a teacher educator and academic researcher. During previous semesters, I developed a trusting professional relationship with the participants enhanced by the fact that I was the Spanish proficiency support coordinator. As part of my role as a coordinator, I conducted workshops and tutorial sessions to help pre-service bilingual teachers to become proficient in academic Spanish. My interest in teaching and researching this community are borne out of my active involvement within this community; a collaboration I cultivated for years. My continuous investment in the success of the teacher preparation program portrayed in this study shows that I was not teaching for teaching's sake (Dixson & Dingus, 2008). The fact that I am a native Spanish speaking teacher educator provided me the credibility to be an expert not only in terms of language proficiency but also in terms of educational expertise.

Being a teacher was not the only passion I had. Parallel to my teacher training, I was an actress and founded my drama company together with some classmates from the drama school I attended. This lasted for some years until I decided I needed to dedicate my time to teaching only. It was refreshing to discover *Theater of the Oppressed*, and it was exciting when I realized I could merge my passions in my own research. Balancing my multiple roles in the research site was not an easy task; being the instructor and drama-based pedagogy facilitator required all my attention to what I was doing to cater to the participants' academic, linguistic and emotional needs before, during and after instruction and improvisational games.

"I Am Both the Oppressed and the Oppressor"

During this specific session, I needed to prepare a writing workshop in which I would help students to write their teaching philosophy in Spanish while at the same time concentrating on the development of their knowledge on grammatical structures, vocabulary, writing conventions and style. As Tejeda, Espinoza, and Gutierrez (2003) stated, I was confronted with two needs: the need to prepare and help the students develop their language skills in Spanish as something fundamental in their professional success as bilingual teachers; and the need to expose my students to urgent issues in bilingual education in which teachers may end up being complicit without problematizing and critical analysis. Since the prescription was in the content of the lesson but not the pedagogical tools in which to deliver the content, I decided to use part of my own teaching philosophy to cover both needs. While at the beginning, the students were somewhat overwhelmed by the prospect of having to write in Spanish due to their feelings of inadequacy (Said-Mohand, 2005; Sutterby, Ayala, & Murillo, 2005), the fact that I was going to share an excerpt of my own teaching philosophy written in Spanish activated their interest:

> The experiences I had as a student, teacher and teacher educator and in general as a human being have shaped myself in different and ever evolving critical stages. I used to believe all the gains I obtained were due to my hard work, and that people should be like "pull themselves up by their bootstraps." I had some privileges I was neither ready nor willing to admit, neither was I prepared to accept my own internalized racism, classism, homophobia, sexism, ableism. This conscientization led me to untangle the ways society positions me as both "the oppressor" and "the oppressed" at the same time.

I made sure students understood that the text contained several errors in Spanish (not shown here), and that we were all going to discuss it both linguistically and critically.

Wanting to disrupt the "all knowing professor" status (Marsh, 2003), I let the students first work on the linguistic features of the text, generating/discovering their own grammatical rules, generalizing characteristics first as a group and then as a whole group. My role as a teacher educator in this context became a text for preservice teachers to read into, not only as a language model but as a teaching model as well. My persistence in the development of Spanish proficiency and the elevation of Spanish as a language of power is present in my speech during the observations since I mostly spoke in that language. As a native speaker of Spanish, separating languages is easy and strategic so I surprised myself when I engaged in what Garcia (2009) calls translanguaging. The surfacing of my translanguaging practices in academic settings were the result of trusting relationships I developed with the participants that blurred the distance between colloquial and academic registers. During the analysis of the excerpt of my teaching philosophy, the engagement in translanguaging bridged English and Spanish for the development of metalinguistic awareness:

Researcher:	aja, y el "how" cuándo se utiliza? / aha, so when do you use "how"?	
Student 1:	con preguntas / in questions	
R:	entonces, es pregunta? Acento? / So is it a question? Accent?	
S2:	y comparando no lleva acento? / does it have an accent if it's a comparison?	
R:	Un simil; se acuerdan? /A simile, do you remember?	
S1:	tus ojos son como el cielo /your eyes are like the skies	
S3:	como la cocacola / like Coke	
R:	ahh tus ojos son como la cocacola (laughter) acento o no acento? /Ahh, your eyes like Coke (laughter). Accent or not accent?	
Unison:	no!	
R:	utilicen sus recursos de inglés para ver qué significa en español. Acuerdense que, como hemos hablado, que el inglés no es un impedimento para que ustedes desarrollen su espanõl. Al contrario; utilicen esos recursos, por ejemplo how and like / Use all your resources in English to understand in Spanish. Remember what we've been talking, using English won't stop you from developing Spanish. On the contrary, use those resources, for example "how" and "like"	

The last example is important since this is an explicit plea for the students to use their linguistic resources to develop their Spanish proficiency. In this case, I used their knowledge of the use of "how" to transfer the rule to its equivalent in Spanish: "cómo." I found my performance as a teacher educator as a rich opportunity to subvert the preconceived notions of how a bilingual teacher speaks (Morgan, 2004). My translanguaging practices showed not only that it is valid for a teacher to use all of their linguistic repertoire, but also my explicit encouragement of the use of students' linguistic toolkits contributed to the possible breakage of the idea that bilingualism means dual monolingualism with this cohort.

However effective this multilingual approach was, it was not exempt from issues. My naming of the grammatical and written conventional mistakes in Spanish as "*problemitas*" (little mistakes) was my way to minimize their effect on students, who see their own writing from a deficit perspective. Nevertheless, by saying this, I failed to acknowledge that their writing is in different developmental stages that are marked by the uniqueness of the interconnection of both their languages (Soltero-Gonzalez, Escamilla, &

Hopewell (2012); therefore, they become language approximations, not mistakes nor errors. This approach to writing development encourages the student to move past the view of bilingualism as a problem but bilingualism as an asset: moving from a monolingual to a multilingual mindset.

As a teacher educator, I would like to provide future teachers the tools to face the challenges and struggles of being a bilingual teacher in a society with a monolingual mindset; which includes empowering practices for the students and varied techniques the authors aforementioned studied in which the use of Spanish empowers students and elevates its status. At the same time, I would like to provide the foundation for an ever-evolving discourse that welcomes students' linguistic practices and strategies and also strives to develop their linguistic repertoire (especially in Spanish) while pointing out the "how, why, for what purposes, with whom, in which varieties of language, at which stage in the individual and community biliteracy cycle" (Cahnmann, 2003, p. 198). While I know these concepts, it is difficult to get rid of an ingrained vocabulary and how learning to listen (Andreotti, 2011) is also applicable to oneself since it is vital to understand the implications and assumptions of what comes out of our mouths.

"So Nobody Wants to Be the Teacher?"

After working on metalinguistic analysis of the excerpt of my teaching philosophy, the students started asking questions about what I meant. One of the students asked me why the word "position" the last sentence of the excerpt ("*untangle the ways society positions me as both at the same time*") was in present and not in past tense. I opened the discussion to the whole class so they could make sense of what I was trying to say. Some of the students discussed their interpretation by saying that I had been the oppressed in the past as a student, and that now I was the oppressor because of the power I currently have as a professional, or that I could rightfully demand and have higher expectations from others. In other words, my success gave me the right to "oppress" others for excellence; therefore, being an "oppressor," for some students, was not something negative, but more akin to using "tough love" to motivate others to reach success. One student raised her hand and added her own interpretation;

> I think it is something about power. Oppressed, because there is always someone above you, telling you what to do and how; and oppressor because you have the power over us to tell us what to do and how.

Even though I planned the lesson and chose the material, I was confronted with my own power (Marsh, 2003) and at the same time with my powerlessness since the outcomes of scrutinizing myself and my urge for them to see beyond teaching are unpredictable (Kumashiro, 2000). Since my goal was to include "disruptive knowledge, not simply more knowledge" (Kumashiro, 2000, p. 34) I changed gears and instead of going on with the analysis of my text—which would have meant discussing issues in abstract ways—I chose a more dialogical way to breach the topic of power (Sleeter, 2012). I contextualized the concepts of "oppressor," "oppressed," "power relations," and the "fluidity of identity depending on context (p. 572) by using an online narrative of a seasoned bilingual teacher (Ahora Si, 2012—translated from Spanish):

> I remember a conversation between my mom and my 5th grade teacher very clearly. It was during parent-teacher conference and my mom would take me to help translate so I was a witness and participant of such conversation. It was one of the first times I felt we were powerless. My teacher told my mom that administration had decided to remove me from the bilingual program and enroll me in mainstream classes as they thought we were ready. My mom kept silent as she felt obliged to listen to the "expert" because she, as many Latino parents, believed that teachers know what's best.

During the two previous sessions, the students became acquainted with *Theater of the Oppressed*, and specifically *Forum Theater* structure so I was able to go straight from the narrative to the reenactment. The narrative used in this part of the class was about the experience of a bilingual teacher who, as a child, was transitioned to mainstream classes before she was ready to exit the bilingual program. The teacher informed her mother of this decision during a parent-teacher conference. Since teachers are generally considered the "experts" by many Latino parents (including my own) the mother agreed even though she and her child (now a bilingual teacher) preferred bilingual classes.

Three students volunteered to be the main characters of the narrative: the teacher, the child and the mother. Following *Forum Theater* structure, the students stopped in the middle of the conflict to allow others to try alternatives to the ending of the story (the child transitioned to a mainstream classroom). I pointed out the complexity of the situation without further explanation knowing that they were trying to make sense of the conflicting discourses the situation posed. One of the students proposed adding the character of the administrator and the students performed again.

Administrator: (to the Teacher) The results I had from last year are very low and the kids need to learn more English. I have a list of children here and I want them to transition to mainstream classes as soon as possible. They need all English classes; the results have to go up. Inform the parents (Teacher turned around to talk to a mother waiting with her daughter)

> Teacher (to the Parent): The administration has just told me we need to transfer your child to mainstream classes to learn more English.

After this intervention, I pointed out how the addition of the administrator—thanks to that students' contribution—painted a bigger picture of how oppression trickled down from the most powerful (school districts driven by score results) to the powerless (the bilingual student). Since the bilingual teacher was part of that inequality chain, the students hesitated to take the part of the teacher since the intervention of this narrative made oppression recognizable. The nature of *Forum Theater* does not allow for any forced intervention so I chose not to insist on anyone taking up any of the characters. I could see the students struggled to reimagine their role in this situation because, as Kumashiro (2000) points out, "we unconsciously desire to learn only that which affirms our sense that we are good people and that we resist learning anything that reveals our complicity with racism, homophobia, and other forms of oppression" (p. 43).

It was almost the end of the session but the students were so engrossed in the roleplay that no one made an attempt to leave the class; no searching for backpacks or computers, just watching the characters, maybe looking for a way to modify the teacher's stance. Instead of volunteering to take part in the roleplay, some students narrated similar stories: one student discussed the need for balance in language acquisition in bilingual classroom as preparation prior to middle school, another student retold a story she overheard during her internship, of a mother who wanted out of the bilingual program because she was worried about her child's proficiency in English. Finally, a student volunteered to replace the mother:

> Mother: (after hearing about the transition) that sounds good, thanks for your effort. But as a mother I have the right to decide where I want my child to be, right? I have done my research and I know my daughter can remain in the bilingual classroom. It is my decision as the mother, but thank you. Maybe you can arrange ways to help or something like that. (snaps her fingers) I know my rights.

After asking what they thought about the intervention, some students argued that the parent could challenge the oppression by being informed of her rights, though not knowing your rights was a common occurrence. One student suggested that maybe the teacher could inform the parent of the school decision but at the same time offer other alternatives, such as the one presented in the last intervention. As I asked for volunteers to try the last suggestions, the students had become aware of the time. The session was well over and the students started to leave for their next class.

Time played against me; I wish I had more time to work on the *Forum Theater*; I thought we did not close the forum properly, though I understand why the students were impatient about leaving; they stayed far longer than they normally did. I also wondered about the middle ground between following the *Forum Theater* structure and "going with the flow." Generally, during *Forum Theater*, the participants are not allowed time to discuss the situation but encouraged to act out what they have in their minds. In the session described, I let them discuss their personal experience because it was important for me that they make connections with their own lives, though I wondered if I made the right decision by letting participants discuss their ideas instead of rehearsing them because we were out of time. Bartolome (1994) and Cochran-Smith and Lytle (1993), reassure me that it is not a matter of method, but it is the political understanding behind it that is important. Fidelity to *Forum Theater* structure in this instance may have prevented students from reflecting on their role as future bilingual teachers in the given situation, and developing deeper connection with their own experiences as bilingual beings. At the same time, this drama-based format allowed my students to engage in a dialogical critique of their role as teacher to either reify or resist oppressive and harmful discourses without the teacher educator (me) imposing my own views (Kumashiro, 2000).

DISCUSSION

It is difficult to ignore how my own identity as a teacher educator becomes a text for preservice teachers to read into, especially as a language model. My persistence in the development of Spanish proficiency and the elevation of Spanish as a language of power is present in my speech during the observations. Even though I mostly taught in Spanish, and did not remind students to remain in that language—I could not find any examples of this behavior—the participants used mostly Spanish, especially during the improvisations. Yet, there was room for translanguaging (Garcia, 2009), and styleshifting (Alim, 2004) in the classroom, something that was even encouraged during the metalinguistic analysis activity. The participants were able to discover grammatical rules by using their entire linguistic repertoire—be it in Spanish or English—as a way to honor their linguistic practices.

More salient, however, was my teaching practice geared towards language development of bilingual teachers aware of the systematic discrimination of the Latino community and its repercussions in the classroom in order for them to be able to respond. The materials, pedagogical tools—especially the use of the body as means of learning/knowing—and political stance were borne out of my own beliefs in education and its connection with racism, linguicism and inequality. Performing concrete situations provided the participants several opportunities to rethink their own stances and responses, reflect on their future practices, and imagine possibilities collectively. Some participants took notice of the pedagogical value of these activities and mentioned they would integrate them into their teaching practice. *Theater of the Oppressed* techniques also provided me with the opportunity to break some boundaries of what a teacher can do in the classroom and even what a bilingual teacher speaks like.

However, my practice was not exempt from issues and became messy at points. While trying to encourage the use of Spanish and welcoming students' linguistic practices and strategies, it was difficult to get rid of an ingrained vocabulary of deficit geared toward double monolingualism. Learning to listen (Andreotti, 2011) is also applicable to oneself since it is vital to understand the implications and assumptions of what comes out of our mouths as teacher educators.

Reflecting on my craft as a teacher educator is a difficult endeavor but a crucial one in order to approximate myself as the kind of educator I want to be, even though I have been teaching for more than two decades. As the critical educator I aspire to be, this teacher/action research made me aware of my own uncertainties and abilities while coming to terms with the fact that I will be more prone to mistakes since I am taking a less traveled path. Universities and colleges may be the last opportunity to provide a space for the development of social consciousness in future teachers, thus furthering a social justice agenda is a moral obligation. After all, future bilingual teachers will be surrounded by a hegemonic and pervasive agenda everywhere they go, so why not create a space for resistance?

REFERENCES

Ahora Si, (2012). Padres unidos mejoran la escuela [Parents united to improve school]. Retrieved from http://archive.ahorasi.com/padres-unidos-mejoran-la-escuela-2/

Alim, H. S., & American Dialect Society. (2004). *You know my steez: An ethnographic and sociolinguistic study of styleshifting in a Black American speech community.* Durham, NC: Duke University Press for the American Dialect Society.

Andreotti, V. (2011). *Actionable postcolonial theory in education*. New York, NY: Palgrave Macmillan.

Bartolome, L. I. (1994). Beyond the methods fetish: Toward a humanizing pedagogy. *Harvard Educational Review*, 64(2), 173–194.

Boal, A. (2000). *Theater of the oppressed*. London, England: Pluto.

Brown, K., Gillespie, D. (1999). Responding to moral distress in the university: Augusto Boal's *Theater of the Oppressed*. *Change: the Magazine of Higher Learning*, *31*(5), 34–39

Bucholtz, M., & Hall, K. (2005). Identity and interaction: A sociocultural linguistic approach. *Discourse Studies*, *7*, 4–5.

Cahnmann, M. (2003) To correct or not to correct bilingual students' errors is a question of continua-ing reimagination. In N. H. Hornberger (Ed.), *Continua of biliteracy: An ecological framework for educational policy, research, and practice in multilingual settings* (pp. 187–204). Clevedon, England: Multilingual Matters.

Cohran-Smith, M. (2009) Toward a theory of teacher education for social justice. *Springer International Handbooks of Education*, *23*, 445–467

Cochran-Smith, M., & Lytle. S. L. (1993). *Inside/outside teacher research and knowledge*. New York, NY: Teachers College Press.

Dixson, A., & Dingus, J. E. (2008). In search of our mothers' gardens: Black women teachers and professional socialization.*Teachers College Record*, *110*(4), 805–837.

Feldman, A. (2002). Bec(o/a)ming a teacher educator. In C. Kosnik, A. R. Freese, & A. P. Samaras (Eds.), *Making a difference in teacher education through self-study. Proceedings of the fourth international conference on self-study of teacher education practices, Herstmonceux Castle, East Sussex, England* (Vol. 1, pp. 66–70). Toronto, ON: OISE, University of Toronto.

García, O. (2009). Education, multilingualism and translanguaging in the 21st century. In A. Mohanty, M. Panda, R. Phillipson, & T. Skutnabb-Kangas (Eds.), *Multilingual education for social justice: Globalising the local* (pp. 128–145). New Delhi: Orient Blackswan (former Orient Longman).

Holland, D., Lachicotte, W. S., Skinner, D., & Cain, C. (2003). *Identity and agency in cultural worlds*. Cambridge, MA: Harvard University Press.

King, J. E. (1991). Dysconscious racism: Ideology, identity, and the miseducation of teachers. *Journal of Negro Education*, *60*(2), 133–146.

Kirshner, D., & Whitson, J. A. (1997). *Situated cognition: Social, semiotic, and psychological perspectives*. Mahwah, NJ: L. Erlbaum.

Korthagen, F. (2004). In search of the essence of a good teacher: Towards a more holistic approach in teacher education. *Teaching and Teacher Education*, *20*, 77–97.

Kumashiro, K. K. (2000). Toward a theory of anti-oppressive education. *Review of Educational Research*, *70*(1), 25–53.

Ladson-Billings, G. (1995). Toward a theory of culturally relevant pedagogy. *American Educational Research Journal*, *32*(3), 465–491.

Lave, J., & Wenger, E. (1991). *Situated learning: Legitimate peripheral participation*. Cambridge, England: Cambridge University Press.

Marsh, M. M. (2003). Examining the discourses that shape our teacher identities. *Curriculum Inquiry*, *32*(4), 453–469.

Menchaca, M. (2011). *Naturalizing Mexican immigrants: A Texas history*. Austin, TX: University of Texas Press.

Morgan, B. (2004). Teacher identity as pedagogy: Towards a field-internal conceptualisation in bilingual and second language education. *International Journal of Bilingual Education & Bilingualism*, *7*, 172–188.

Nieto, S. (1999). Critical multicultural education and students' perspectives. In S. May (Ed.), *Critical multiculturalism* (pp. 191–215). London, England: Falmer.

Palmer, D., Martínez, R., Mateus, S., & Henderson, K. (2014). Reframing the debate on language separation: toward a vision for translanguaging pedagogies in the dual language classroom. *The Modern Language Journal, 98*(3), 757–772.

Said-Mohand, A. (2005). La enseñanza del discurso academico a estudiantes bilingues en los Estados Unidos: Reflexion y estado de la cuestión [The teaching of academic discourse to bilingual students in the United States: Reflection and state of the issue]. *Bilingual Research Journal, 29*(3), 699–710.

Schaedler, M. (2010). Boal's theater of the oppressed and how derail real-life tragedies with imagination In D. Sommer & A. Sanín (Eds.), *Cultural agents and creative arts* (pp. 141–151). San Francisco, CA: Jossey-Bass/Wiley.

Sleeter, C. E. (2008) Preparing white teachers for diverse students. In M. Cochran-Smith, S. Feiman-Nemser, & J. McIntyre (Eds.), *Research in teacher education: Enduring issues in changing contexts* (3rd ed., pp. 559–582). New York, NY: Routledge Press.

Sleeter, C. E. (2012). Confronting the marginalization of culturally responsive pedagogy. *Urban Education, 47*(3), 562–584.

Soltero-Gonzalez, L., Escamilla, K., & Hopewell, S. (2012). Changing teachers' perceptions about the writing abilities of emerging bilingual students: Towards a holistic bilingual perspective on writing assessment. *International Journal of Bilingual Education and Bilingualism, 15*(1), 71–94.

Souto-Manning, M. (2009). Negotiating culturally responsive pedagogy through multicultural children's literature: Towards critical democratic literacy practices in a first grade classroom. *Journal of Early Childhood Literacy, 9*(1), 50–74.

Sutterby, J. A., Ayala, J., & Murillo, S. (2005). "El Sendero torcido al espanol" [The twisted path to Spanish]: The development of bilingual teachers' Spanish-language proficiency. *Bilingual Research Journal, 29*(2), 435–452.

Tejeda, C., Espinoza, M., & Gutierrez, K. (2003) Toward a decolonizing pedagogy: Social justice reconsidered. In P. P. Trifonas (Ed.), *Pedagogies of difference: Rethinking education for social justice* (pp. 9–38). New York, NY: Routledge Press.

Varghese, M. (2004). Professional development for bilingual teachers in the United States: A site for articulating and contesting professional roles. *Bilingual Education and Bilingualism, 47*, 130–145.

Valenzuela, A. (1999). *Subtractive schooling: Issues of caring in education of U.S.-Mexican youth*. Albany, NY: State University of New York Press

Wenger, E. (1998). *Communities of practice: Learning, meaning, and identity*. Cambridge, England: Cambridge University Press.

CHAPTER 12

TRANSFORMING TEACHER EDUCATION

Nurturing Innovative Pathways of Collaboration Essential to Democratizing Teacher Education

Edward Podsiadlik and Michelle Parker-Katz

Transforming college and university teacher education demands a rethinking of teacher preparation epistemology in the United States. Hidden curricula embedded in existing models of teacher education too often trump public calls for infusion of content and experiences pertaining to equity and cultural and linguistic sensitivity (Jeffrey & Polleck, 2013; Zeichner, 2014). Since its formal establishment in the mid-1900s, the purposes of teacher education have ranged widely from cultural assimilation to social transformation, from job preparation to teaching as a form of agency for change, and from the transmission of information to the development of critical thinking (Milam, 2015). The competing purposes of teaching education in part mirror those of teaching practices in schools as parents, teachers, students, politicians, and citizens at large debate what defines an effective teacher. That divisive landscape leaves contemporary

---

Transformative Pedagogies for Teacher Education:
Critical Action, Agency, and Dialogue in Teaching and Learning Contexts, pp. 197–212
Copyright © 2019 by Information Age Publishing
All rights of reproduction in any form reserved.

teacher education vulnerable to charges challenging its relevancy, professionalism, and capacity.

One consequence of this climate is the growing demand for accountability per the use of standardized measures of achievement as the "primary engine of educational reform" (Sloan, 2010). One such major measure widely used with consequences for state licensure is the edTPA (Education Teacher Performance Assessment). Currently implemented in over 30 states, this assessment reflects a push towards greater national alignment and accountability among teacher candidates, teachers, government agencies, and schools of education. The focus is on future teachers' competency to prepare, teach, and assess student learning. While its advocates cite the soundness of the assessment in terms of construct validity and its alignment to a prescribed set of measured performance outcomes, opponents operating from progressive and constructivist perspectives argue that individual, cultural, political, and social nuances need to be considered, not minimized (Sato, 2014). From this latter perspective, teacher education tools that rely too strongly on quantitative measurement and accountability threaten to support a "system that obliterates school communities, diminishes knowledge, and discourages democratic participation in the construction of schooling" (Grumet, 2010).

In an ever-changing national and global climate, teachers and teacher educators need capacities to examine multiple systems and dynamics that form societal ecosystems. Doing so can enable educators to construct understandings of the wide and conflicting range of knowledge, views, values, and life circumstances of the students and communities served. In turn, schools can better adapt the curriculum and instruction to more closely align to local needs, strengths, and concerns. We call this democratizing teacher education.

Accomplishing this kind of a paradigm shift requires meaningful opportunities for multiple discourses among the diverse voices within schools and surrounding communities. The inclusiveness of this kind of expansive discourse counters power dynamics that can potentially silence the voices of some (though they are often the majority) while emboldening the more powerful minority frequently in positions of authority. Hence, the very nature of what we mean by "community" and who defines it needs to be critiqued and expanded.

This chapter is rooted in the idea that teacher education practitioners must be diligent in protecting, nurturing, and strengthening practices and curricula that ignite and support sustained community engagement. Preparation of teachers for a democratic society in the 21st century demands spaces of collaboration wherein three sets of knowledge intersect: knowledge of practice, knowledge of the multiple and at times competing values of community members in which schools reside, and knowledge of one's own evolving identity as an educator. Through thoughtful and strategic collaboration among stakeholders, transformative teacher education can emerge in the spirit of William Pinar's (2004) vision of an educational experience "in which curriculum and teaching are understood as complicated conversations toward the construction of a democratic public sphere" (p. 229).

We analyze two teacher education initiatives that embody this collaborative and transformative vision. Teacher Candidates without Borders (TCB) and Community Conversations (CC) rely on networks of collaboration, meaningful discourse and reflection among multiple stakeholders, and shared responsibility to transform and democratize teacher education toward outcomes that better meet the challenges of our increasingly diverse society. Both initiatives rely on the belief that effective teacher education needs to acknowledge, support, and strengthen the capacity of individual voices to impact systems of teaching and learning.

Moreover, individual teachers need to work with a collective that includes persons in and out of the school, defining that discourse community broadly as work with family members, students and former students, administrators, community, religious and business leaders, and various community agencies that can enhance the capacities of schools and local conjointly. In so doing, teacher education takes on the role of explicitly laying the foundation of such experiences to better enable advocacy for new policies as well as develop critical pathways toward democratizing teacher education. For as Dewey (1915) wrote, "Only by being true to the full growth of all the individuals who make it up, can society by any chance be true to itself" (p. 7).

Descriptions of the Initiatives

Teacher Candidates without Borders. Situated in an undergraduate program for those becoming urban elementary teachers, "Teacher Candidates without Borders" (TCB) aims to nurture personal and professional connectedness by restructuring the roles of teacher candidates, host school and community members, and university teacher educators with the purpose of altering traditional hierarchies of power. Breaking down these borders means embracing a philosophy that replaces linear modes of thinking and practice with a greater emphasis on nurturing the intrinsic growth and development of teacher candidates including their emerging and evolving professional identities (Smith, Villegas, Abrams, Chavez-Moreno, Mills, & Stern, 2015). Networks of collaboration and introspective assignments are designed to *both* build professional skills *and* to support the personal journey of the candidates. While still preparing students for required standardized measures of performance (e.g., edTPA and state exams), the TCB initiative concurrently builds opportunities for them to realize, reflect upon, and embrace personal challenges and demands incumbent to emerging professional teacher identities.

The TCB assignments, projects, and activities described in this chapter attempt to balance the scales between external and internal growth, inner and outer development, and intrinsic and extrinsic understanding. The intentionally integrated structures build on Hopkins (1954) who differentiated subject-specific learning as linear action and personal-needs learning as circular action. Integrating the linear with the circular, he writes, is a dualism that demands "integrating the emerging action into a better unity of the self.... What takes place inside of [the teacher] rather than what he gives back to the environment, is what counts in growing" (pp. 63, 66). Strategically embracing this dualism between the personal and the professional is critical to developing the emotional and interpersonal capacities of educators integral to enriching our personal freedoms and hence our larger democracy.

Community Conversations (CC). This initiative is part of a capstone experience for post-baccalaureate students already licensed and practicing as special educators. Emerging from the international structure called World Café (Brown, Isaacs, & Wheatley, 2005), the community conversation is an assets-based process for inviting discourse among persons holding varied responsibilities and doing so in varied roles. In those structured conversations, people with diverse viewpoints stemming from roles as family member, current or former student, educator, administrator, and/or community member, part of religious, business, leisure or community groups gather to discuss one issue with great relevance to the varied stakeholders. The conversation goal is to construct action-oriented results to manage or resolve the issue. Focus and discussion outcomes matter to attendees because the content, intent and import grow organically. In this way, collective knowledge, problem-solving, and implications for action emerge authentically, and are co-created at multiple levels throughout the event.

Practicing teachers not only participate in the community conversation, but learn to plan, conduct and analyze them for use in their own teaching settings. The event, typically 1–2 hours long, adheres to clearly delineated components. First, attendees review the principles and structure of the CC and examine focal question(s) to be discussed. Talks begin with one round of small groups (approximately 10–15 minutes) after which some persons move to new tables while others stay for a second round of discourse. Key words, notes, or pictures are recorded so that participants leave behind their thoughts for others to see and add onto. The next round of conversation is therefore deepened with reflections on what previous and current participants propose as issues and action steps related to the focal question.

After three rounds of conversation, key points are collected on poster paper or an electronic document to facilitate whole group discourse. Follow-up includes a newsletter and at times events that help move attendees toward individual and collective action. Community conversations have been used in education to enhance high school transition programming (Carter & Bumble, 2018; Dutta et al., 2016; Trainor, Carter, Swedeen, & Pickett, 2012). Outside of education, the structure has also been used in areas related to health administration and other social reforms (Campbell et al., 2013; Halsall & Marks-Maran, 2014).

While research has focused on results of community conversations in terms of enhancing community participation, through the CC initiative we move teachers and teacher educators into gaining specific capacity to implement it. We collected and made available online a repository of materials (e.g., sample invitations, sample questions from past events, a planning checklist) from former students. We show guidelines from the World Café website (http://www.theworldcafe.com/). Peers and former students share online and in person about their planning, implementation and results. Additionally, we teach teachers ways to analyze the data from their conversations to identify central themes and disseminate the information to those who did and did not attend (see Parker-Katz, Cushing, & Athamanah, 2018).

Analyses of the Initiatives

The conjoint purpose of the initiatives is to facilitate explicit and strategic ways for preservice and in-service teachers to deeply reflect upon the scope, depth and potential of teaching while concurrently learning to integrate a wide array of community assets, values, and challenges. The initiatives purport to effect a careful link between the more objective and empirical components of teacher education with equally relevant intrinsic considerations. In this way, participants are nurtured to develop *adaptive expertise* (Bransford, Brown, & Cocking, 2000) and wisdom of practice when implementing research and evidence-based practices (Cook, Tankersley, & Harjusola-Webb, 2008). In so doing they can create a caliber of teaching and learning that goes beyond assessment rubrics and standardized protocols. They learn to focus closely as well on building meaningful relationships with students and parents, thereby planning and delivering instruction that can reflect the specific context of students, their backgrounds and their communities that include families. Likewise, they learn to adapt and mediate instructional practices that better align to student and community strengths and needs.

We use three binary polemics as lenses through which to better demonstrate how the TCB and CC initiatives are avenues to build a curriculum of teacher education in which teachers study how to draw on and become part of the naturalistic contexts in which they work. Instead of being product-oriented and measured primarily on external and homogenized criteria, these initiatives nurture the situated dynamic processes of collaboration, discourse, and reflection. The TCB and CC initiatives rely on creating organic spaces that honor the processes naturally inherent in teaching and learning. In doing so, these initiatives demonstrate ways to transform spaces—for teacher educators and for teachers of K–12 pupils.

Organic Versus Regimented Practices

In this polemic, we argue that transformation happens by revisiting and prioritizing the more organic aspects of teaching and learning. By that we mean prioritizing the assets, challenges and interests of individual learners and their local communities, thereby helping make teaching and learning increasingly culturally relevant and responsive. By contrast, Cochran-Smith (2005) argued that the current thrust in teacher education represented a shift toward a knowledge economy, a market approach to education policy, and more stringent accountability requirements and accreditation standards. The TCB initiative aims against that dialectic, and instead focuses on nurturing teachers' personal beliefs and developmental dimensions that intrinsically drive teaching and learning.

We begin by acknowledging and building upon the personal attributes of teacher candidates (i.e., language, talents, backgrounds, values), and having them learn to investigate the lived experiences of their students and communities they service. In the TCB, students visit community events, local student sports gatherings, services at area worship centers, libraries, recreation centers, and neighborhood stores. These experiences deepen student understandings of the social, political and economic contexts of the school and the community. How these factors affect teaching and learning in the classroom then becomes a major focus at weekly university seminars in terms of strengthening—and personalizing—lesson plans and classroom activities.

These kinds of community-based experiences are intended to validate and strengthen teacher candidates' understanding of the more deeply rooted role parents and community stakeholders play in the education of children. Teacher candidates are encouraged to observe firsthand the underlying economic, social, political, linguistic, and cultural concerns, assets, and priorities that are intricately linked to the lives of students. These experiences outside the classroom walls are not in addition to regular teacher preparation tasks, but are integral to those tasks. The TCB initiative prioritizes these local assets as critical tools for designing lessons and selecting learning resources that are more culturally relevant to the students. When these community connections are integrated into daily instruction, we reason that student engagement deepens and existing curriculum becomes more relevant to their daily lives.

Since the TCB initiative began, there has been a substantial increase in teacher candidates seeking out local artists and community leaders to visit classrooms as primary sources and organizing field trips to local museums, public murals, and cultural centers. These are concrete examples of how existing curriculum can be transformed by recognizing and embracing students' cultures through word, deed, and personal connections. In this way, teacher preparation seminars focus on discussion topics, content area projects, and classroom activities closely aligned to the needs, assets, and interests of the individual learners and communities they service.

Similarly, the CC initiative aims to help teachers identify and investigate the circumstances of students, families, colleagues and other local community stakeholders in order to prioritize that as they plan instruction and plan, implement and revise the Individual Education Plan (IEP) mandated for all students with disabilities. The CC teacher education initiative provides explicit skills and resources for teachers to listen with clearly identified purpose to multiple persons whose observations and experiences could add to the education of a student with disabilities. The CC provides ways to ascertain background outside school life that could help educators develop a holistic profile of a student. That is especially key when helping prepare youth with disabilities to be successful when they finish school, especially since adult outcomes for persons with disabilities are markedly less successful than those for persons without disabilities (Newman, Wagner, Cometo, & Knokey, 2009).

Learning to create the CC, conduct it, and then analyze the discussion consequences situates teachers in the communities in which their students reside and/or in which the school is located. For instance, in order to arrange the conversation event in terms of the time, dates and place, teachers need to be aware of issues outside school staff and administrators. The very act of inviting persons and gaining their attendance demands consideration of diverse ideas and beliefs. Dissemination of ideas is also key to continued conversation and could become vehicles for inviting additional members into the conversations.

While supports are provided for teachers to enact the CC, the nonregimented nature of the focus question or who is invited or where the conversation happens remains key. That fluidity is at times, though, a struggle. Learning about the purposes and varied consequences that could emerge from a CC while also actually implementing it can be a heavy load.

Understandably, teachers seek guidelines while wondering about best ways to adapt them for their local settings. Enacting a new routine, also, often means bringing assumptions to the table as well. Teachers are encouraged to hold their assumptions up to the light to be critiqued, remolded, and at the very least, questioned.

Intrinsic Versus Extrinsic Measures of Teaching Effectiveness

In this polemic, we argue that transformation happens by traversing linear borders of space and time in order to deepen the pathways of reflection and to extend the expanse of personal, cultural, and ethical understanding. Such linear pathways, furthermore, might need criss-crossing as practices in teacher education and teaching build on personalize aspects of motivational and inspiration. That will mean that in addition to the array of quantitative tools used to measure teacher candidate and teacher performance, instructional effectiveness can be investigated in multiple qualitative ways that can enable highlighting the intrinsic intersection of personal and professional changes. Traversing beyond extrinsic measures necessitates maintaining a depth of reflection that encompasses the more deep-rooted examination of our emerging and evolving personal and professional values.

Using literature in teacher education, just like using literature in K–12 schooling, has great value in showing multiple kinds of effectiveness intrinsically and extrinsically. In the TCB initiative we have integrated Stephen Crane's *The Red Badge of Courage* (1895/1970) into required reading. Students meet protagonist Henry Fleming, a 19th century American Civil War new recruit. Externally, Fleming faces the challenges of the battlefield, but internally he battles the discrepancies between his vision of war and the reality of his situation; between the external demands of his commanding officers and his intrinsic values. Similarly, teacher candidates face the external challenges of the classroom, while internally they battle discrepancies between their personal vision of teaching and professional demands of their settings. Teacher preparation that invests time reflecting on these kinds of intrinsic challenges serves more than the immediate concerns of the day; it is a long-term investment in their growing teacher identities and values.

Specific seminar discussions facilitated by Crane's text have evolved around these intrinsically-driven questions (Podsiadlik, 2014):

- As a teacher, to what extent are you perpetuating what Henry Fleming called the "iron laws of tradition and law?" What are some of the significant teaching moments you've had that promoted free

will versus what Crane called a "mob-like mentality?" In what ways have these experiences influenced your role as educator?
- Try to recall experiences (as a teacher and as a student) in which you, like Henry Fleming, seemed lost within in the "deep thickets" of deeper personal reflection and awareness. To what extent do you feel these events play a role in your emerging and evolving teacher identity?
- Once Henry cast off his obedience to the external demands of his commander, he felt that "his brain emerged from clogged clouds, and at last he was enabled to more closely comprehend himself and his circumstance" (p. 125). To what extent do you think it would be possible to re-focus curricula away from extrinsically quantitative, fact-based information and toward a more intrinsically personal, and qualitative perspective? What would be gained? What would be lost?
- How much of our lives as teachers and individuals revolve around societal values imposed externally and how much revolves around the values and character of our own individual beings? From which 'reality' (the externally-imposed one or the internally derived one) does our personal and collective mission and vision find its sustenance?
- As a teacher (and a person), how much time is spent, like Henry Fleming, responding to immediate external stimuli and expectations rather than using one's journey as teacher to develop a deeper sense of possibility and understanding of one's self and one's students?

Additional literary texts were also utilized to help teacher candidates examine their growth including Ralph Ellison's *Invisible Man* (1947), Mary Shelley's *Frankenstein* (1818/2000); and Elie Wiesel's *Night* (1960/1982). The novels allow us to transcend the borders of space and time while facilitating discussions, reflections, and debates pertaining to deeply and intrinsically rooted ethical, philosophical, political, and social challenges and aspirations. Having these kinds of discourse in a teacher preparation setting is a testimonial to the transforming quality (and potential) of education.

Similarly, the CC provides multiple measures of teacher and learning effectiveness. The very meaning of "intrinsic" and "extrinsic" elements of teacher education are embedded in learning about the CC. The extrinsic nature of learning in the sense of looking outside the self is key to the CC. For example, deciding who to invite to a CC and how to gather a wide range of people who work both in and out of schools provides access to several viewpoints that can push and pull teachers to examine their own beliefs. Also, as they talk, CC attendees give voice to their own intrinsic ideas while listening to and potentially altering their knowledge and beliefs from others' voices. Intrinsic and extrinsic meaning-making come into a playful dance together.

To help teachers facilitate this, a variety of supports are provided including checklists for planning and implementation of a CC. As teachers create their invite list, for example, they are encouraged to include former students and their families so that they create opportunities for teachers to hear their voices and what successes and challenges they have faced. The same is true for community members who might employ former students, or teach them, or see them in recreational activities. After the CC, teachers use the knowledge gained as they integrate it into action through changes in school programming and instruction. Examples of this can include: Creating new events like visits from eighth grade students to their high schools, develop new employment internships while students are in high school, and implementing additional resources to support students during the transition from high school to entry level college testing and early coursework.

Drawing together the views that are naturally aligned (and those which at times are competing) enables both educators and a range of community stakeholders to question assumptions and deepen empathic responses. Identifying and acknowledging those can become a kind of internal measure of success. Additionally, the articulation of these more intrinsically-driven thoughts and ideas helps expand, deepen, and often-times challenge individuals' opinions. That could be associated with increased empathy and mutual respect that emerge from compassion that could complement extrinsic measures.

Reconciling Personal Vision Versus Professional Mandates

In this polemic, we argue that transformation happens by strategically embedding teacher education with opportunities to collectively and individually examine the thoughts, visions, and values that underlie and, at times, challenge one's professional work. As entities to be considered, the personal and the professional are used here akin to what Ayers (2004) called the 'quarreling twins' of humanization and dehumanization (p. 16). Acknowledging the ongoing investigation of the personal and professional dilemmas in teaching can transform teacher education into an endeavor that helps teachers realize the humanizing mission of education that in part relies on one's values, vision, and inspiration.

In TCB we designate one question in the final year of preparation: *to what extent are you being or becoming the educator you've aspired to become?* This query honors the emerging professional voice of the teacher candidates. It aims to confront head-on the discrepancies that frequently arise between one's intrinsic personal vision and externally-imposed professional mandates. Over an extended period of time, it demands collective and individual reflection and discourse intended to free teaching and learning from the dehumanizing trappings of mathematical assessment scores and curricula that threaten to ignore or devalue the social, cultural, linguistic, political, and economic realities of the students. Instead, using this question as a guiding (and evolving) checkpoint grounds the teacher preparation experience in terms that acknowledge and respect the experiences, languages, and unique aspirations of the teacher candidates.

Iterations of this essential question have taken many forms over the past three years of the TCB initiative. A sample of its discourse and reflection has involved these intrinsically-driven queries:

- As an educator, where do you stand in terms of infusing your personal values and ideals into your instruction? Reflect on times when the school's curriculum and your own values were at odds. As a professional, how can these dilemmas be addressed?
- Focus on your own school or educational situation. Where in the daily curriculum do your personal values reside? For instance, do humility, patience, and charity have a place in your work with children? How might curriculum or learning experiences embrace such areas?
- To what extent does our work with children align to our personal mission and vision of teaching? Are we teaching students what they need to be citizens who abide exclusively to societal regulations, restrictions, and obligations or are we empowering them with the tools they need to function positively in society without losing a conscience?
- What would need to be done to help educators better balance the external demands of one's public professional life with one's more intrinsic priorities and values?

In the CC initiative, teachers honor their personal values within their professional work as well. There is an interplay of personal stance and professional mandates that can be mediated by attention to the dynamics of background, experience and culture that shape a child's education. As Bronfenbrenner (1975) theorized, different levels of environmental influences and interactions will affect a child's development. Knowing about those factors and dynamics is integral to special educators' professional responsibilities as they work with others to design and implement the IEP.

That IEP is aimed at helping youth reach goals in school that will help prepare them for being successful members of multiple communities.

Many questions asked in the TCB are parallel to what teachers ask as they plan and conduct a CC and analyze the results. CC participants are invited to reflect upon and discuss questions that call for an integration of their personal beliefs and professional demands. For example, where in the values of the communities in and outside school walls do my personal values reside? Within the external demands of multiple and often competing values, where do my ideas and practices coincide? How might professional practices and programming be revised to reflect personal values of the teacher and important "others" key to an individual's life and future?

Over the last five years of the CC initiative, we have encouraged teachers to pose CC questions to investigate ideas at levels larger than their classrooms or programs so that CC results have far-reaching impacts. The focuses they choose and questions they ask demonstrate the potential for how personal and professional identities can be melded and co-constructed with community members. Examples of CC focuses and questions used to guide the conversations range from development of programming for students (e.g., use of comprehensive literacy that includes community-based education) to parental participation and overall increase in parents experiencing a welcomed feeling at schools and how to invite that, to wider influences in the community such as job training or preparation for postsecondary education. Several teachers have had focus questions about school inclusion and strategies to facilitate it, for example, how does this school define "inclusive education," how do we genuinely invite Lationx parents' perceptions in order to include that in decision making and how do we create after-school or leisure activities to enhance inclusive opportunities for all youth. Some questions have focused on facilitating transitions from elementary to middle and from middle school to high school. Examples from a subset of special educators studying to become specialists in postsecondary transition shows the wide array of questions teachers have posed in their community conversations:

- What can we do as a community to facilitate successful transition from high school?
- How can we engage the community to see the strengths and challenges youth with disabilities have?
- What resources might we identify in our community to help youth?
- What could we teach in school courses that could transfer to employment?
- How could we increase and enhance opportunities for job training?

These questions are indicative of the overall democratic aim of the CC, that is, to have attendees hear multiple views and identify actionable next steps. Those implications emerge from a fusion of personal visions into a collective vision of possibility. That is the core of democracy, the understanding that the collective achievement is only as valuable as the achievement of each individual.

Conclusion

In both teacher preservice and in-service teacher education, we have shown innovative ways to have students explicitly develop opportunities to authentically interface with multiple kinds of communities in which they teach. By so doing, teachers become increasingly linked to the lives of their students in and out of school, and teachers themselves change in personal and professional ways. Additionally, through TCB and CC, teacher educators attend to what Kathryn Strom (2015) terms an "ontological turn in teacher education" in which we focus on the processes of teaching work rather than only the outcomes. Drawing on work by Lather and St. Pierre (2013), she concludes

> We can investigate and document the fundamentally relational, non-linear nature of teaching and refute the reductionist conceptions that undergird current educational policy and reforms. (p. 331)

Intentionally framing teacher education with these kinds of democratically-infused processes and strategies further increases a more expansive ownership of the overall educational experiences. As meaningful educational engagement increases in thoughtful ways, the dynamics of top-down control over curriculum and instruction can be transformed into opportunities for a more democratic discourse and for relevant collective action. communities. Teachers are indeed key players to connect what happens in the school building to the intrinsic assets and challenges of the many who are invested in the education of our youth. Teachers will be part of validating community voices. In this way, meaningful educational engagement is inextricably linked with others' voices in and out of school.

In both the TCB and CC initiatives, the teaching endeavor itself is seen as a blurring of school walls and "outside of school" life. Participants engage in grass-roots experiences and conversations that can enhance meaningful teaching and learning. In this way, the work of teacher education is transformed from a curriculum of prescribed methods and strategies into a process that relies upon shared values, empathy, and joint opportunities for growth. Individuals and community stakeholders engaging in collective work and the communities engaging within it exemplify democratic values. People in multiple roles find common ground and purpose, and can operate collaboratively to break down traditional separations.

Moreover, through initiatives like TCB and CC teachers also learn ways to investigate and to become critical of individual and collaborative work as it aims toward the common good. Preservice and in-service teachers come to better recognize issues of power that privilege some and not others, and ways to question personal and professional beliefs as they learn from multiple voices. By doing that in teacher education, teacher educators implement a series of organic processes useful in any number of future teachers' settings. The narrow focus on homogenized outcomes criteria is broadened to better reflect the assets and challenges representative of all learners. We seek to teach teachers to value the challenges of maintaining one's personal vision while critically examining it, and doing the same critical examination of policies that mandate practices aimed to support all learners with little adaptation. We hope that the TCB and CC initatives help teacher education rely more closely on what William James (1899/2008) called a "democratic respect for the sacredness of the individual" (p. 8).

In conclusion, the TCB and CC experiences provide preservice teachers and teachers with (1) a set of lenses to better understand community values, (2) an empathy that serves to increase meaningful engagement in schools that more closely aligns to local assets and challenges, and (3) an more informed commitment to develop relevant instruction and curriculum rooted democratically in the fabric of the lives, values, and aspirations of the youth and the families and communities in which teachers serve. As Richmond (2017) argues, "the knowledge that exists within community-settings, and the norms and practices which are valued by them, have the potential to inform programs and their participants in powerful and educative ways" (p. 7). It remains incumbent on teacher educators to set a path for such actions.

REFERENCES

Ayers, W. (2004). *Teaching toward freedom*. Boston, MA: Beacon Press.

Bransford, J., Brown, A., & Cocking, R. R. (Eds.). (2000). *How people learn: Mind, experience, and school* (Expanded ed.). Washington DC: National Academy Press.

Bronfenbrenner, U. (1979). *The Ecology of Human Development: Experiments by Nature and Design*. Cambridge, MA: Harvard University Press.

Brown, J., Isaacs, D., & Wheatley, M. (2005). *The world café: Shaping our futures through conversations that matter*. Oakland, CA: Berrett-Koehler.

Campbell, C., Nhamo, M., Scott, K., Madanhire, C., Nyamukapa, C., Skovdal, M., & Gregson, S. (2013). The role of community conversations in facilitating local HIV competence: Case study from rural Zimbabwe. *BMC Public Health, 13*, 354–369. doi:10.1186/1471-2458-13-354

Carter, E. W., & Bumble, J. L. (2018). The promise and possibilities of community conversations: Expanding employment opportunities for people with disabilities. *Journal of Disability Policy Studies*.

Cochran-Smith, M. (2005). The new teacher education: For better or for worse? *Educational Researcher, 34*(7), 3–17.

Cook, B. G., Tankersley, M., & Harjusola-Webb, S. (2008). Evidence-based special education and professional wisdom: Putting it all together. *Intervention in School and Clinic, 44*(2), 105–111. doi:10.1177/1053451208321566

Crane, S. (1970). *The red badge of courage and selected stories* (R. W. Stallman, Ed.). New York, NY: Signet. (Original work published 1895)

Dewey, J. (1915). *School and society*. Chicago, IL: University of Chicago Press.

Dutta, A., Kundu, M., Johnson, E., Chan, F., Trainor, A., & Christy, R. (2016). Community conversations: Engaging stakeholders to improve employment-related transition services for youth with emotional and behavioral disabilities. *Journal of Vocational Rehabilitation, 45*, 53–61. doi:10.3233/JVR-1608

Ellison, R. (1947). *Invisible man*. New York, NY: Random House.

Grumet, M. (2010). The public expression of citizen teachers. *Journal of Teacher Education. 61*(1-2), 66–76.

Halsall, S., & Marks-Maran, D. (2014). Welcome to my café: Facilitating a domestic abuse workshop for midwives. *British Journal of Midwifery, 22*, 806–812. doi:10.12968/bjom.2014.22.11.806

Hopkins, L. T. (1954). *The emerging self in home and school*. Westport, CT: Greenwood Press.

James, W. (2008[1899]). *Talks to teachers on psychology: And to students on some of life's ideals*. Rockville, MD: Arc Minor.

Jeffrey, J. V., & Polleck, J. (2013). Transformations in site-based teacher preparation courses: The benefits and challenges. In J. Noel (Ed.), *Moving teacher education into urban schools and communities* (pp. 105–119). New York, NY: Routledge.

Lather, P., & St. Pierre, E. A. (2013). Post-qualitative research. *International Journal of Qualitative Studies in Education, 26*(6), 629–633.

Milam, J. (2015). Teacher education curriculum. In M. F. He, B. Schultz, & W. H. Schubert (Eds.), *The SAGE guide to curriculum in education* (pp. 198–206). Los Angeles, CA: SAGE.

Newman, L., Wagner, M., Cometa, R., & Knokey, A. (2009). *The post-high school outcomes of youth with disabilities up to 4 years after high school: A report from the National Longitudinal Transition Study-2 (NLTS2)*. Menlo Park, CA: SRI International.

Podsiadlik, E. (2014). *Anecdotes and afterthoughts: Literature as a teacher's curriculum*. Rotterdam, the Netherlands: Sense.

Parker-Katz, M., Cushing, L. S., Athamanah, L. (2018). Fostering transitional leadership to promote partnerships with families and communities. *Journal of Disability Policy Studies*.

Pinar, W. F. (2004). *What is curriculum theory?* New York, NY: Routledge.

Richmond, G. (2017) The power of community partnership in the preparation of teachers. *Journal of Teacher Education, 68*(1), 6–8.

Sato, M. (2014). What is the underlying conception of teaching of the edTPA? *Journal of Teacher Education, 65*(5), 421-434.

Shelley, M. (2000). *Frankenstein, or the modern prometheus.* New York, NY: Signet. (Original work published 1818)

Sloan, K. (2010). Meeting the challenges of high-stakes testing: Toward a culturally-relevant assessment literacy. In V. Hill-Jackson & C. W. Lewis (Eds.), *Transforming teacher education: What went wrong with teacher training, and how we can fix it* (pp. 178–198). Sterling, VA: Sylus.

Smith, M., Villegas, A., Abrams, L., Chavez-Moreno, L., Mills, T., & Stern, R. (2015). Critiquing teacher preparation research: An overview of the field. *Journal of Teacher Education, 66*(2), 109–121.

Strom, K. (2015). Teaching as assemblage: Negotiating learning and practice in the first year of teaching. *Journal of Teacher Education. 66*(4), 321–333.

Trainor, A. A., Carter, E. W., Swedeen, B., & Pickett, K. (2012). Community conversations: An approach for expanding and connecting opportunities for employment for adolescents. *Career Development for Exceptional Individuals, 35,* 50–60. doi: 10.1177/0885728811419166

Wiesel, E. (1982). *Night* (S. Rodway, Trans.). New York, NY: MacGibbon & Kee. (Original work published 1960)

Zeichner, K. (2014). The struggle for the soul of teaching and teacher education in the USA. *Journal of Education for Teaching, 40*(5), 551–568.

CHAPTER 13

WE DON'T DO THIS WORK ALONE

How Practitioner Demos Develop Digital Praxis in Teacher Education

Cherise McBride, Lanette Jimerson, and Jabari Mahiri

Teacher education programs are charged with training teachers who are able to address the 21st century learning needs of students (Darling-Hammond, 2012, 2006). Key to this training is a collaboration with experienced practitioners. Within teacher education the most notable collaboration between practitioners and preservice teachers is the field placement. Field placements allow preservice teachers to observe experienced practitioners, engage students and curriculum, and discuss aspects of teaching. Although field placements provide for clear collaboration, there is often a disconnect between the university course work preservice teachers engage in and the field placement experience (Zeichner, 2010). To address this disconnect, university programs have attempted to create more intentional connections between coursework and classroom contexts by adjusting the role of practitioners within university courses (Ball & Cohen, 1999, Borthwick et al., 2004; Darling-Hammond, 2012). Experienced practitioners are invited

---

Transformative Pedagogies for Teacher Education:
Critical Action, Agency, and Dialogue in Teaching and Learning Contexts, pp. 213–229
Copyright © 2019 by Information Age Publishing
All rights of reproduction in any form reserved.

by teacher education programs to participate as instructors in teacher education courses.

However, inviting practitioners to engage as instructors in university courses, is not in and of itself a solution. Rather the engagement must unveil the practitioner's content and pedagogical decision-making process (Darling-Hammond, 2012; Zeichner, 2010). In conjunction with access to practitioners' thinking, preservice teachers must also be able to engage in experiential learning wherein they have the opportunity to reflect upon the cognitive, affective, and motivational factors for taking up experienced practitioners' practice (Korthagen, 2010). This need is necessary in every aspect of teaching and in dire need when assessing preservice teachers' uptake of technology within their practice.

RESEARCH CONTEXT

This chapter is concerned with exploring how teaching demonstrations by experienced practitioners might support the bridging of preservice teachers' knowledge from theory to practice. It is part of a larger study of working with teachers to develop digital pedagogy, a central component of which includes the ability to use technological tools in their instruction in conjunction with critical literacy. While central to teaching are several elements of knowledge, including the requisite disciplinary and pedagogical content knowledge (Shulman, 1987), as well as cultural knowledge (Mahiri, 2011), also important is supporting teachers' intellectual growth through professional development (Cochran-Smith & Lytle, 2001), often in combination with their own reflective work (Pedro, 2005). The research team here is concerned with how teaching demonstrations might support the work of preparing teachers to develop and implement a digital pedagogy that is robust to support student learning in meaningful ways.

As such, the central inquiry question explored in this part of the study was: how might technology demonstration lessons by experienced practitioners help bridge theory to practice with the preservice teachers (PSTs)? We sought to identify technological pedagogical and content knowledge, as well as critical praxis, within in the teacher demonstration lessons.

TECHNOLOGY INTEGRATION AND TEACHER EDUCATION

Effectively training preservice teachers to integrate technology within their practice has required that teacher education programs increase focus on teacher educators' technological expertise and how that expertise is made visible in university courses (Borthwick et al., 2004; Brush & Saye, 2009;

Dexter, Doring, & Riedel, 2006; Gomez, Sherin, Griesdorn & Finn, 2008). As Dexter and colleagues (2006) found in their five-year study of a college-wide teacher education technology integration study, whether or not teacher educators integrate technology into their courses greatly depends on their own prior knowledge and experience with technology. Additionally, even when teacher education programs include a focus on technology integration, there are few opportunities for preservice teachers to engage in what Ertmer (2005) calls vicarious exploration—the opportunity for preservice teachers to observe practitioners model technology integration. Vicarious exploration also provides preservice teachers moments for reflection on their beliefs about the uses of technology in instruction.

TECHNOLOGICAL AND PEDAGOGICAL CONTENT KNOWLEDGE

For preservice teachers to integrate technology within a content-specific frame they must exercise technological content knowledge (TCK), defined as "an understanding of the manner in which technology and content influence and constrain one another" (Koehler & Mishra, 2009, p. 63). Due to the ever-changing nature of technology it follows that preservice teachers must also become early adopters of new technology (Straub, 2009) and engage in continued professional development to not only increase their technological knowledge but also their pedagogical content knowledge (Brzycki & Dudt, 2005). Pedagogical content knowledge demands both a facility with technology tools and an understanding of how particular tools afford deeper content understandings (Darling-Hammond, 2006; Kleiner, Thomas, & Lewis, 2007). Thus, technology tools cannot simply be added to literacy instruction; rather, technology must be integrated in ways such that it transforms the learning experience while being responsive to the diverse contexts of schools and student populations (Hicks, Turner, & Fink, 2013; Mahiri, 2011; National Council of Teachers of English [NCTE], 2013). Additionally, because literacy development is deeply situated within sociocultural contexts, preservice teachers must also implement instruction that is critical of how knowledge is constructed through the use of technological tools (Morrell, 2005, 2015).

TECHNOLOGY AS A TOOL FOR CRITICAL PRAXIS

Preservice teachers must develop what we have termed a "critical praxis." A "critical praxis" stance integrates inquiry with critical literacy. Such a stance is necessary for preservice teachers to be able to evaluate technology tools for content understanding and for how the tool (re)constructs knowledge. Inquiry should occur not just in a theoretical sense within the university course, but also through authentic modeling via interaction with practitioners who implement technology tools to evaluate and refine their own critical praxis. In a contemporary context, the learning analytic affordances of digital technology to capture teacher and students' responses (Siemens & Long, 2011) is one example of the robust environment for the integration of inquiry and critical literacy. As texts are increasingly multimodal and global (Kress, 2009; New London Group, 1996), digitally-mediated and participatory (Jenkins, Purushotma, Weigel, Clinton, & Robison, 2009), opportunities for "learning to ask important questions about whatever you see, watch or read" (Thoman & Jolls, 2004, p. 24) abound. These ways of questioning provide useful frames for developing a of critical praxis and allowing preservice teachers to consider how they might apprentice students into asking questions such as "Who created this message?" and "What lifestyles, values, and points of view are represented in—or omitted from—this message?"

MUSE PROGRAM TECHNOLOGY COURSE REDESIGN

To provide a context wherein preservice teachers develop technological content knowledge and critical praxis, the Multicultural Urban Secondary English Master's and Credential Program (MUSE) at the University of California, Berkeley, faculty redesigned its technology course to more explicitly focus on the knowledge, skills, and experiences necessary to design transformative technology-integrated lessons (Schmidt et al., 2009; NCTE, 2013). The three core team members who planned the redesign were the faculty director of the credential program, the credential program director, and two doctoral students. It is worth noting that three of the core members of the redesign team have worked with the National Writing Project, which is the originator of the teaching demonstrations cited later in this chapter.

The redesign team came together for two meetings to identify the key components of an effective technology course for preservice teachers. Additionally, the core team reviewed prior syllabi and surveyed alumni of the program to identify their experience and self-identified competency in integrating technology in their current classrooms. The result of these research actions was a redesigned, semester-long technology course that centered literacy content and pedagogy alongside development of technological tools.

The redesigned course had three central components: (a) practitioner demonstrations from experienced teachers with a history of effective strategies for implementing technology tools, (b) tinkering time for preservice teachers to explore a variety of technology tools, and (c) an inquiry focus to support preservice teachers' ability to bridge educational theory into practice. These components served to create a learning community that would not only support the development of preservice teachers, but also provide learning opportunities for practitioners and teacher educators both within and outside of the program to draw upon the full potential of expertise, innovation, and resources. Lastly, as the MUSE program is rooted within a social justice frame, the course required preservice teachers to consider how a critical media literacy framework (Center for Media Literacy, 2003; Thoman & Jolls, 2004) and a push against the "digital native" rhetoric (Prensky, 2001) implicated necessarily critical understandings about technology tools and overall learning goals.

This study focuses on the first component of the course redesign: the practitioner demos, particularly how they served as a space for PSTs to engage theories presented in the course with guided expertise of experienced practitioners (Lieberman & Wood, 2003). Technology-centered demonstrations build upon and extend this practice by offering opportunities for reflections on not only the content and pedagogical knowledge, but also the respective intersections with technology. Practitioners begin a demonstration by sharing their rationale for the lesson and the content-area (in this case, literacy) research that informed the lesson design and student learning trajectory. The practitioner then facilitates the lesson that the pre-service teachers experience as students, allowing them to consider their own learners' perspective. Finally, the demonstrations close with a review of the practitioner's student work and a dialogue about the affordances and constraints of the lesson and technological tool (NCTE, 2013).

METHODOLOGY

We used qualitative methods for data collection and analysis. Our goal during the teaching demonstrations was to trace the practitioners' engagement of the kinds of knowledge shown in the literature to be important to effectively integrate technology into instruction.

Site

The technology course, Education 295C: Integrating Technology into Secondary English Instruction, from here on referred to as the "tech course," met once a week for three hours during the spring semester. Held in a modern microcomputing facility the meeting space contained 18 Mac computers, a projector and screen, and a master computer for displaying information on the projector screen. In addition to the microcomputing lab, students met in a classroom adjacent to the lab to engage in group work, one-on-one conferencing, and for the culminating course showcase. The tech course also had a digital space—a private Google Plus site and a public Twitter feed.

Participants

In this paper, we use three critical cases, a purposive sample that we expect to provide insight on other like cases (Miles, Huberman, & Saldana, 2013). These critical cases exemplify how experienced practitioners supported the tech course. Each of the practitioners have been given pseudonyms to protect anonymity. All of the experienced practitioners were invited to present based on their history of literacy-teaching in urban schools, have taught English at the secondary level for 10 years or more, and teach in the geographic area where most MUSE preservice teachers will go on to be employed. All of the tools presented in the demonstrations had to be web-based—such that PSTs could access them in their own practice without having to purchase or install software—and accessible from netbooks as these are a common, affordable hardware in secondary classrooms. Both cohorts of students had a range of technological experience as detailed in their pre-course technology survey.

Data

Data was collected in three stages. Prior to the demonstration, practitioners were asked to upload their lesson plan and materials to the course's Google Drive folder. The use of the Google Drive folder to house documents allowed the researchers to share materials with the PSTs. During the practitioner demonstrations, the research team video-recorded classroom interactions and took field notes. Observation notes were also generated from the automatic tracking of PSTs interactions with web-based materials during the demonstration lesson embedded within Google Documents software. These notes included timestamps generated by the software. In addition to monitoring PSTs' interaction, the research team collected PSTs' in-class work, written responses, blog posts, final projects and social media posts from the course's digital spaces. To effectively track content within the digital space, PSTs were asked to tag all artifacts they created related to the course using the hashtag #MUSEDigPed. While a starting place for indexing their relevant online activity, this does not represent a comprehensive digital ethnography of all their online activity related to teaching or developing a digital pedagogy. It is possible that other activity was missed, or left untagged intentionally or unintentionally by the PSTs. Finally, at the conclusion of each demonstration, the PSTs were asked to compose a written response to gauge their understanding of the tool presented in the demonstration and self-assess their potential to integrate both the lesson design and technology tool into their practice.

Data Analysis

Across all data sources we looked for evidence that the demonstrations provided participants with grounded examples of the concepts and theories covered in the course. We analyzed the data using video analysis (Erickson, 2006) and qualitative coding (Miles, Huberman, & Saldana, 2013), looking specifically through the lenses of the practitioners' knowledge and practice. Teacher knowledge was coded for the following: technology knowledge, content knowledge, pedagogical content, pedagogical content knowledge, and technological content knowledge. These elements comprise the component parts of TPCK (Koehler & Mishra, 2009). Teacher practice was coded specifically through the lens of critical praxis, with the five subcodes: advocacy, resource management, against the grain reading, collegiality, inquiry. These codes were applied to both the talk produced by the experienced practitioners during the demonstrations and the evidence of uptake by preservice teachers in their interactions with the materials, the work they submitted, and social media posts. Due to the varied nature of engagement, particularly within digital spaces, ambiguous data that could not be triangulated by student work, researcher memos, or talk produced by the practitioner was omitted.

Researcher Positionality

As designers and instructors of the course, our familiarity with the course and the PSTs potentially shaped our interpretation of the findings. Given the frequency and relative proximity of our interactions as instructors and students, we had a wide range of naturally-occurring experiences with the PSTs from which to draw in terms of data. The course instructors were in class with the PSTs three hours weekly with the students, in addition to asynchronous discussions outside class via the social media channels.

During the teacher-demonstrations, the course instructors sat at the back of the room, or off to the side. Hence the third-person illustrative accounts presented in a style as they were witnessed. While the university researchers also perform the role of university instructors, it is also important to note that we draw upon our identities as former high school teachers in a significant way. Each week, PSTs were made aware that the presenting practitioners were professional colleagues connected to the instructors directly, meaning that we had worked with them in some capacity before. We clarified in our articulation of "collegiality," that these are the ways in which we build and activate our networks to support one another as teachers.

FINDINGS

The findings are reported in three separate vignettes. The presenting practitioners seamlessly weave elements of TPCK (specifically: technological content knowledge, technological knowledge, and content knowledge), and critical praxis into their demonstrations. Each vignette provides an overall summary of the demonstration and the connection between the practitioner's demo and one or more of the theoretical frames introduced earlier in the chapter. Evidence for these findings came from across several data sources: field notes, video transcripts of the demonstrations, and the PSTs' classwork.

Vignette 1: Ms. Matthews Introduces Socrative

Aware that the PSTs, like her, have just finished a long day, Ms. Matthews dives directly into her presentation of the technology tool Socrative with a playful survey. "Come enter my classroom," she announces with a laugh as she displays the number 732101 on the projector screen. She waits for the PSTs to join her in the virtual room. Desktops and a few laptops click loudly as the PSTs rush to log in. After a few moments they start responding to the survey about how they are feeling. "You got four choices," Ms. Matthews announces. "Tired, confused, hungry, or extremely upset." The majority chooses option b: "Hungry" and d: "Tired." Ms. Matthews asks one more personal question to get a sense of the PSTs' day and then ends the intro of her demo with a simple, "OK, so this is Socrative." Next, Ms. Matthews shifts to describing her use of the tool within a ninth-grade course to address misogyny and feminism.

She shares how she and her high school-based teaching team used the affordances of Socrative's capturing of student responses to respond to instances of harm during classroom dialogue. Following several instances of behavior that she describes as "patriarchal and misogynistic," she and her teaching team developed an inquiry question: "How do we create a space where dominant young men learn, our silenced young men have space to speak, and our young women have space to verbalize their opinion?" Using Socrative to mediate the discussion, they gave each of the three high school student groups isolated time to contribute to the conversation via Socrative before each group reviewed the discussion of the other two student groups. She shares how the use of the tool opened the discussion in ways that a regular classroom discussion would not have:

> We were able to create that space where they were engaging with other people's positionality, hearing each other's pain. And we did not get the same reality with just the fishbowl discussion. Tech gave the chance for them to voice things. (Video Recording, 2015)

Together the teaching team reviewed the transcripts of the Socrative conversations, triangulated them with their field notes, and analyzed them. Ms. Matthews shares that the use of the transcripts as inquiry allowed the teaching team to notice moments in which students opted-out of the conversation or when a teacher's response shifted the tenor of the room and constrained the perspective of the students. They used the transcripts in the ninth grade as texts for follow-up discussions and ultimately, a written reflection assignment. She ends the demo with an open Q&A for the PSTs to ask questions.

Technological Tools for Critical Praxis

The use of technology as a tool for critical praxis in Ms. Matthews' demonstration was identified by PSTs in their survey responses. The week after Ms. Matthews' demonstration, we asked PSTs to respond to the question: "How can technology be used as a tool toward social justice/equity in our English instruction?" PST responses highlighted:

> It was also awesome to see how technology can be used to point out silent (or not so silent) trends in a classroom that may otherwise go unaddressed (technology can maximize "teachable moments" outside of/in addition to the formal lesson). (Student Reflection, 2/18/2015)

Another PST made a direct connection to instruction writing "technology can also promote social justice/equity in that it can facilitate differentiation for students of different skill levels and needs." (Student Reflections, 2/18/2015). Finally, the effect that technology can have on voice and power relations emerged as PSTs reflected: "Technology allows students to have a voice in places and with audiences that they might normally be silenced," and "Technology can position students as teachers, and has the power to reverse traditional power relations (especially when students are more educated about tech than teachers!)" (Student Reflections, 2/18/2015).

PSTs' consideration of use of Socrative in instruction was not constrained to these reflections on Ms. Matthew's demonstration. Several PSTs integrated Socrative within their field placement or as part of the final project. One PST, the same PST, later identified Socrative on a list of technology tools she would like to continue exploring throughout the course. Her self-identified fluency level and personal goals were: "Some practice. I want to use Socrative in order to gage [sic] student opinions, understandings, and interest levels. I also want to use Socrative in order to facilitate class discussions." (Student classwork, 2/25/2015).

Months later, Kelly continued to use Socrative with fiction and nonfiction texts in her "Digital Mapping Project." She had her middle school students use the platform to discuss motivation and place and record the author's claims, evidence, and their personal responses to an article on motivation (Blackwell, 2002). (PST Final Project, 5/18/2015)

Vignette 2: Ms. Evans Introduces the Slave Voyages Database

To start her demo lesson on the tool Slave Voyages (SV), Ms. Evans lets the PSTs know that her migration unit was designed with her school's context in mind: a public charter middle school with a high proportion of English language learners and special populations—many of her students have individual educational plans or individual behavioral support plans. Ms. Evans explains that the SV database appeals to visual learners because while the traditional unit presents a challenge with its large amount of technical language, using the database allows her students to benefit from the variety of maps, making the content "more accessible."

Using the interactive Google document, the PSTs, in groups of three, work through the guided worksheet. Ms. Evans reminds the PSTs that the learning goal is for students to: "think critically about the scope of the Trans-Atlantic Slave Trade, the humanity of those involved, and the language we use to teach and write about it" (Field notes, 3/16/2016). They are directed to "play with the data table" and speculate on why estimates may not be complete. In the work period, PSTs explore more maps and timelines, identify which period had the most people transported, interpret the difference in numbers between "embarked" and "disembarked," and experiment with queries in the African names database. At the end of the work time, Ms. Evans asks the PSTs for ideas of how they might use the SV database in their respective classrooms. One PST proposes collaborating with a math teacher to have their students examine the data through both quantitative and qualitative lenses. Another suggests using the SV database during a unit on poetry to explore "poetries from different countries" and looking at "big historical events that had effects on people" (Field notes, 3/16/2016).

Ms. Evans closes the demonstration by passing around samples of her middle school students' creative writing, generated from their work with the SV database. This offers an opportunity for PSTs to examine veritable student work generated in a particular disciplinary context.

Technological Content Knowledge

Ms. Evans demonstrates TCK in her use of the SV databases to bridge the needs of various learners by drawing upon the affordances of the tool to visually convey the required content of history and English in a way that responded to the learning modalities of her students. Ms. Evans highlights how the interactive nature of the variety of SV maps allowed her students to "read" multiple sources of information, thus offering them multiple entry points through which they could engage with the historical content. She also identified and described accessibility not only in terms of the number of maps but also how the ability to interactively navigate the maps exceeds the functionality of a traditional textbook. The guided worksheet highlights these affordances in its design. Each affordance of the interactive maps is listed as a separate response section for students to attend to: navigation of the maps, sources, tables, timetables, names database. This approach isolates the technological affordances of the database—supporting students' more thorough navigation of the tool and potentially a more robust learning of the content through these varied lenses of data.

Technological Tools for Critical Praxis

Ms. Evans' demonstration lesson embodies an expectation of the enactment of critical literacy through the way she positions her middle school students as critical consumers of information. The Slave Voyage database presents raw historical data, however, Ms. Evans' inquiry questions were designed such that they presented an opportunity for students to engage in a counter-reading of the data. Questions such as: "Read the section on Estimates. Why are the records not complete?" and "How might you interpret the difference in numbers between embarked and disembarked?" required that students not take the numbers at face value. Rather than asking recall questions about the information that was presented, the questions asked students to inquire about missing information, read between the lines, and further their analytical skills to interrogate the sociohistorical conditions that may have accounted for discrepancies in primary source information.

Ms. Evans' inclusion of students' creative writing in the demonstration also served as an example of critical literacy as students synthesized and extended the given quantitative data (maps, names, dates, country information) to compose supplementary qualitative narratives, thereby probing the question of: "Which voices are not reflected?" This critical reading, question-asking, and generative inquiry also demonstrate critical praxis.

Vignette 3: Ms. Burroughs Introduces LucidChart

Ms. Borroughs starts by letting the preservice teachers (PSTs) know that she uses technology in her classroom all of the time. "More than I should maybe?" she offers with a chuckle. She points out that her school, like many under-resourced schools, has seen cuts in its arts programs. "So here, we're using tech as an art tool. It's a creative tool." With that, Ms. Borroughs displays a slide with a list: online whiteboards, Padlet, blogs, LucidChart, and Pixlr.[1] The software programs are ones that some of the PSTs nod in acknowledgement of having seen prior to today's class.

To launch into LucidChart, Ms. Borroughs asks, "What is a sandbox? Who is it for? Who gets to play in it?" She shares that these questions tap into the schema of her middle school students to help them imagine what a sandbox typically represents: playtime, openness, and making things. She then displays a slide with directions for her Sandbox technique. They call for PSTs in pairs to figure out how to complete a range of tasks in Lucid-Chart, from basic functions such as dragging and deleting shapes to more complicated functions such as adding an image from the web. The slide also features a short list of "advanced skills" including adding text onto the connecting lines and discovering five additional functions of LucidChart that were not included on the slide. Before the PSTs get started, Ms. Burroughs points out familiar buttons within the program: the color palette, image icon, and eraser.

For the next 10 minutes, the PSTs explore LucidChart. Ms. Burroughs points out that she will not answer any questions; instead she wants them to ask each other for help. Although LucidChart is a tool that none of the PSTs have seen prior to today, they dive into the tool with ease. Once the allotted sandbox time has elapsed, Ms. Borroughs spends the remaining 40 minutes sharing student work while guiding the PSTs through what happened in class when her students had the opportunity to complete similar open-ended projects.

Ms. Borroughs ends the demo with an open discussion of how the pedagogical approach might be used in the PSTs' field placements, asking several "thought questions" such as: "How could you use the sandbox method to introduce a program or app in your classroom?" and "What are potential issues/confusion students could have with open-ended projects?"

Technological Content Knowledge

Ms. Borroughs' open-ended LucidChart project evidences her technological content knowledge. Using the blank canvas of the technological platform, her students created, in various flowchart formats, a representation of their learning. Ms. Borroughs' student work also showcased the diversity of linkages between ideas within King Lear through the use of coded-color schemes, shapes, fonts and other visual cues. She noted that students' selections—for example white boxes for family members, or yellow connector lines to indicate unrequited love—afforded her insight into how students processed what they understood. In this way, the openness (freeform) of the technology and the layered design choices of students allowed her to assess how they were engaging with the content.

Following Ms. Borroughs' demo, in response to the prompt: "What should 21st century learners be able to do?" PST reflected on Ms. Borroughs' demonstration lesson and how within technology integration "learners should be able to 'tinker' with new platforms and technologies," and "should be equipped with strategies and skills to explore and independently learn new technology" (Google+ blog post, 3/6/2016). Exploration and tinkering were highlighted as important in light of "new technologies [that] continue to roll out" (Google+ blog post, 3/6/2016). The PST also noted in their post that "without the skill to independently tinker [their] way to understanding, learners sacrifice the opportunity to full [sic] engage with new tech" (Google+ blog post, 3/6/2016).

Subsequently, a veteran English teacher with over 20 years of experience and member of the networked community commented on the post with an affirmation of the sandbox tool, noting that he is a "Big fan of the sandbox," (Google+ blog comment 3/10/2016). They moved forth in a dialogue as the PST asked for recommendations of "any other strategies for introducing new tech." (Google+ blog comment, 3/12/2016). The exchange on the #MUSEDigPed blog presents a window for the PST and the audience of the post, including the PSTs in the course, to witness collegiality enacted among practitioners across levels of expertise.

DISCUSSION

Each of the three practitioners augmented the teacher education course content with her unique blend of pedagogical priorities. While the tech course covers principles of technology integration, experienced practitioners who effectively integrate technology in their instruction have important knowledge to offer PSTs. The practitioner demonstrations highlighted here called upon PSTs to not simply engage with the tools, but to intentionally consider the technological and pedagogical content knowledge required for their own students' successful engagement with the learning goal. This framing reinforces that technology integration is not just about technological fluency with the tools, but the meaning these tools bear respective to their pedagogical and content applications, and the intersection of technological fluency with critical literacy.

As shown in Ms. Matthews' example, technological tools that afford transcripts, usage logs, and other artifacts—which can be analyzed by teachers and students—provide not only learning data about students' content knowledge, but information about student engagement, discussion patterns, and their related impact. This range of affordances is significant as PSTs may be familiar with technological tools for a variety of personal and professional uses, yet they may not be as familiar with their use for content mastery and inquiry into one's practice.

Not only must PSTs move beyond the familiar, teacher educators must extend their own thinking beyond the narrative of the preservice teachers as "digital natives," which assumes a degree of fluency of preservice teachers by virtue of exposure to and/or immersion in technology. This move beyond a presumptive narrative is crucial if teacher educators desire to prepare PSTs with disciplinary facility with technology tools. Allotting technology tinker time in teacher education courses is one means towards that end (McBride, 2019).

CONCLUSION

Preservice teachers need multiple points at which they can engage in learning, including both theory and practice of that theory. Technology demonstrations create a hands-on opportunity to meet and engage with other educators, and most importantly to do so in a way that integrate technology and literacy instruction in practical ways. Through the demonstrations of their practice, the practitioners revealed robust thinking, a history of inquiry into their own practice, and approaches to pedagogy for aspiring educators. An important consideration is how to facilitate continued space for tinkering once PSTs have matriculated into their own classrooms as teachers of record. While technology continues to proliferate, and universities and schools experience various resource constraints, teacher education programs must channel the resources within reach, particularly access to experienced practitioners, to appropriately equip the next generation of educators. When done in ways that are humanizing and affirming, such partnerships can extend learning for involved stakeholders and professionalize the teacher development process through teachers themselves.

NOTE

1. Various online educational technology tools. All on the list have collaborative features. Online whiteboards are virtual spaces for drawing and writing, Padlet is a collaborative space for sharing links and resources with a team, blogs are digital publication platforms, LucidChart is a visual chart creator (also referenced in data section above), and Pixlr is a web-based photo editor.

REFERENCES

Ball, D. L., & Cohen, D. K. (1999). Developing practice, developing practitioners: Toward a practice-based theory of professional education. *Teaching as the Learning Profession: Handbook of Policy and Practice*, *1*, 3–22.

Blackwell, L. (2002). You can grow your intelligence: New research shows the brain can be developed like a muscle. *Health & Science News You Can Use*, 6–9.

Borthwick, A. C., Pierson, M. E., Anderson, C. L., Morris, J. L., Lathem, S. A., & Parker, H. B. (2004). Building learning communities to increase faculty and preservice teacher use of technology. *Journal of Computing in Teacher Education*, *21*(1), 23–32. Retrieved June 19, 2019, from https://www.learntechlib.org/p/55253/

Brush, T., & Saye, J. (2009). Strategies for preparing preservice social studies teachers to effectively integrate technology: Models and practices. *Contemporary Issues Intechnology and Teacher Education*, *9*(1), 46–59.

Brzycki, D., & Dudt, K. (2005). Overcoming barriers to technology use in teacher preparation programs. *Journal of Technology and Teacher Education*, *13*(4), 619.

Center for Media Literacy. (2003). Literacy for the 21st Century. An overview & orientation guide to media literacy education. Retrieved from: http://www.medialit.org/reading_room/article540.html

Cochran-Smith, M., & Lytle, S. L. (2001). Beyond certainty: Taking an inquiry stance on practice. *Teachers Caught in the Action: Professional Development That Matters*, 45–58.

Darling-Hammond, L. (2006). Constructing 21st-century teacher education. *Journal of Teacher Education*, *57*(3), 300–314.

Darling-Hammond, L. (2012). *Powerful teacher education: Lessons from exemplary programs*. Hoboken, NJ: John Wiley & Sons.

Dexter, S., Doering, A. H., & Riedel, E. S. (2006). Content area specific technology integration: A model for educating teachers. *Journal of Technology and Teacher Education*, *14*(2), 325.

Erickson, F. (2006). Definition and analysis of data from videotape: Some research procedures and their rationales. *Handbook of Complementary Methods in Education Research, 3*, 177–192.

Ertmer, P. A. (2005). Teacher pedagogical beliefs: The final frontier in our quest for technology integration? *Educational technology research and development, 53*(4), 25–39.

Gomez, L. M., Sherin, M. G., Griesdorn, J., & Finn, L. E. (2008). Creating social relationships: The role of technology in preservice teacher preparation. *Journal of Teacher Education, 59*(2), 117–131.

Hicks, T., Turner, K. H., & Fink, L. S. (2013). No longer a luxury: Digital literacy can't wait. *English Journal, 102*(6), 58.

Jenkins, H., Purushotma, R., Weigel, M., Clinton, K., & Robison, A. J. (2009). *Confronting the challenges of participatory culture: Media education for the 21st century.* Cambridge, MA: MIT Press.

Kleiner, B., Thomas, N., & Lewis, L. (2007). *Educational technology in teacher education programs for initial licensure* (Statistical Analysis Report. NCES 2008-040). Washington, DC: National Center for Education Statistics.

Koehler, M. J., & Mishra, P. (2009). What is technological pedagogical content knowledge? *Contemporary Issues in Technology and Teacher Education, 9*(1), 60–70.

Korthagen, F. A. (2010). Situated learning theory and the pedagogy of teacher education: Towards an integrative view of teacher behavior and teacher learning. *Teaching and Teacher Education, 26*(1), 98–106.

Lieberman, A., & Wood, D. R. (2003). *Inside the National Writing Project: Connecting network learning and classroom teaching* (Vol. 35). New York, NY: Teachers College Press.

Kress, G. (2009). *Multimodality: A social semiotic approach to contemporary communication.* New York, NY: Routledge.

Mahiri, J. (2011). *Digital tools in urban schools: Mediating a remix of learning.* Ann Arbor, MI: University of Michigan Press.

McBride, C. C., & Mahiri, J. (2019). OMG can I have your meme lesson? TY: Affective literacies and collegial meaning-making in digitally-mediated participatory networks. *Universitas Tarraconensis. Revista de Ciències de l'Educació, 1*(2), 28–42.

Miles, M. B., Huberman, A. M., & Saldana, J. (2013). *Qualitative data analysis: A methods sourcebook.* Thousand Oaks, CA: SAGE.

Mishra, P., & Koehler, M. (2006). Technological pedagogical content knowledge: A framework for teacher knowledge. *Teachers College Record, 108*(6) 1017–1054.

Morrell, E. (2005). Critical English education. *English Education, 37*(4), 312–321.

National Council of Teachers of English. (2013). NCTE Definition of 21st Century Literacies. Retrieved January 15, 2017, from http://www2.ncte.org/statement/21stcentdefinition

New London Group. (1996). A pedagogy of multiliteracies: Designing social futures. *Harvard Educational Review, 66*(1), 60–93.

National Writing Project (2003). Retrieved from https://www.nwp.org/cs/public/print/doc/about.csp

Pedro, Y. (2005). Reflections in teacher education: Exploring pre-service teachers' meanings of reflective practice. *Reflective Practice, 6*(1) 49–66.

Prensky, M. (2001). Digital natives, digital immigrants part 1. *On the Horizon, 9*(5), 1-6.

Schmidt, D. A., Baran, E., Thompson, A. D., Mishra, P., Koehler, M. J., & Shin, T. S. (2009). Technological pedagogical content knowledge (TPACK) the development and validation of an assessment instrument for preservice teachers. *Journal of Research on Technology in Education, 42*(2), 123–149.

Shulman, L. (1987). Knowledge and teaching: Foundations of the new reform. *Harvard Educational Review, 57*(1), 1–22.

Siemens, G., & Long, P. (2011). Penetrating the fog: Analytics in learning and education. *EDUCAUSE Review, 46*(5), 30.

Straub, E. T. (2009). Understanding technology adoption: Theory and future directions for informal learning. *Review of Educational Research, 79*(2), 625–649.

Thoman, E., & Jolls, T. (2004). Media literacy—A national priority for a changing world. *American Behavioral Scientist, 48*(1), 18–29.

Zeichner, K. (2010). Rethinking the connections between campus courses and field experiences in college-and university-based teacher education. *Journal of Teacher Education, 61*(1–2), 89–99.

ABOUT THE AUTHORS

Lisa A. Borgerding is an Associate Professor of Science Education at Kent State University. She presently coordinates secondary science teacher education at KSU and teaches undergraduate and graduate science teacher education courses. Lisa taught high school biology in a rural Midwestern school district and became ensconced in the challenges of teaching and learning biological evolution and other societally-denied science. Her research centers on evolution teaching and learning as a multicultural issue and also focuses on science teacher recruitment, preservice education, and professional development.

Blanca Caldas Chumbes is an assistant professor in Second Language Education and Elementary Education—College of Education and Human Development at The University of Minnesota Twin Cities. Her research focuses on bilingual education, preservice bilingual/language teacher education, and minoritized language practices and pedagogies. Her recent research has appeared in *International Journal of Bilingual Education and Bilingualism, Teaching Education,* and *Arts Education Policy Review.*

Amanda Jo Cordova is an experienced social worker and K–12 teacher. Her research agenda is focused on social justice, transformation, and the use of decolonizing methodologies to re-shape education from the voices of a diverse society. She is an Assistant Professor at Iowa State University.

ABOUT the AUTHORS

Encarnación Garza is a Professor at the University of Texas at San Antonio in the Department of Educational Leadership and Policy Studies. His major emphasis in teaching is the preparation of future school principals and superintendents that will serve primarily minority children. Dr. Garza's research is focused on the preparation of school leaders who serve in schools with predominately minority student populations. His experiences as a K–12 educator (teacher, counselor, principal, and superintendent) provide him with heuristic knowledge that is critical to his research. As a scholar-practitioner whose scholarship employs a critical theory perspective, his research is focused on four themes: (1) the study of minority student success rooted in critical pedagogy, (2) the preparation of principals as leaders for social justice, (3) the exploration of school district/university partnerships with respect to preparing principals as social justice advocates, and (4) international study of successful school principalship with the International Successful School Principals Project (ISSPP). Dr. Garza is coordinator of the nationally recognized Urban School Leaders Collaborative, which received the 2013 UCEA Exemplary Educational Leadership Preparation Program Award.

Xenia Hadjioannou is associate professor of Language and Literacy Education at the Harrisburg campus of Penn State University. A former elementary teacher, Xenia holds a bachelor's degree in the Sciences of Education from the University of Cyprus; a master of Education from the University of Florida; and a PhD in Instruction and Curriculum also from the University of Florida. In her teaching, Dr. Hadjioannou works with pre- and in-service teachers in various courses on language and literacy methodology. Her research focuses on the study of classroom discourse that supports student thinking and learning; the analysis of exemplary practices in the language arts classroom; and the preparation of teachers to effectively work with diverse students, including emergent bilinguals. Xenia's work has appeared in various journals such as the *American Educational Research Journal*, the *Early Education and Development Journal*, *Current Issues in Language Planning*, and the *International Journal of Multicultural Education*.

Todd S. Hawley is an Associate Professor of Social Studies Teacher Education at Kent State University where he is the Coordinator for both the Social Studies Education and the Curriculum and Instruction Programs. Todd works to support classroom teachers as professionals and to change the national narrative that schools and teachers are failing students and communities. His research focuses on transformative, rationale-based social studies teacher education and the power of social issues to engage and prepare activist, socially-just citizens. Todd is the coeditor of *Race Lessons:*

Using Inquiry to Teach about Race in Social Studies and the coauthor of the Southern Schooling column for the *Bitter Southerner*. Before earning his PhD at the University of Georgia, Todd taught high school social studies at North Atlanta High School and at Oglethorpe County High School, both in his home state of Georgia.

Nina Helgevold is a professor in pedagogy at the University of Stavanger, Norway. She works as a teacher educator in teacher education and is also involved with teachers' professional development in schools, with a special focus on Lesson Study. Her research interest are inclusive education, teacher education and teachers' professional development.

Mary Hutchinson is an associate professor in ESL Education at Penn State University. She holds a bachelor's degree in English with a minor in business from Susquehanna University, a master's degree in ESL from the Universidad de Turabo in Puerto Rico, and a doctorate in education from Penn State University. As a community-engaged scholar, Dr. Hutchinson's research has been dedicated to strengthening the theoretical knowledge and practice for teachers working with culturally and linguistically diverse students. She has served as the principal investigator for two major U.S. Department of Education, Office of English Language Acquisition grants focused on preparing teachers to work with English learners. In addition, she has published and presented both nationally and internationally on this topic.

Lanette Jimerson is an assistant professor in the College of Education at University of Houston. Her research is situated at the intersection of literacy theory, writing studies, and writing instruction and assessment. In particular, she considers how writing competency impacts the academic and career outcomes of youth and adult learners from communities of color. Lanette has over 20 years of experience in urban schools as a former English teacher and literacy specialist. Lanette also serves as an assistant editor for the journal English Education and is a member of the California Statewide English Language Arts Intervention Advisory Board

Jennifer Lock is a Professor and the Associate Dean of Teaching and Learning in the Werklund School of Education at the University of Calgary. Her current research interests are in the following five areas: (1) Building capacity of online educators; (2) Technology integration in education and teacher education; (3) Change and innovation in education; (4) Scholarship of teaching and learning in higher education; and (5) Experiential learning through making and makerspaces.

ABOUT the AUTHORS

Ann E. Lopez is a faculty member in the Department of Leadership, Higher and Adult Education at the Ontario Institute for Studies in Education, University of Toronto. She is also the Director of the Center for Leadership and Diversity and Advisor to the Provost on Access Programs. She has wide experience in public education in Canada as a secondary school administrator and teacher in one of the Canada's largest school boards. Born and raised in Jamaica, Dr. Lopez's teaching and research focuses on issues of equity and diversity, student engagement, school leadership across contexts, transformative decolonizing leadership and education. Her most recent publications include *Culturally Responsive and Socially Just Leadership in Diverse Contexts: From Theory to Action*; *Disruptive Pedagogy: Critical Approach to Diversity in Teacher Education*; *Walk steady, keep going: Navigational moves of empowerment, resistance and sustenance in the academy* as well journal articles in *Multicultural Perspectives, Multicultural Education Review, Mentoring and Tutoring, Canadian Journal of Educational Administration and Policy* and *Journal of Cases in Educational Administration*. Dr. Lopez is the current President of the National Association for Multicultural Education. She is an editorial board member of the *Journal of Cases in Educational Leadership* and the *International Journal of Educational Policy & Leadership*.

Jabari Mahiri is a professor in the Graduate School of Education at UC Berkeley and the Brinton Family Endowed Chair in Urban Teaching. He is Chair of the Leadership Education Advisory and Development Group, the P.I. and Faculty Advisor for the Bay Area Writing Project, a Board Member of the National Writing Project, and a Faculty Fellow of Berkeley's HAAS Institute for a Fair and Inclusive Society. He has been a high school English teacher for seven years in Chicago Public Schools, and he has published six academic books. His latest publication *Deconstructing Race* (2017) has won several major awards.

Cherise McBride is a PhD Candidate in Language, Literacy and Culture at University of California, Berkeley's Graduate School of Education. Her research draws from her extensive work with pre- and -inservice teachers. She has taught courses on Urban Education, blended learning, and technology at UC Berkeley and Stanford as well as facilitated professional development workshops for the Bay Area Writing Project and the National Writing Project. Her dissertation explores how preservice teachers came to understand, reveal and apply sociocultural knowledge about their students and new media technologies in their designs of digitally-mediated learning. She explores teacher learning and new relationships for meaning making in her recent article, "OMG, can I have your meme lesson? TY: Affective literacies and collegial meaning making in digitallymediated participatory networks." Prior to her doctoral studies, Cherise taught English at the high school, adult school, and community college levels.

Aki Murata is an associate professor of mathematics and teacher education at University of Florida. She studies how teachers learn to teach by understanding student learning. She has conducted numerous research studies in elementary school classrooms, and worked with teachers globally. She is best known for her work with lesson study for the international audience, and her publication is considered to be seminal work in the area.

Juan Manuel Niño is an assistant professor at the University of Texas at San Antonio. Niño's public educator experience include: secondary science teacher, ESL teacher, athletic coach, campus and district leader. His primary research focus on school leadership for school improvement. Current research interests center on school district leadership, leadership preparation for social justice, Latino leadership and intersectionalities. Niño's preferred method of inquiry is qualitative research to better understand the complexities of schools as evolving systems. Other interests include instructional supervision for diverse students, instructional leadership and multicultural studies.

Elsie Lindy Olan, associate professor and track coordinator for Secondary English Language Arts in the School of Teacher Education at the University of Central Florida, researches the role of language and writing, literacy, literature and diversity in learning and teaching in Language Arts education and cross-disciplinary education, and teachers' narratives, inquiry and reflective practices in (national and international) teaching environments and professional development settings. Her work has been published in *English Education, English Leadership Quarterly, Research in the Teaching of English, Education and Learning Research Journal, Argentinian Journal of Applied Linguistics*, and *Language Arts*. Her current research on teacher education and diversity is shared in a coedited book series, *Transformative Pedagogies for Teacher Education*, from Information Age Publishing, Inc. Elsie L. has presented her work and research at conferences in Mexico, Spain, United Kingdom, Canada, and United States.

Michelle Parker-Katz is Clinical Professor in the Department of Special Education at the University of Illinois at Chicago where she also coordinates the master's programs and clinical fieldwork. She teaches masters and doctoral level courses that include supervising clinical internships and student teaching in Chicago Public Schools. She is a fellow with the UIC Honors College and teaches in the UIC Foundations of College Teaching Certificate program. Dr. Parker-Katz's courses focus on teacher learning and teacher education, which also align with her three major related research agendas. One focuses on the structures, nature, and possibilities of building authentic collaborative engagement amongst educators, students, families and a range of community members. A second and related focus is how teachers develop cultural competencies and literacies related to their students. A related third agenda is how to build and support teacher leadership. She is or has been co-PI on a number of projects funded by the Institute of Education Sciences, Office of Special Education Programs, and National Science Foundation. She publishes widely in general and special education journals as well as in books and online venues. She provides professional support to several non-profit community groups and is active in state and national organizations. In addition to teaching awards, Parker-Katz most recently earned the INSPIRE! award for her ongoing efforts to recruit, sustain and nurture students at the University of Illinois at Chicago as they learn and continuously develop their teacher practices

Edward Podsiadlik III, PhD, is currently a Clinical Assistant Professor at the University of Illinois at Chicago in the College of Education. He has over 20 years experience in urban public education as a middle school teacher, literacy coach, and administrator. His research interests include qualitative explorations of what informs and defines authentic teacher identity. His book, *Anecdotes and Afterthoughts: Literature as a Teacher's Curriculum*, was published in July 2014 by Sense Publishers.

Kristine E. Pytash is an Associate Professor in Teaching, Learning and Curriculum Studies at Kent State University's College of Education, Health, and Human Services (EHHS) where she directs the secondary Integrated Language Arts teacher preparation program. She is a former high school English teacher. Her research focuses on the literacy practices of youth in juvenile detention facilities. In addition, she studies disciplinary writing and how to prepare teachers to teach writing. An underlying theme across all her lines of inquiry is how technology significantly influences young adults' literacy practices and their literacy instruction. Kristine is a regular contributor to the International Literacy Association's TILE-SIG blog. She recently published, *Writing from the Margins: Exploring the Writing Practices of Youth in the Juvenile Justice System*.

Enrique A. Puig taught 24 years in Orange County Public Schools (OCPS) with experiences varying from classroom teacher to literacy coach district trainer with the Ohio State University's Literacy Collaborative project. Enrique has worked as an education consultant for numerous school districts from Maryland to Oregon and major publishing companies. He has presented on various aspects of literacy acquisition and instruction at state, regional, national and international conferences. In addition, he has worked at the Ohio State University, Texas Tech University and Purdue University with Literacy Collaborative. He is the Chair of the Board of the Florida Literacy Association. Currently, Enrique is the director of the College of Education and Human Performance–Morgridge International Reading Center at the University of Central Florida. He teaches graduate and undergraduate courses on diagnostic reading and reading in the content areas. He is author and co-author of several articles and chapters; in addition to T*he Literacy Coach: Guiding in the Right Direction, 2nd ed.* (Allyn & Bacon/ Pearson) and *The Literacy Leadership Team: Sustaining and Expanding Success* (Allyn & Bacon/ Pearson). His research interest is on coherence and improving literacy acquisition and instruction for low-progress learners. Enrique continues to work with students to further his knowledge of learning and teaching.

Amy Rector-Aranda is a Visiting Assistant Professor of Teacher Education and Urban/Multicultural Education in the Department of Teaching, Learning, and Culture at Texas A&M University. Her scholarship examines matters of equity, relational culture, care and compassion, critical consciousness, and student agency and voice in pre-K–12 and teacher education. Her current research interrogates how we can better prepare future educators for their essential roles in a pluralistic society, including recruiting and supporting more teachers of color, providing training in critical and culturally sustaining pedagogies, and otherwise ensuring that all teachers are empowered to enact transformative, responsive, and equitable practices.

Petrea Redmond is an associate professor of Educational Technology in the School of Teacher Education and Early Childhood at the University of Southern Queensland. Her research is situated in interrelated fields of educational technology including: blended and online learning and teaching; online collaboration; online communities of inquiry; online mentoring; gender and STEM; community of inquiry; and the integration of technology to enhance learning and teaching in the school and higher education contexts. She has published and copublished in a number of international refereed books, journals and conference proceedings. Petrea has received six outstanding conference paper awards at international conferences; along with industry, faculty and university awards for research and teaching. She is also a lead editor for *Australasian Journal of Educational Technology* (AJET).

Kathy Sanford is a senior scholar at the University of Victoria whose educational research draws from critical feminist theory, understanding the need to address issues of power and acknowledging existent gender inequities worldwide. Kathy is a member of the board of the Community Based Research Canada (CBRC) national network and is the current president of the Canadian Association for the Study of Women and Education (CASWE). She has taught graduate courses in Teacher Education as well as Gender and Pedagogy and is a strong advocate of inclusion of gender issues in formal and informal education. Her research utilizes theoretical and methodological approaches related to community engagement, collaboration, and critical discourse analysis. Her national and international networks (e.g., World Educational Research Association, International Congress of School Effectiveness and Improvement) demonstrate her ability to engage with scholars from diverse contexts.

Lisa J. Starr is an Assistant Professor at McGill University in the Department of Integrated Studies in Education (DISE) and the Past President of the Canadian Association for the Study of Women and Education (CASWE). She completed her doctoral degree in the Department of Curriculum and Instruction at the University of Victoria. Dr. Starr's teaching career led her from Canada to Pakistan, Kuwait, Mongolia and back to Canada. Her travels created a passion for the study of the relationship between identity and culture, particularly in relation to pedagogy, preparation of teachers and 21st century learning, as well as leadership, and gender equity. Her current research focus is innovative approaches to high school eduction using design thinking as a response to the Action Canada (2013) call to prioritize teacher education by integrating 21st century learning into preservice teachers' academic training as well as to model innovative and collaborative pedagogy to create flexible, interdisciplinary learning environments. Dr. Starr also advocates for the use of autoethnography as means to investigate, understand, and make meaning of the intersections inherent in 21st century leading and learning.

CPSIA information can be obtained
at www.ICGtesting.com
Printed in the USA
BVHW040254191019
561550BV00007B/7/P